K. Deighton

The Life and Death Of King John

K. Deighton

The Life and Death Of King John

ISBN/EAN: 9783348011723

Printed in Europe, USA, Canada, Australia, Japan

Cover: Foto ©ninafisch / pixelio.de

More available books at **www.hansebooks.com**

SHAKESPEARE

THE LIFE AND DEATH OF
KING JOHN

WITH

AN INTRODUCTION AND NOTES

BY
K DEIGHTON

London
MACMILLAN AND CO.
AND NEW YORK
1893

First Edition, 1890
Reprinted 1891.

CONTENTS.

INTRODUCTION.

INTERNAL evidence as to structure of verse tone of Date of Composition
thought, style of composition, as well as allusions, real or
supposed, to contemporary events, have all been appealed
to in the endeavour to fix the date at which *King John*
was written, but all we know is that it is first mentioned by Meres in his *Palladis Tamia*, published in 1598

Apart from history, the play is founded on an earlier Source
one, by an unknown writer, entitled *The Troublesome
Raigne of Iohn King of England, with the discouerie of King
Richard Cordelions base sonne (vulgarly called, The Bastard
Fauconbridge) also the death of King Iohn at Swinstead
Abbey, etc*, which was first printed in 1591

The play opens at Northampton, with the demand made Outline of the Play Act I
by the King of France, through his ambassador, that
John should relinquish, in favour of Arthur, the throne of
England and Ireland, as well as the French fiefs of
Poictiers, Anjou, Touraine, Maine   This demand is
accompanied by the threat of war in case of refusal, a
threat which John meets with haughty defiance and
preparation for the invasion of France   On the departure
of the ambassador, we are introduced to a quarrel between two brothers, the reputed sons of Sir Robert
Faulconbridge, the younger of whom claims his father's

estate on the ground that his brother was an illegitimate
son of his mother by Richard Cœur de lion On their
being brought before the King to have their dispute
decided, both John and his mother, Elinor, remark upon
the strong likeness which the younger brother bears to
Richard, and he, on being asked by the latter whether
he is willing to forsake his fortune and follow her, joy-
fully assents, having apparently been long convinced of
his true parentage He is then knighted by John as Sir
Richard Faulconbridge, in place of his baptismal name
Philip Almost immediately afterwards his mother, who
had heard of the quarrel between the brothers, and
angrily followed them to assert her good name, is
brought to confess that she had been seduced by Richard
during her husband's absence in Germany, and that her
eldest son was the result of the intrigue

Act II At the beginning of the second Act, Philip, King of
France, with his son, Lewis, and the Archduke of
Austria, is preparing to besiege the city of Angiers,
which refuses to acknowledge Arthur's right when John
appears on the scene with an English army After
mutual recriminations, each king appeals to the citizens
of the place to admit his claim, John for himself, Philip
on behalf of Arthur On their refusal, an indecisive
engagement takes place between the two armies at the
close of which the Bastard suggests that, uniting their
powers, the two kings should first bring the city into
submission, and then continue the contest to decide to
which of them the city shall belong The suggestion is
approved, but while preparations are being made to
carry the agreement into effect, one of the chief citizens
proposes a settlement of the quarrel by the marriage of

Blanch, niece to John, with Lewis, the Dauphin   To
this proposal Philip and John assent, the latter agreeing
to bestow Anjou, Touraine, Maine, and Poictiers upon
Blanch, as a dowry, while, as a sop to Constance and his
own conscience, he proposes to create Arthur Duke of
Bretagne and Earl of Richmond, and to make over to
him the city of Angiers   The Act then closes with
preparations for the wedding

The third Act introduces Salisbury bearing to Con- Act III
stance the tidings of the agreement that had been
entered into , and upon the entrance of the two Kings,
Elinor, etc , a fierce contest of words takes place between
the mother and the grandmother of Arthur, the former
bitterly reproaching Philip and Austria for having
abandoned her son's cause   While these recriminations
are going on, Pandulph, the Pope's legate, appears upon
the scene, demanding of John his reason for refusing to
acknowledge Stephen Langton as Archbishop of Canterbury   The King, defying the Pope, is at once excom-
municated by the legate, while Philip is bidden, on pain
of the Church's curse, to break off all league with him,
and to show his obedience to the Pope by making war
upon the " arch-heretic "   Philip reluctantly obeys, and
the first Scene ends with preparation on both sides for
the conflict   The second Scene merely brings in the
Bastard, bearing the head of the Archduke whom he had
killed ; and John, who in the engagement had taken
Arthur captive, making him over to the custody of
Hubert de Burgh, a Norman knight devoted to the
King   In the third Scene the Bastard is commissioned
by John to return to England and wring from the clergy
their hoarded treasures in order to meet the expenses of

the war. On his departure, the king breaks with Hubert as to Arthur's murder, which with little demur Hubert undertakes to bring about. The fourth Scene is mainly taken up with Constance's lamentations for her son, now torn from her, and with Pandulph's persuasion of Lewis to invade England.

Act IV. With the fourth Act we come to the Scene between Hubert and Arthur, whose eyes the former is preparing to have burnt out in order to render impossible his coming to the throne. Arthur's pleadings, however, soften Hubert's heart, and he renounces his project. In the second Scene John, newly re-crowned, is urged by Pembroke and Salisbury to give Arthur his liberty, and has scarcely promised to do so, when Hubert, entering, tells him privately of Arthur's death. On his announcing these tidings to the lords, they throw off their allegiance and quit his presence. A messenger then appears with news of the French invasion under Lewis, and immediately afterwards the Bastard returns to report the result of his commission to plunder the abbeys, bringing with him a hermit whom he had arrested for prophesying that before Ascension Day the King would yield up his crown. John, having ordered the hermit to be taken to prison, and to be put to death on the day to which his prophecy referred, gives the Bastard the task of trying to reconcile the revolted peers. On his departure, Hubert enters, and, telling the King that Arthur is still alive, is ordered to communicate the fact to the peers with all possible speed. The third Scene opens with Arthur's death in his attempted escape from prison. The peers in consultation about joining Lewis are met by the Bastard, who calls upon them to return to the

King   He has hardly delivered his message, when they come upon Arthur's dead body outside the castle walls, and Hubert, entering, is accused by them of the deed An angry colloquy ensues, at the end of which Hubert is ordered to take up Arthur's body for burial, and the Bastard proceeds to rejoin the King

By this time John, frightened out of his obstinacy by _{Act v} the menacing attitude of his subjects, determines to make submission to the Pope, and yields up his crown, which is then returned to him by the legate   The Bastard enters with news that the nobles refuse to return, and that the people are welcoming the Dauphin   At the King's entreaty, Pandulph goes off with the object of persuading Lewis to make peace, while John, utterly unnerved, leaves the Bastard to make preparations for the defence of the country   The second Scene describes the compact between the revolted lords and the Dauphin, and the legate's unsuccessful endeavour to persuade the latter to return to France   In the third Scene, John enters from the field of battle, prostrate with fever, and is borne off in a litter to Swinstead Abbey   In the fourth Scene, another part of the field is shown, in which the French lord, Melun, persuades Salisbury, Pembroke, and Bigot, to abandon Lewis, whose intention is to put them to death at the close of the battle, and to return to the King   In the fifth, the Dauphin, boasting of his success in the battle, is informed of the falling off of these lords, and of the wreck of his expected reinforcements on the Goodwin Sands   Meanwhile the King has been poisoned by a monk, and Hubert, in the death scene, seeks out the Bastard to inform him of this fact Together they hasten to Swinstead, when, in the seventh

Scene, the revolted lords, with Prince Henry, are found
assembled round John's death bed as he expires in great
agony. The Play closes with the news that the Dauphin is setting out on his return, and with preparations
for the King's funeral and his son's accession to the
throne

Deviations   Having now traced the course of the Play, it will be
from history   convenient for us to notice the main deviations from
history which, for one cause or other, Shakespeare has
chosen to make

In the first place, Arthur's title to the throne, which was
without doubt a sound one, is represented in the Play as in-
disputable, though in reality John had this much in his
justification that in those days the rule of lineal descent
was not as distinctly recognized as it later on came to be,
that in the second of Richard's two wills he is named as
successor to the throne; and that his accession was con-
firmed by election   In the next place, though Arthur's
right was the cause of the wars between Philip and
John, it was not in his murder that the real troubles of
John's reign, continuing to its end, had their origin
These were due to his ill treatment of his subjects, but
for which the Pope's interference would probably have
had but little effect Again, "The great quarrel between
John and the Pope, with reference to the election of
Stephen Langton, did not take place till 1207, about
six years after Arthur was taken prisoner at Mirebeau
Pandulph was not sent 'to practise with the French
king' against John till 1211, and the invasion of England by the Dauphin (which is suggested by Pandulph
as likely to be supported by the indignation of the English on the death of Arthur) did not take place till 1216,

the year of John's death" (Knight, *Pictorial Shakspere*, p 57) In regard to Arthur, Shakespeare has made several more or less important deviations from history. When we first meet with him, as also at the time of his death, he is represented as little more than a child, while in reality he lived to be nearly eighteen years old In the second place, his confinement and death are represented as taking place in England In point of fact, he was first confined at Falaise, and afterwards at Rouen, where he died Further, the scene between Hubert and Arthur has no historical authority, Hubert having, according to Holinshead, saved Arthur from the men sent to murder him In the Play, Angiers refuses to acknowledge as its lord either John or Arthur until the question of right to the throne of England should be decided by battle, whereas in reality Anjou, Touraine, Maine, were from the first loyal to Arthur Shakespeare's Constance is a widow, the real Constance was at this time married to her third husband, Guy De Thouais Moreover, she died the year before Arthur fell into John's hands The Austrian Archduke, who had confined Richard in a dungeon, is made to live five or six years after the date of his actual death, and is represented as one and the same person with Vidomai, Viscount of Limoges, in besieging whose castle of Chaluz, Richard was mortally wounded The four wars between John and Philip are compressed into two, and at the close of the Play the Dauphin's return to France makes it appear that all idea of trying to conquer England had been abandoned, though in reality Philip's efforts were continued for two years longer Finally, though Holinshed, on the authority of Caxton, speaks of John as having been poisoned by a monk, he, according to the best authorities, died at Newark of a fever, not at Swinstead

For the more important of the foregoing deviations from history, Hudson finds a reason in the conception of John's character and of the events of his reign which the older play of the *Troublesome Raign*, etc, and Bishop Ball's pageant of *King John*, had established in the popular mind "The King John of the stage,' he remarks, "striking in with the passions and interests of the time, had become familiar to the people, and twined itself closely with their feelings and thoughts A faithful version would have worked at great disadvantage in competition with the theatrical one thus established This prepossession of the popular mind Shakespeare may well have judged it unwise to disturb (In other words, the current of popular association being so strong, he probably chose rather to fall in with it than to stem it; We may regret that he did so, but we can hardly doubt that he did it knowingly and on principle nor should we so much blame him for not stemming that current as thank him for purifying it" Again, in regard to the behaviour of Angiers and the circumstances of Arthur's imprisonment and death, "These, however, are immaterial points in the course of the drama, save as the latter has the effect of bringing Arthur nearer to the homes and hearts of the English people ; who would naturally be more apt to resent his death if it occurred at their own doors" ,The representation of Constance as a widow, and the prolongation of her life beyond its actual date, Hudson considers "a breach of history every way justifiable, since it gives an occasion, not otherwise to be had, for some noble outpourings of maternal grief

and tenderness   And the mother's transports of sorrow
might well consist with a second marriage, though to
have represented her thus would have impaired the
pathos of her situation, and at the same time have been
a needless embarrassment of the action   It is enough
that so she would have felt and spoken had she been still
alive , her proper character being thus allowed to tran-.
spire in circumstances which she did not live to see "
The same reason, viz , that greater pathos could be given
to the scenes in which Arthur appears, led Shakespeare
to make him out much younger than he really was   The
Austrian Archduke, like Constance, is shown as alive
some years after his actual death "for no other purpose
than that Richard's natural son may have the honour of
revenging his father's wrongs and death "   In following
Holinshed's account of the cause of John's death,
Shakespeare may have done so because he believed the
fact to be as represented, or his object may have been to
enhance the hatred in which John's subjects held him
Furnivall, noticing that in the older play the monk is
prompted to the deed by John's anti-papal patriotism,
considers that Shakespeare in setting this story aside has
"left a serious blot on his drama which it is impossible
to remove "   To me it seems more in keeping with his
attitude in this play towards religious questions that he
has omitted the question of motive on the monk's part,
and Holinshed's account can scarcely be said to bear out
the idea that religious fanaticism had anything to do
with the action   His words are, "There be which have
written that after he had lost his army, he came to the
abbey of Swinestead, in Lincolnshire, and there under-
standing the cheapness and plenty of corn, shewed him-

-self greatly displeased therewith as that he for the
hatred which he bare to the English people, that had so
traitorously revolted from him unto his adversary Lewis,
wished all misery to light upon them, and thereupon said
in his anger, that he would cause all kind of grain to be
at a far higher price ere many days should pass   Whereupon a monk who heard him speak such words, *being
moved with zeal for the oppression of his country*, gave the
King poison in a cup of ale, whereof he first took the
assay, to cause the king not to suspect the matter, and so
they both died in manner at one time"   ,

The general
question of
literal
accuracy in
historical
dramas con
sidered

On the subject of literal accuracy in historical dramas,
Knight remarks, "It would appear scarcely necessary
to entreat the reader to bear in mind   that the
'Histories' of Shakspere are Dramatic Poems   And yet,
unless this circumstance be watchfully regarded, we shall
fall into the error of setting up one form of truth in con-
tradiction to, and not in illustration of, another form of
truth   It appears to us to be worse than useless employment to be running parallels between the poet and the
chronicler, for the purpose of showing that for the liberal
facts of history the poet is not so safe a teacher as
the chronicler   The 'lively images' of the poet
present a general truth much more completely than the
tedious narratives of the annalist   The ten magnificent
'histories' of Shakspere   stand in the same relation to the contemporary historians of the events they
deal with, as a landscape does to a map. The
principle, therefore, of viewing Shakspere's history
through another medium than that of his art, and pro-
nouncing, upon this view, that his historical plays cannot
be given to our youth 'as properly historical,' is nearly

as absurd as it would be to derogate from the merits of
Mr Turner's beautiful drawings of coast scenery, by
maintaining and proving that the draughtsman had not
accurately laid down the relative positions of each bay
and promontory   There may be, in the poet, a
higher truth than the literal, evolved in spite of, or
rather in combination with, his minute violations of
accuracy, men may in the poet better study history, 'so
to speak after nature,' than in the annalist,—because the
poet masses and generalizes his facts, subjecting them,
in the order in which he presents them to the mind, as
well as in the elaboration which he bestows upon them,
to the laws of his art, which has a clearer sense of fitness
and proportion than the laws of a dry chronology   But,
at any rate, the structure of an historical drama and of
an historical narrative are so essentially different, that the
offices of the poet and the historian must never be confounded   It is not to derogate from the poet to say that
he is not an historian, it will be to elevate Shakspere
when we compare his poetical truth with the truth of
history   We have no wish that he had been more exact
and literal"   Hudson, too, in noticing the anticipation
by several years of the papal instigation as the cause of
the war in which Arthur was taken prisoner, observes
that " The laws of dramatic effect often require that the
force and import of divers actual events be condensed
and massed together   To disperse the interest over
many details of action involves such a weakening of it
as poetry does not tolerate   So that the Poet was
eminently judicious in this instance of concentration
The conditions of right dramatic interest clearly re-
quired something of the kind   United, the several events

might stand in the drama, divided, they must fall.
Thus the course of the play in this matter was fitted to
secure as much of actual truth as could be told *dramati-
cally* without defeating the purpose of the telling.
Shakespeare has many happy instances of such condensa-
tion in his historical pieces"

Spirit of the Play In dealing with the general spirit of the Play, Gervinus
points out that Shakespeare has throughout "softened
for the better the traits of the principal political characters, and has much obliterated the bad His John, his
Constance, his Arthur, his Philip Augustus, even his
Elinor, are better people than they are found in history
The ground of this treatment, which is not usual to him,
is not merely that in this instance he did not draw
directly from the sources of the Chronicle, his design in
it was also that the vehicles of the political story
should be merely men of ordinary stamp, deriving their
motives for their actions from no deep lying passions,
men neither of a very noble nor of a very ignoble sort,
but, as is generally the case in the political world, men
acting from selfishness and common interest" Shakespeare has also shown a wide difference from the older
play, and Bishop Bail's pageant, in the way in which he
treats the question of opposing religion His feelings
towards the Papal power and towards Protestantism
have no bitterness on the one hand or enthusiasm on the
other, but, as Hudson points out, are "only the natural
beatings of a sound, honest English heart, resolute to
withstand alike all foreign encroachments, whether from
kings, or emperors, or popes." And while "giving full
vent to the indignation of the English at Popish rule and
intrigue, encroachment and oppression," Shakespeare,

remarks Gervinus, "did not go so far as to make a farce
of Faulconbridge's extortion from the clergy, the old
piece offered him here a scene in which merry nuns and
brothers burst forth from the opened coffers of the
'hoarding abbots,' a scene certainly very amusing to the
fresh Protestant feelings of the time, but to our poet's
impartial mind the dignity of the clergy, nay even the
contemplativeness of cloister-life, was a matter too sacred
for him to introduce it in a ridiculous form into the
seriousness of history" Another noticeable feature in
the spirit of the play is the light in which Shakespeare,
in accordance with historical truth, represents the feelings of his countrymen in John's time towards the Papal
interference   On this point Green, *History of the
English People,*[*] remarks, "In after times men believed
that England thrilled at the news [of Pandulph's inter-
vention on John's behalf] with a sense of national shame,
such as she had never felt before   'He has become the
Pope's man,' the whole country was said to have mur-
mured, 'he has forfeited the very name of king, from
a free man he has degraded himself into a serf'   But
this was the belief of a time still to come, when the
rapid growth of national feeling, which this step and its
issues did more than anything to foster, made men look
back on the scene between John and Pandulph as a
national dishonour   We see little trace of such a feeling
in the contemporary accounts of the time   All seem rather
to have regarded it as a complete settlement of the difficulties in which king and kingdom were involved   As a
political measure, its success was immediate and complete.
The French army at once broke up in impotent rage"

* Volume I, page 236

The Char
acters in the
Play

John

The more prominent characters in the play are John, Constance, the Bastard, and Pandulph   John, as has been pointed out, though cruel and weak, is not, at all events in the earlier scenes, portrayed in colours as dark as those used by the historians   Hume [*] says, " The character of King John is nothing but a complication of vices equally mean and odious, and alike ruinous to himself and destructive to his people   Cowardice, inactivity, folly, levity, licentiousness, ingratitude, treachery, tyranny, and cruelty—all these qualities appear too evidently in the several incidents of his life to give us room to suspect that the disagreeable picture has been anywise overcharged by the prejudices of the ancient historians'   According to Stubbs,[*] " John trusted no man, and no man trusted him " Macaulay [*] calls him " a trifler and a coward "   Green [*] alone has a good word to say for him, declaring that " with all his vices, he yet possessed all the quickness, vivacity, cleverness, good humour, and social charm which distinguished his House "   At the opening of the Play he is represented as blustering a good deal, though at the same time resolute,—a resolution no doubt largely due to his mother's strong will,—and showing in his invasion of France both promptitude and personal courage   He is, of course, ready enough to enter into an unholy compact with Philip, but the facility of compromise is due rather to a consciousness of the doubtful nature of the title by which he holds the crown than to any promptings of physical cowardice   Again, in his defiance of the Pope, Shakespeare gives him something like real dignity of purpose, while his retreat from

* Quoted by Canning, Hist Thoughts, etc

France is acknowledged by Philip and Lewis to have been conducted with masterly generalship It may be that a good deal of the determination he displays is only such as would be evoked in anyone so highly placed when amid the excitement of war, for no sooner is that excitement past, than he enacts the most shameless scene in the play, that in which he would tempt Hubert to the murder of Arthur, though not daring to put his temptation into anything but hints. Still, Dowden, as it seems to me, somewhat exaggerates when he says, "The show of kingly strength and dignity in which John is clothed in the earlier scenes of the play must . be recognised (although Shakspere does not obtrude the fact), as no more than a poor pretence of true regal strength and honour " On the other hand, if this be the very rigour of the law, Gervinus appears to discover in John qualities which Shakespeare would hardly acknowledge as his gift "He is not," [i e at the opening of the play] that critic remarks, "the image of a brutal tyrant, but only the type of the hard manly nature, without any of the enamel of finer feelings, and without any other motives for action than those arising from the instinct of this same inflexible nature and of personal interest Severe and earnest, an enemy to cheerfulness and merry laughter, conversant with dark thoughts, of a restless, excited temperament, he quickly rises to daring resolves, he is uncommunicative to his best advisers, laconic and reserved, he does not agree to the good design of his evil mother that he should satisfy Constance and her claims by an accommodation; it better pleases his warlike manly pride to bear arms against threatened arms, in his campaigns against

Constance and her allies the enemy himself feels that the 'hot haste,' managed with so much foresight, and the wise order in so wild a cause, are unexampled." Here it seems to me that we have a nearer approach to nobility of nature than the play warrants; and, further, that Shakespeare would not be likely to invest with such firmness of backbone a character so soon to be shown as the very impersonation of weakness. For whatever John's behaviour in the earlier scenes, from the time of his return to England we see in him nothing but meanness, the most piteous vacillation, grovelling humility, and an utter absence of anything like courage in adversity. These may be the essential qualities of his nature which stirring events have for a time obscured while brightening, or it may be that 'coward conscience,' after the manner threatened by the ghosts in Richard the Third's dream, paralyses whatever activity of mind he once possessed, whatever resolution he had in France nerved himself to display. In order to strengthen his position with his own countrymen, he on his return goes through the farce of being crowned again (in reality for the fourth time), he yields, plainly out of fear, to the demand made by Pembroke for Arthur's liberation, he hypocritically laments Arthur's death when the news of it is brought to him, is terror-stricken by the report of the Dauphin's invasion, with incredible meanness reproaches Hubert for the crime which had been his own suggestion, apologizes as unreservedly when told by Hubert that his order has not been carried out, yields up to Pandulph the crown which he had boastfully declared he would maintain "without the assistance of a mortal hand", beseeches him in the very spirit of

cringing servility to negotiate peace with the Dauphin ;
in absolute prostration of mind leaves it to the Bastard
to make preparations for defence, is seen hastening from
the battle-field to nurse his fever at Swinstead, and
finally in his death agony parades his facility of quibbling
out maudlin lamentations for himself

Constance's action in the play is so small that it is not Constanc
necessary to trace it , while for an analysis of her character I would refer all students of the play to Mr Jameson's
Characteristics of Women, with the single remark that
Hudson seems to me to be justified in thinking that the
critics are inclined to pitch too high their praise, not as
to the conception of the character, but as to the style of
execution

The Bastard, on the other hand, pervades the play The Bast
with a presence ever active   The first Act is almost all
Faulconbridge, with his good-humoured jests during the
dispute, his readily-given adherence to John, his amusing
self-complacency on being knighted, and his affectionate
patronage of his mother   In the second, his impudent
banter of the Austrian Archduke relieves the contentious
mouthings of the two kings, his is the practical suggestion that Angiers should be brought to its bearings by
the combined attack of the opposing forces, and from
him, though pretending to no more exalted a morality
than the pursuit of selfish expediency, we have a caustic
commentary on the hypocrisy and treachery of Philip
and John   It is he who is prominent in the battle of
the third Act, to him, instinctively assured of his fidelity,
John gives the important and difficult commission of
wringing from the abbots some of their hoarded wealth ,
through his agency John, on the news of the Dauphin's

invasion, hopes to bring back to their allegiance the
revolted lords from his lips we have the sternest con
demnation of Arthur's murder, a condemnation pro
nounced in spite of his well knowing that Hubert, if
guilty, had only so acted out of misguided loyalty to the
King In his outspoken honesty, he shrinks not from
freely chiding John when entreating the legate to help
him to effect peace with Lewis, in his embassy to that
prince, his fearlessness teaches him a language of defiance
which John had not dared to use, in the ensuing battle
he "alone upholds the day"; to him Hubert hastens
upon the poisoning of the King, and into his ear John
pours his last querulous accents, persuaded that from
him, if from none else, he will receive a genuine sym
pathy The Bastard's general position in the play is
thus set out by Swinburne "Considering this
play in its double aspect of tragedy and history, we
might say that the English hero becomes the central
figure of the poem as seen from the historic side, while
John remains the central figure of the poem as seen
from its tragic side; the personal interest that depends
on personal crime and retribution is concentrated on the
agony of the king, the national interest which he, though
eponymous hero of the poem, was alike inadequate as a
craven and improper as a villain to sustain and represent
in the eyes of the spectators was happily and easily
transferred to the one person of the play who could
properly express within the compass of its closing act at
once the protest against papal pretension, the defiance of
foreign invasion, and the prophetic assurance of self-
dependent life and self-sufficing strength inherent in the
nation then fresh from a fiercer trial of its quality, which

an audience of the days of Queen Elizabeth would justly
expect from the poet who undertook to set before them
in action the history of the days of King John " And,
again, speaking of him more in his personal character, he
observes, "As far beyond the reach of any but his
Maker's hand is the pattern of a perfect English warrior,
set once for all before the eyes of all ages in the figure of
the noble Bastard. The national side of Shakespeare's
genius, the heroic vein of patriotism that runs like a
thread of living fire through the world-wide range of his
omnipresent spirit, has never, to my thinking, found
vent or expression to such glorious purpose as here
Not even in Hotspur or Prince Hal has he mixed with
more god like sleight of hand all the lighter and graver
good qualities of the national character, or compounded
of them so lovable a nature as this " .

Pandulph, from his point of action, plays nearly as large a part as the Bastard From Philip, though the
most powerful of continental sovereigns, he will brook
no wavering in the fulness of obedience to be rendered
to the Church by its eldest son , though, knowing how
important to the Papacy is his support, he condescends
to put forth every subtlety of persuasion, while in the
case of the recalcitrant John he scorns all argument, and
at once pronounces his excommunication Upon Lewis
he works by appeals to his ambition, in order to use him
as a tool for the subjugation of John , and this end
attained, he has no object in further humiliating that
King, no interest in further giving his countenance to the
Dauphin's invasion That Prince may bluster for awhile
and refuse to be a puppet in the legate's hands , but his
hesitation is not of much longer duration than was his

father's, and he retires to France in abandonment of a project which he had flattered himself was so soon to be crowned with success. Pandulph is a hard, unlovely character, but he is what his profession made him, and we cannot altogether refuse a kind of admiration to the stern consistency of purpose with which, in the service of the Church, he sweeps away all obstacles, even though among his weapons unblushing casuistry and chicane are those most frequently used.

Style and subject matter

In style, at all events in the three first Acts, *King John* is closely allied with *Richard the Second*, there is the same love of conceits, of antithesis, of rhetorical language, and empty declamation. And though Shakespeare has now shaken himself free from the fetters of rhyme which so hampered him in *Richard the Second*, we have none of that rich prose which occupies so large a part in the later historical plays, and gives them a vigour that is wanting in *King John*. Furnivall points out the similarity in subject matter with *Richard the Third* "In both plays," he says, "we have cruel uncles planning their nephew's murder because the boys stand between them and the crown. In both we have distracted mothers overwhelmed with grief. In both we have prophecies of ruin and curses on the murderers, and in both the fulfilment of these. In both we have the kingdom divided against itself, and the horrors of civil war. In both we have the same lesson of the danger of division taught to the discontented English parties of Shakespeare's own day. *Richard III* is the example of the misgovernment of a cruel tyrant, *King John* of the misgovernment of a selfish coward. The temptation scene of John and Hubert repeats that of Richard and Tyrrel. The

Bastard's statement of his motive, 'Gain, be my lord,' etc, is like that of Richard the Third's about his villany" The scope, however, of *King John* is much larger than that of *Richard the Third*, for while the latter is but the history of the unscrupulous ambitions of one man and of the struggle for power between the two rival houses of York and Lancaster, *King John* deals with matters affecting more deeply the vital interests of England as a nation, and foreshadows the independence of spirit in regard to religious questions which at a later time was to be the accompaniment to political independence

THE LIFE AND DEATH OF

KING JOHN.

DRAMATIS PERSONÆ.

KING JOHN
PRINCE HENRY, son to the king
ARTHUR, Duke of Bretagne, nephew to the king
The Earl of PEMBROKE
The Earl of ESSEX
The Earl of SALISBURY
The Lord BIGOT
HUBERT DE BURGH
ROBERT FAULCONBRIDGE, son to Sir Robert Faulconbridge
PHILIP the BASTARD, his half-brother
JAMES GURNEY, servant to Lady Faulconbridge
PETER of Pomfret, a prophet

PHILIP, King of France
LEWIS, the Dauphin
LIMOGES, Duke of Austria
CARDINAL PANDULPH, the Pope's legate
MELUN, a French Lord
CHATILLON, ambassador from France to King John

QUEEN ELINOR, mother to King John
CONSTANCE, mother to Arthur
BLANCH of Spain, niece to King John.
LADY FAULCONBRIDGE

Lords, Citizens of Angiers, Sheriff, Heralds, Officers, Soldiers, Messengers, and other Attendants

SCENE   *Partly in England, and partly in France*

THE LIFE AND DEATH OF

KING JOHN.

ACT I

Scene I King John's *palace*

Enter King John, Queen Elinor, Pembroke, Essex, Salisbury, *and others, with* Chatillon

K John Now, say, Chatillon, what would France with us?
Chat Thus, after greeting, speaks the King of France
In my behaviour to the majesty,
The borrow'd majesty, of England here
  Eli A strange beginning 'borrow'd majesty!'
  K John Silence, good mother, hear the embassy
  Chat Philip of France, in right and true behalf
Of thy deceased brother Geffrey's son,
Arthur Plantagenet, lays most lawful claim
To this fair island and the territories,   10
To Ireland, Poictiers, Anjou, Touraine, Maine,
Desiring thee to lay aside the sword
Which sways usurpingly these several titles,
And put the same into young Arthur's hand,
Thy nephew and right royal sovereign
  K John What follows if we disallow of this?
  Chat The proud control of fierce and bloody war,
To enforce these rights so forcibly withheld

K. John Here have we war for war and blood for
blood,
Controlment for controlment   so answer France   20
  Chat Then take my king's defiance from my mouth,
The farthest limit of my embassy
  K. John Bear mine to him, and so depart in peace
Be thou as lightning in the eyes of France
For ere thou canst report I will be there,
The thunder of my cannon shall be heard
So hence ! Be thou the trumpet of our wrath
And sullen presage of your own decay
An honourable conduct let him have
Pembroke, look to 't   Farewell, Chatillon   30
                     [*Exeunt Chatillon and Pembroke*
  Eli What now, my son ' have I not ever said
How that ambitious Constance would not cease
Till she had kindled France and all the world,
Upon the right and party of her son ?
This might have been prevented and made whole
With very easy arguments of love,
Which now the manage of two kingdoms must
With fearful bloody issue arbitrate
  K. John Our strong possession and our right for us
  Eli Your strong possession much more than your right,
Or else it must go wrong with you and me   41
So much my conscience whispers in your ear,
Which none but heaven, and you and I shall hear

           Enter a Sheriff

  Essex My liege, here is the strangest controversy
Come from the country to be judged by you
That e'er I heard   shall I produce the men ?
  K. John Let them approach
Our abbeys and our priories shall pay
This expedition's charge

Enter ROBERT FAULCONBRIDGE, *and* PHILIP *his bastard brother*

What men are you ?

Bast Your faithful subject I, a gentleman   50
Born in Northamptonshire and eldest son,
As I suppose, to Robert Faulconbridge,
A soldier, by the honour giving hand
Of Cœur-de lion knighted in the field
  K John What art thou ?
  Rob The son and heir to that same Faulconbridge
  K John. Is that the elder, and art thou the heir ?
You came not of one mother then, it seems.
  Bast Most certain of one mother, mighty king ,
That is well known , and, as I think, one father   60
But for the certain knowledge of that truth
I put you o'er to heaven and to my mother
Of that I doubt, as all men's children may.
  Eli Out on thee, rude man ! thou dost shame thy mother
And wound her honour with this diffidence. *Constant ! `   `*
  Bast I, madam ? no, I have no reason for it ,
That is my brother's plea and none of mine ,
The which if he can prove, a' pops me out
At least from fair five hundred pound a year
Heaven guard my mother's honour and my land ?   70
  K John A good blunt fellow   Why, being younger born,
Doth he lay claim to thine inheritance ?
  Bast I know not why, except to get the land.
If old Sir Robert did beget us both
And were our father, and this son like him,
O old Sir Robert, father, on my knee
I give heaven thanks I was not like to thee !
  K John. Why what a madcap hath heaven lent us here !
  Eli He hath a trick of Cœur-de-lion's face ,
The accent of his tongue affecteth him   80
Do you not read some tokens of my son

C

In the large composition of this man?

K. John. Mine eye hath well examined his parts
And finds them perfect Richard.—Sirrah, speak,
What doth move you to claim your brother's land?

Bast. Because he hath a half-face like my father.
With half that face would he have all my land:
A half faced groat five hundred pound a year!

Rob. My gracious liege, when that my father lived,
Your brother did employ my father much,—   90
And once despatch'd him in an embassy
To Germany, there with the emperor
To treat of high affairs touching that time.
The advantage of his absence took the king
And in the mean time sojourn'd at my father's;
Where how he did prevail I shame to speak,
But truth is truth: large lengths of seas and shores
Between my father and my mother lay,
As I have heard my father speak himself,
When this same lusty gentleman was got.   100
Upon his death-bed he by will bequeath'd
His lands to me, and took it on his death
That this my mother's son was none of his;
Then, good my liege, let me have what is mine,
My father's land, as was my father's will.

K. John. Sirrah, your brother is legitimate;
Your father's wife did after wedlock bear him,
And if she did play false, the fault was hers,
Which fault lies on the hazards of all husbands
That marry wives.   110
My mother's son did get your father's heir,
Your father's heir must have your father's land.

Rob. Shall then my father's will be of no force
To dispossess that child which is not his?

Bast. Of no more force to dispossess me, sir,
Than was his will to get me, as I think.

Eli. Whether hadst thou rather be a Faulconbridge

And like thy brother, to enjoy thy land,
Or the reputed son of Cœur-de-lion,
Lord of thy presence and no land beside ?   120
   Bast. Madam, an if my brother had my shape,
And I had his, sir Robert his, like him ;
And if my legs were two such riding-rods,
My arms such eel-skins stuff'd, my face so thin
That in mine ear I durst not stick a rose
Lest men should say ' Look, where three-farthings goes ! '
And, to his shape, were heir to all this land,
Would I might never stir from off this place,
I would give it every foot to have this face ,
I would not be sir Nob in any case   130
   Eli. I like thee well   wilt thou forsake thy fortune,
Bequeath thy land to him and follow me ?
I am a soldier and now bound to France
   Bast. Brother, take you my land, I 'll take my chance
Your face hath got five hundred pound a year,
Yet sell your face for five pence and 'tis dear
Madam, I follow you unto the death
   Eli. Nay, I would have you go before me thither
   Bast. Our country manners give our betters way
   K. John. What is thy name ?   140
   Bast. Philip, my liege, so is my name begun ;
Philip, good old sir Robert's wife's eldest son
   K. John. From henceforth bear his name whose form thou
    bear'st
Kneel thou down Philip, but rise more great,
Arise Sir Richard and Plantagenet
   Bast. Brother by the mother's side, give me your hand
My father gave me honours, yours gave land
Now blessed be the hour, by night or day,
When I was got, sir Robert was away !
   Eli. The very spirit of Plantagenet !   150
I am thy grandam, Richard , call me so
   Bast. Madam, by chance but not by truth , what though ?

K. John. Go, Faulconbridge now hast thou thy desire,
A landless knight makes thee a landed squire
Come, madam, and come, Richard, we must speed
For France, for France, for it is more than need

Bast. Brother, adieu good fortune come to thee,
For thou wast got i' the way of honesty

[Exeunt all but Bastard

A foot of honour better than I was,
But many a many foot of land the worse   160
Well, now can I make any Joan a lady
'Good den, sir Richard'—'God-a-mercy, fellow!'—
And if his name be George, I'll call him Peter,
For new-made honour doth forget men's names;
'Tis too respective and too sociable
For your conversion Now your traveller,
He and his toothpick at my worship's mess,
And when my knightly stomach is sufficed,
Why then I suck my teeth and catechize
My picked man of countries 'My dear sir,   170
Thus, leaning on mine elbow, I begin,
'I shall beseech you'—that is question now,
And then comes answer like an Absey book
'O sir,' says answer, 'at your best command;
At your employment, at your service, sir'
'No, sir,' says question, 'I, sweet sir, at yours'
And so, ere answer knows what question would,
Saving in dialogue of compliment,
And talking of the Alps and Apennines,
The Pyrenean and the river Po,   180
It draws towards supper in conclusion so
But this is worshipful society
And fits the mounting spirit like myself
For he is but a bastard to the time
That doth not smack of observation,
And so am I, whether I smack or no
And not alone in habit and device,

Exterior form, outward accoutrement,
But from the inward motion to deliver
Sweet, sweet, sweet poison for the age's tooth   190
Which, though I will not practise to deceive,
Yet, to avoid deceit, I mean to learn ,
For it shall strew the footsteps of my rising
But who comes in such haste in riding-robes ?
What woman-post is this ? hath she no husband
That will take pains to blow a horn before her ?

Enter LADY FAULCONBRIDGE *and* JAMES GURNEY

O me ! it is my mother   How now, good lady !
What brings you here to court so hastily ?
   Lady F Where is that slave, thy brother ? where is he,
That holds in chase mine honour up and down ?   200
   Bast My brother Robert ? old sir Robert's son ?
Colbrand the giant, that same mighty man ?
Is it sir Robert's son that you seek so ?
   Lady F Sir Robert's son !   Ay, thou unreverend boy,
Sir Robert's son   why scorn'st thou at sir Robert ?
He is sir Robert's son, and so art thou
   Bast James Gurney, wilt thou give us leave awhile ?
   Gur Good leave, good Philip
   Bast   Philip ! sparrow   James,
There 's toys abroad   anon I 'll tell thee more. [*Exit Gurney*
Madam, I was not old sir Robert's son   210
Sir Robert might have eat his part in me
Upon Good-Friday and ne'er broke his fast
To whom am I beholding for these limbs ?
Sir Robert never holp to make this leg
   Lady F Hast thou conspired with thy brother too,
That for thine own gain shouldst defend mine honour ?
What means this scorn, thou most untoward knave ?
   Bast Knight, knight, good mother, Basilisco-like
What ! I am dubb'd ! I have it on my shoulder

But, mother, I am not sir Robert's son,   220
I have disclaim'd sir Robert and my land,
Legitimation, name and all is gone
Then, good my mother let me know my father,
Some proper man, I hope   who was it, mother?
   Lady F Hast thou denied thyself a Faulconbridge?
   Bast As faithfully as I deny the devil
   Lady F King Richard Cœur-de lion was thy father
Heaven lay not my transgression to my charge
Thou art the issue of my dear offence,
Which was so strongly urged past my defence   230
   Bast Now, by this light, were I to get again,
Madam, I would not wish a better father
Needs must you lay your heart at his dispose,
Subjected tribute to commanding love,
Against whose fury and unmatched force
The aweless lion could not wage the fight,
Nor keep his princely heart from Richard's hand
He that perforce robs lions of their hearts
May easily win a woman's.   Ay, my mother,
With all my heart I thank thee for my father!   240
Who lives and dares but say thou didst not well
When I was got, I'll send his soul to hell
Come, lady, I will show thee to my kin,
   And they shall say, when Richard me begot,
If thou hadst said him nay, it had been sin
   Who says it was, he lies, I say twas not   [*Exeunt*

ACT II

SCENE I.   *France   Before Angiers*

*Enter AUSTRIA and forces, drums, etc on one side · on the
other KING PHILIP of France and his power, LEWIS,
ARTHUR, CONSTANCE and attendants*

K Philip Before Angiers well met, brave Austria
Arthur, that great forerunner of thy blood,
Richard, that robb'd the lion of his heart
And fought the holy wars in Palestine,
By this brave duke came early to his grave
And for amends to his posterity
At our importance hither is he come,
To spread his colours, boy, in thy behalf,
And to rebuke the usurpation
Of thy unnatural uncle, English John   10
Embrace him, love him, give him welcome hither.
  Arth God shall forgive yon Cœnr-de-lion's death
The rather that you give his offspring life,
Shadowing their right under your wings of war
I give you welcome with a powerless hand,
But with a heart full of unstained love
Welcome before the gates of Angiers, duke
  K Phi A noble boy ! Who would not do thee right ?
  Aust Upon thy cheek lay I this zealous kiss,
As seal to this indenture of my love,   20
That to my home I will no more return,
Till Angiers and the right thou hast in France,
Together with that pale, that white-faced shore,
Whose foot spurns back the ocean's roaring tides
And coops from other lands her islanders,
Even till that England, hedged in with the main,
That water-walled bulwark, still secure
And confident from foreign purposes,

Even till that utmost corner of the west
Salute thee for her king: till then, fair boy,   39
Will I not think of home, but follow arms.

Const O take his mother's thanks, a widow's thanks,
Till your strong hand shall help to give him strength
To make a more requital to your love!

Aus The peace of heaven is theirs that lift their swords
In such a just and charitable war.

K Phi Well then to work our cannon shall be bent
Against the brows of this resisting town.
Call for our chiefest men of discipline
To cull the plots of best advantages: 40
We'll lay before this town our royal bones,
Wade to the market place in Frenchmen's blood,
But we will make it subject to this boy.

Const Stay for an answer to your embassy,
Lest unadvised you stain your swords with blood
My Lord Chatillon may from England bring
That right in peace which here we urge in war
And then we shall repent each drop of blood
That hot rash haste so indirectly shed

Enter CHATILLON

K Phi A wonder, lady! lo, upon thy wish   50
Our messenger Chatillon is arrived!
What England says, say briefly, gentle lord,
We coldly pause for thee, Chatillon, speak.

Chat Then turn your forces from this paltry siege
And stir them up against a mightier task
England, impatient of your just demands,
Hath put himself in arms: the adverse winds
Whose leisure I have stay'd, have given him time
To land his legions all as soon as I,
His marches are expedient to this town,   60
His forces strong, his soldiers confident
With him along is come the mother-queen,

An Ate, stirring him to blood and strife
With her her niece, the Lady Blanch of Spain ;
With them a bastard of the king's deceased ,
And all the unsettled humours of the land,
Rash, inconsiderate, fiery voluntaries,
With ladies' faces and fierce dragons' spleens,
Have sold their fortunes at their native homes,
Bearing their birthrights proudly on their backs,   70
To make a hazard of new fortunes here
In brief, a braver choice of dauntless spirits
Than now the English bottoms have waft o'er
Did never float upon the swelling tide,
To do offence and scath in Christendom   [Drum beats
The interruption of their churlish drums
Cuts off more circumstance   they are at hand,
To parley or to fight , therefore prepare
　K Phi How much unlook'd for is this expedition !
　Aust By how much unexpected, by so much   80
We must awaken endeavour for defence ;
For courage mounteth with occasion
Let them be welcome then , we are prepared

　Enter KING JOHN, ELINOR, BLANCH, *the* Bastard, Lords,
　　　and forces

　K John Peace be to France, if France in peace permit
Our just and lineal entrance to our own ,
If not, bleed France, and peace ascend to heaven,
Whiles we, God's wrathful agent, do correct
Their proud contempt that beats His peace to heaven
　K Phi Peace be to England, if that war return
From France to England, there to live in peace   90
England we love , and for that England's sake
With burden of our armour here we sweat
This toil of ours should be a work of thine ,
But thou from loving England art so far,
That thou has under-wrought his lawful king,

Cut off the sequence of posterity,
Out-faced infant state and done a rape
Upon the maiden virtue of the crown.
Look here upon thy brother Geffrey's face .
These eyes, these brows, were moulded out of his :   100
This little abstract doth contain that large
Which died in Geffrey, and the hand of time
Shall draw this brief into as large a volume
That Geffrey was thy elder brother born,
And this his son , England was Geffrey's right
And this is Geffrey's in the name of God
How comes it then that thou art call'd a king,
When living blood doth in these temples beat
Which owe the crown that thou o'ermasterest ?

   K John From whom hast thou this great commission,
     France,   110
To draw my answer from thy articles?

   K Phi From that supernal judge, that stirs good thoughts
In any breast of strong authority,
To look into the blots and stains of right
That judge hath made me guardian to this boy
Under whose warrant I impeach thy wrong
And by whose help I mean to chastise it.

   K John Alack, thou dost usurp authority
   K Phi Excuse , it is to beat usurping down
   Eli Who is it thou dost call usurper, France?   120
   Const Let me make answer ; thy usurping son
   Eli Out, insolent ' thy bastard shall be king,
That thou mayst be a queen, and check the world '

   Const My bed was ever to thy son as true
As thine was to thy husband , and this boy
Liker in feature to his father Geffrey
Than thou and John in manners , being as like
As rain to water, or devil to his dam
My boy a bastard ' By my soul, I think
His father never was so true begot   130

It cannot be, an if thou wert his mother

   Eli There 's a good mother, boy, that blots thy father

   Const There 's a good grandam, boy, that would blot thee

   Aust Peace '

   Bast   Hear the cher

   Aust   What the devil art thou ?

   Bast One that will play the devil, sir, with you,

An a' may catch your hide and you alone

You are the hare of whom the proverb goes, *t* -

Whose valour plucks dead lions by the beard

I 'll smoke your skin-coat, an I catch you right ,

Sirrah, look to 't , i' faith, I will, i' faith   140

   Blanch O, well did he become that lion's robe

That did disrobe the lion of that robe '

   Bast It lies as sightly on the back of him

As great Alcides' shows upon an ass

But, ass, I 'll take that burthen from your back,

Or lay on that shall make your shoulders crack

   Aust What cracker is this same that deafs our ears

With this abundance of superfluous breath ?

King,—Lewis, determine what we shall do straight

   K Phi Women and fools, break off your conference   150

King John, this is the very sum of all ,

England and Ireland, Anjou, Touraine, Maine,

In right of Arthur do I claim of thee

Wilt thou resign them and lay down thy arms?

   K John My life as soon , I do defy thee, France

Arthur of Bretagne, yield thee to my hand ,

And out of my dear love I 'll give thee more

Than e'er the coward hand of France can win

Submit thee, boy

   Eli   Come to thy grandam, child

   Const Do, child, go to it grandam, child ,   160

Give grandam kingdom, and it grandam will

Give it a plum, a cherry, and a fig

There 's a good grandam

Arth   Good my mother, peace!
I would that I were low laid in my grave
I am not worth this coil that 's made for me

    Eli His mother shames him so, poor boy, he weeps

    Const Now shame upon you, whether she does or no!
His grandam's wrongs, and not his mother's shames,
Draws those heaven moving pearls from his poor eyes,
Which heaven shall take in nature of a fee,   170
As, with these crystal beads heaven shall be bribed
To do him justice and revenge on you

    Eli Thou monstrous slanderer of heaven and earth!

    Const Thou monstrous injurer of heaven and earth!
Call not me slanderer, thou and thine usurp
The dominations, royalties and rights
Of this oppressed boy this is thy eld'st son's son,
Infortunate in nothing but in thee
Thy sins are visited in this poor child;
The canon of the law is laid on him,   180
Being but the second generation
Removed from thy sin conceiving womb

    K John Bedlam, have done

    Const   I have but this to say,
That he 's not only plagued for her sin
But God has made her sin and her the plague
On this removed issue, plagued for her
And with her plague, her sin his injury,
Her injury the beadle to her sin,
All punish'd in the person of this child,
And all for her, a plague upon her!   190

    Eli Thou unadvised scold, I can produce
A will that bars the title of thy son

    Const Ay, who doubts that? a will! a wicked will,
A woman's will, a canker'd grandam's will!

    K Ph Peace, lady! pause, or be more temperate
It ill beseems this presence to cry aim!
To these ill-tuned repetitions

Some trumpet summon hither to the walls
These men of Angiers   let us hear them speak
Whose title they admit, Arthur's or John's   200

Trumpet sounds.   Enter certain Citizens upon the walls

First Cit Who is it that hath warn'd us to the walls ?
K Phi. Tis France, for England
K John   England, for itself
You men of Angiers, and my loving subjects,—
   K Phi You loving men of Angiers, Arthur's subjects,
Our trumpet call'd you to this gentle parle—
   K. John For our advantage, therefore hear us first
These flags of France, that are advanced here
Before the eye and prospect of your town,
Have hither march'd to your endamagement
The cannons have their bowels full of wrath,   210
And ready mounted are they to spit forth
Their iron indignation 'gainst your walls .
All preparation for a bloody siege
And merciless proceeding by these French
Confronts your city's eyes, your winking gates ;
And but for our approach those sleeping stones,
That as a waist doth girdle you about,
By the compulsion of their ordinance
By this time from their fixed beds of lime
Had been dishabited, and wide havoc made   220
For bloody power to rush upon your peace
But on the sight of us your lawful king,
Who painfully with much expedient march
Have brought a countercheck before your gates,
To save unscratch'd your city's threatened cheeks,
Behold, the French amazed vouchsafe a parle ,
And now, instead of bullets wrapp'd in fire,
To make a shaking fever in your walls,
They shoot but calm words folded up in smoke,
To make a faithless error in your ears   230

Which trust accordingly, kind citizens,
And let us in, your king, whose labour'd spirits,
Forwearied in this action of swift speed,
Crave harbourage within your city walls.

K. Phi. When I have said, make answer to us both.
Lo, in this right hand, whose protection
Is most divinely vow'd upon the right
Of him it holds, stands young Plantagenet,
Son to the elder brother of this man,
And king o'er him and all that he enjoys   240
For this down-trodden equity, we tread
In warlike march these greens before your town,
Being no further enemy to you
Than the constraint of hospitable zeal
In the relief of this oppressed child
Religiously provokes. Be pleased then
To pay that duty which you truly owe
To him that owes it, namely this young prince
And then our arms, like to a muzzled bear,
Save in aspect, hath all offence seal'd up ,   250
Our cannons' malice vainly shall be spent
Against the invulnerable clouds of heaven ,
And with a blessed and unvex'd retire,
With unhack'd swords and helmets all unbruised,
We will bear home that lusty blood again
Which here we came to spout against your town,
And leave your children, wives and you in peace
But if you fondly pass our proffer'd offer,
'Tis not the roundure of your old-faced walls
Can hide you from our messengers of war,   260
Though all these English and their discipline
Were harbour'd in their rude circumference.
Then tell us, shall your city call us lord,
In that behalf which we have challenged it ?
Or shall we give the signal to our rage
And stalk in blood to our possession ?

First Cit In brief, we are the king of England's subjects
For him, and in his right, we hold this town

   K John Acknowledge then the king, and let me in

   First Cit That can we not , but he that proves the king,
To him will we prove loyal   till that time   271
Have we ramm'd up our gates against the world

   K John Doth not the crown of England prove the
      king ?
And if not that I bring you witnesses,
Twice fifteen thousand hearts of England's breed,—

   Bast Bastards, and else

   K John To verify our title with their lives

   K Phi. As many and as well-born bloods as those,—

   Bast Some bastards too

   K Phi Stand in his face to contradict his claim   280

   First Cit Till you compound whose right is worthiest,
We for the worthiest hold the right from both

   K John Then God forgive the sin of all those souls
That to their everlasting residence,
Before the dew of evening fall, shall fleet,
In dreadful trial of our kingdom's king !

   K Phi Amen, amen !   Mount, chevaliers ! to arms !

   Bast Saint George, that swinged the dragon, and e'er
      since
Sits on his horse back at mine hostess' door,
Teach us some fence ! [*To Aust*] Sirrah, were I at home,
At your den, sirrah, with your lioness,   291
I would set an ox-head to your lion's hide,
And make a monster of you

   Aust   Peace ! no more

   Bast O, tremble, for you hear the lion roar

   K John Up higher to the plain , where we 'll set forth
In best appointment all our regiments

   Bast Speed then, to take advantage of the field

   K Phi It shall be so , and at the other hill
Command the rest to stand   God and our right   [*Exeunt*

Here after excursions, enter the Herald of France, with
trumpets, to the gate

F Her Young men of Angiers, open wide your gates,
And let young Arthur, Duke of Bretagne, in.   301
Who by the hand of France this day hath made
Much work for tears in many an English mother,
Whose sons lie scatter'd on the bleeding ground
Many a widow's husband grovelling lies,
Coldly embracing the discolour'd earth,
And victory, with little loss, doth play
Upon the dancing banners of the French,
Who are at hand, triumphantly display'd,
To enter conquerors and to proclaim   310
Arthur of Bretagne England's king and yours

Enter English Herald, with trumpet

E Her Rejoice, you men of Angiers, ring your bells,
King John, your king and England's, doth approach,
Commander of this hot malicious day .
Their armours, that march'd hence so silver bright,
Hither return all gilt with Frenchmen's blood ,
There stuck no plume in any English crest
That is removed by a staff of France ,
Our colours do return in those same hands
That did display them when we first march'd forth ,   320
And, like a jolly troop of huntsmen, come
Our lusty English, all with purpled hands,
Dyed in the dying slaughter of their foes
Open your gates and give the victors way

First Cit Heralds, from off our towers we might behold,
From first to last, the onset and retire
Of both your armies , whose equality
By our best eyes cannot be censured
Blood hath bought blood and blows have answer'd blows ,

Strength match'd with strength, and power confronted
    power.   330
Both are alike, and both alike we like.
One must prove greatest: while they weigh so even,
We hold our town for neither, yet for both.

Re-enter the two Kings with their powers, severally.

K. John. France, hast thou yet more blood to cast away?
Say, shall the current of our right run on?
Whose passage, vex'd with thy impediment,
Shall leave his native channel and o'erswell
With course disturb'd even thy confining shores,
Unless thou let his silver water keep
A peaceful progress to the ocean.   340

K. Phi. England, thou hast not saved one drop of blood,
In this hot trial, more than we of France;
Rather, lost more. And by this hand I swear,
That sways the earth this climate overlooks,
Before we will lay down our just-borne arms,
We'll put thee down, 'gainst whom these arms we bear,
Or add a royal number to the dead,
Gracing the scroll that tells of this war's loss
With slaughter coupled to the names of kings.

Bast. Ha, majesty! how high thy glory towers,   350
When the rich blood of kings is set on fire!
O, now doth Death line his dead chaps with steel;
The swords of soldiers are his teeth, his fangs;
And now he feasts, mousing the flesh of men,
In undetermin'd differences of kings.
Why stand these royal fronts amazed thus?
Cry 'havoc!' kings; back to the stained field,
You equal potents, fiery-kindled spirits!
Then let confusion of one part confirm
The other's peace; till then, blows, blood and death!   360

K. John. Whose party do the townsmen yet admit?
K. Phi. Speak, citizens, for England; who's your king?

First Cit The king of England, when we know the king
K Phi Know him in us, that here hold up his right
K John In us that are our own great deputy,
And bear possession of our person here,
Lord of our presence, Angiers, and of you
  First Cit A greater power than we denies all this,
And till it be undoubted, we do lock   370
Our former scruple in our strong-barr'd gates,
King'd of our fears, until our fears, resolved,
Be by some certain king purged and deposed
  Bast By heaven, these scroyles of Angiers flout you,
      kings,
And stand securely on their battlements,
As in a theatre, whence they gape and point
At your industrious scenes and acts of death
Your royal presences be ruled by me
Do like the mutines of Jerusalem,
Be friends awhile and both conjointly bend
Your sharpest deeds of malice on this town   380
By east and west let France and England mount
Their battering cannon charged to the mouths,
Till their soul-fearing clamours have brawl'd down
The flinty ribs of this contemptuous city
I 'ld play incessantly upon these jades,
Even till unfenced desolation
Leave them as naked as the vulgar air
That done, dissever your united strengths,
And part your mingled colours once again,
Turn face to face and bloody point to point,   390
Then, in a moment, Fortune shall cull forth
Out of one side her happy minion,
To whom in favour she shall give the day,
And kiss him with a glorious victory
How like you this wild counsel, mighty states?
Smacks it not something of the policy ?
  K John Now, by the sky that hangs above our heads,

I like it well   France, shall we knit our powers
And lay this Angiers even with the ground ,
Then after fight who shall be king of it ?   400
    Bast An if thou has the mettle of a king,
Being wrong'd as we are by this peevish town,
Turn thou the mouth of thy artillery,
As we will ours, against these saucy walls ,
And when that we have dash'd them to the ground,
Why then defy each other, and pell-mell
Make work upon ourselves, for heaven or hell
    K Phi Let it be so   Say, where will you assault ?
    K John We from the west will send destruction
Into this city's bosom   410
    Aust I from the north
    K Phi.   Our thunder from the south
Shall rain their drift of bullets on this town
    Bast. O prudent discipline '   From north to south
Austria and France shoot in each other's mouth
I'll stir them to it   Come, away, away !
    First Cit Hear us, great kings   vouchsafe awhile to stay,
And I shall show you peace and fair-faced league ,
Win you this city without stroke or wound ,
Rescue those breathing lives to die in beds,
That here come sacrifices for the field   420
Persever not, but hear me, mighty kings
    K John. Speak on with favour , we are bent to hear
    First Cit That daughter there of Spain, the Lady Blanch,
Is niece to England   look upon the years
Of Lewis the Dauphin and that lovely maid
If lusty love should go in quest of beauty,
Where should he find it fairer than in Blanch ?
If zealous love should go in search of virtue,
Where should he find it purer than in Blanch ?
If love ambitious sought a match of birth,   430
Whose veins bound richer blood than Lady Blanch ?
Such as she is, in beauty, virtue, birth,

Is the young Dauphin every way complete
If not complete, O, say he is not she;
And she again wants nothing, to name want,
If want it be not that she is not he:
He is the half part of a blessed man,
Left to be finished by such as she;
And she a fair divided excellence,
Whose fulness of perfection lies in him   410
O, two such silver currents, when they join,
Do glorify the banks that bound them in.
And two such shores to two such streams made one,
Two such controlling bounds shall you be, kings,
To these two princes, if you marry them
This union shall do more than battery can
To our fast-closed gates, for at this match,
With swifter spleen than powder can enforce,
The mouth of passage shall we fling wide ope,
And give you entrance   but without this match,   450
The sea enraged is not half so deaf,
Lions more confident, mountains and rocks
More free from motion, no, not Death himself
In mortal fury half so peremptory,
As we to keep this city

    Bast   Here's a stay
That shakes the rotten carcass of old Death
Out of his rags!   Here s a large mouth, indeed,
That spits forth death and mountains, rocks and seas,
Talks as familiarly of roaring lions
As maids of thirteen do of puppy-dogs!   460
What cannoneer begot this lusty blood?
He speaks plain cannon fire, and smoke and bounce,
He gives the bastinado with his tongue
Our ears are cudgell'd, not a word of his
But buffets better than a fist of France
Zounds! I was never so bethump'd with words
Since I first call'd my brother's father dad

Eli Son, list to this conjunction, make this match ,
Give with our niece a dowry large enough
For by this knot thou shalt so surely tie   470
Thy now unsured assurance to the crown,
That you green boy shall have no sun to ripe
The bloom that promiseth a mighty fruit
I see a yielding in the looks of France ,
Mark, how they whisper   urge them while their souls
Are capable of this ambition,
Lest zeal, now melted by the windy breath
Of soft petitions, pity and remorse,
Cool and congeal again to what it was
   First Cit Why answer not the double majesties   480
This friendly treaty of our threaten'd town ?
   K Phi Speak England first, that hath been forward
      first
To speak unto this city   what say you ?
   K John. If that the Dauphin there, thy princely son,
Can in this book of beauty read ' I love,'
Her dowry shall weigh equal with a queen
For Anjou and fair Touraine, Maine, Poictiers,
And all that we upon this side the sea,
Except this city now by us besieged,
Find liable to our crown and dignity,   490
Shall gild her bridal bed and make her rich
In titles, honours and promotions,
As she in beauty, education, blood,
Holds hand with any princess of the world
   K Phi What say'st thou, boy ? look in the lady's face
   Lew I do, my lord ; and in her eye I find
A wonder, or a wondrous miracle,
The shadow of myself form'd in her eye ,
Which, being but the shadow of your son,
Becomes a sun and makes your son a shadow .   500
I do protest I never loved myself
Till now infixed I beheld myself

Drawn in the flattering table of her eye

                        [Whispers with Blanch

Bast Drawn in the flattering table of her eye!

  Hang'd in the frowning wrinkle of her brow!

And quarter'd in her heart he doth espy

  Himself love's traitor this is pity now,

That, hang'd and drawn and quarter'd, there should be

In such a love so vile a lout as he

    Blanch My uncle's will in this respect is mine: 510

If he see aught in you that makes him like,

That any thing he sees, which moves his liking,

I can with ease translate it to my will,

Or if you will, to speak more properly,

I will enforce it easily to my love

Further I will not flatter you, my lord,

That all I see in you is worthy love,

Than this, that nothing do I see in you,

Though churlish thoughts themselves should be your
        judge,

That I can find should merit any hate   520

    K John What say these young ones? What say you, my
      niece?

    Blanch That she is bound in honour still to do

What you in wisdom still vouchsafe to say

    K John Speak then, prince Dauphin, can you love this
      lady?

    Lew Nay, ask me if I can refrain from love,

For I do love her most unfeignedly

    K John Then do I give Volquessen, Touraine, Maine,

Poictiers and Anjou, these five provinces,

With her to thee, and this addition more,

Full thirty thousand marks of English coin   530

Philip of France, if thou be pleased withal,

Command thy son and daughter to join hands

    K Phi It likes us well, young princes, close your
      hands

Aust And your lips too , for I am well assured
That I did so when I was first assured   ⌐łſ⌐ ˙

K Phi Now, citizens of Angiers, ope your gates,
Let in that amity which you have made ,
For at St Mary's chapel presently
The rites of marriage shall be solemnized
Is not the Lady Constance in this troop?   540
I know she is not, for this match made up
Her presence would have interrupted much
Where is she and her son ? tell me, who knows

Lew She is sad and passionate at your highness' tent

K Phi And, by my faith, this league that we have made
Will give her sadness very little cure
Brother of England, how may we content
This widow lady ?   In her right we came ,
Which we, God knows, have turn'd another way,
To our own vantage

K John   We will heal up all ,   550
For we 'll create young Arthur Duke of Bretagne
And Earl of Richmond , and this rich fair town
We make him lord of   Call the Lady Constance ,
Some speedy messenger bid her repair
To our solemnity   I trust we shall,
If not fill up the measure of her will,
Yet in some measure satisfy her so
That we shall stop her exclamation
Go we, as well as haste will suffer us,
To this unlook'd for, unprepared pomp   560
                        [*Exeunt all but the Bastard*

Bast Mad world ! mad kings ! mad composition !
John, to stop Arthur's title in the whole,
Hath willingly departed with a part,
And France, whose armour conscience buckled on,
Whom zeal and charity brought to the field
As God's own soldier, rounded in the ear
With that same purpose-changer, that sly devil,

That broker, that still breaks the pate of faith,
That daily break vow, he that wins of all,
Of kings, of beggars, old men, young men, maids,   570
Who, having no external thing to love
But the word 'maid,' cheats the poor maid of that
That smooth fac'd gentleman, tickling Commodity,
Commodity, the bias of the world,
The world, who of itself is poised well,
Made to run even upon even ground,
Till this advantage, this vile-drawing bias,
This sway of motion, this Commodity,
Makes it take head from all indifferency,
From all direction, purpose, course, intent   580
And this same bias, this Commodity,
This bawd, this broker, this all changing word,
Clapp'd on the outward eye of fickle France,
Hath drawn him from his own determined aid,
From a resolved and honourable war,
To a most base and vile concluded peace.
And why rail I on this Commodity ?
But for because he hath not woo'd me yet.
Not that I have the power to clutch my hand,
When his fair angels would salute my palm ;   590
But for my hand, as unattempted yet,
Like a poor beggar, raileth on the rich
Well, whiles I am a beggar, I will rail
And say there is no sin but to be rich ;
And being rich, my virtue then shall be
To say there is no vice but beggary
Since kings break faith upon commodity,
Gain, be my lord, for I will worship thee   [Exit

ACT III

SCENE I   *The French King's pavilion*

Enter CONSTANCE, ARTHUR, *and* SALISBURY

Const. Gone to be married ! gone to swear a peace !
False blood to false blood join'd ! gone to be friends !
Shall Lewis have Blanch, and Blanch those provinces ?
It is not so , thou hast mispoke, misheard ,
Be well advised, tell o'er thy tale again
It cannot be , thou dost but say 'tis so
I trust I may not trust thee , for thy word
Is but the vain breath of a common man
Believe me, I do not believe thee, man ,
I have a king's oath to the contrary   10
Thou shalt be punish'd for thus frighting me,
For I am sick and capable of fears,
Oppress'd with wrongs and therefore full of fears,
A widow, husbandless, subject to fears,
A woman, naturally born to fears ;
And though thou now confess thou didst but jest,
With my vex'd spirits I cannot take a truce,
But they will quake and tremble all this day
What dost thou mean by shaking of thy head ?
Why dost thou look so sadly on my son ?   20
What means that hand upon that breast of thine ?
Why holds thine eye that lamentable rheum,
Like a proud river peering o'er his bounds ?
Be these sad signs confirmers of thy words ?
Then speak again ; not all thy former tale,
But this one word, whether thy tale be true
    Sal As true as I believe you think them false
That give you cause to prove my saying true
    Const O, if thou teach me to believe this sorrow,
Teach thou this sorrow how to make me die,   30

And let belief and life encounter so
As doth the fury of two desperate men
Which in the very meeting fall and die
Lewis marry Blanch! O boy, then where art thou?
France friend with England, what becomes of me?
Fellow, be gone   I cannot brook thy sight
This news hath made thee a most ugly man

    Sal   What other harm have I, good lady, done,
But spoke the harm that is by others done?

    Const Which harm within itself so heinous is   40
As it makes harmful all that speak of it.

    Arth   I do beseech you, madam, be content.

    Const If thou, that bid'st me be content, wert grim,
Ugly and slanderous to thy mother's womb,
Full of unpleasing blots and sightless stains,
Lame, foolish, crooked swart, prodigious,
Patch'd with foul moles and eye offending marks,
I would not care, I then would be content,
For then I should not love thee, no, nor thou
Become thy great birth nor deserve a crown   50
But thou art fair, and at thy birth, dear boy,
Nature and Fortune join'd to make thee great
Of Nature's gifts thou mayst with lilies boast
And with the half-blown rose   But Fortune, O,
She is corrupted, changed and won from thee,
She adulterates hourly with thine uncle John,
And with her golden hand hath pluck'd on France
To tread down fair respect of sovereignty,
And made his majesty the bawd to theirs.
France is a bawd to Fortune and King John,   60
That strumpet Fortune, that usurping John
Tell me, thou fellow, is not France forsworn?
Envenom him with words, or get thee gone
And leave those woes alone which I alone
Am bound to under-bear
   Sal.   Pardon me, madam,

I may not go without you to the kings
    Const Thou may'st, thou shalt, I will not go with thee
I will instruct my sorrows to be proud,
For grief is proud and makes his owner stout.
To me and to the state of my great grief   70
Let kings assemble, for my grief's so great
That no supporter but the huge firm earth
Can hold it up   here I and sorrows sit,
Here is my throne, bid kings come bow to it
                                  [Seats herself on the ground

Enter KING JOHN, KING PHILIP, LEWIS, BLANCH, ELINOR, *the*
      BASTARD, AUSTRIA, *and* Attendants

    K Phi 'Tis true, fair daughter, and this blessed day
Ever in France shall be kept festival ·
To solemnize this day the glorious sun
Stays in his course and plays the alchemist,
Turning with splendour of his precious eye
The meagre cloddy earth to glittering gold   80
The yearly course that brings this day about
Shall never see it but a holiday
    Const A wicked day, and not a holy day !   *[Rising*
What hath this day deserved ? what hath it done,
That it in golden letters should be set
Among the high tides in the calendar ?
Nay, rather turn this day out of the week,
This day of shame, oppression, perjury
Or, if it must stand still, let wives with child
Pray that their burthens may not fall this day,   90
Lest that their hopes prodigiously be cross'd
But on this day let seamen fear no wreck,
No bargains break that are not this day made
This day, all things begun come to ill end,
Yea, faith itself to hollow falsehood change !
    K Phi By heaven, lady, you shall have no cause
To curse the fair proceedings of this day .

Have I not pawn'd to you my majesty?

Const You have beguiled me with a counterfeit
Resembling majesty, which, being touch'd and tried,　　100
Proves valueless: you are forsworn, forsworn;
You came in arms to spill mine enemies' blood,
But now in arms you strengthen it with yours:
The grappling vigour and rough frown of war
Is cold in amity and painted peace,
And our oppression hath made up this league.
Arm, arm, you heavens, against these perjured kings!
A widow cries, be husband to me, heavens!
Let not the hours of this ungodly day
Wear out the day in peace, but, ere sunset,　　　110
Set armed discord 'twixt these perjured kings!
Hear me, O, hear me!

Aust　　　　　　Lady Constance, peace!

Const War! war! no peace! peace is to me a war.
O Lymoges! O Austria! thou dost shame
That bloody spoil: thou slave, thou wretch, thou coward!
Thou little valiant, great in villany!
Thou ever strong upon the stronger side!
Thou Fortune's champion that dost never fight
But when her humorous ladyship is by
To teach thee safety! thou art perjured too,　　　120
And soothest up greatness. What a fool art thou,
A ramping fool, to brag and stamp and swear
Upon my party! Thou cold-blooded slave,
Hast thou not spoke like thunder on my side,
Been sworn my soldier, bidding me depend
Upon thy stars, thy fortune and thy strength,
And dost thou now fall over to my foes?
Thou wear a lion's hide! doff it for shame,
And hang a calf's-skin on those recreant limbs.

Aust O, that a man should speak those words to me!　130

Bast And hang a calf's-skin on those recreant limbs.

Aust Thou darest not say so, villain, for thy life.

Bast And hang a calf's-skin on those recreant limbs
K John We like not this, thou dost forget thyself

Enter PANDULPH.

K Phi Here comes the holy legate of the pope.
Pand Hail, you anointed deputies of heaven !
To thee, King John, my holy errand is
I Pandulph, of fair Milan cardinal,
And from Pope Innocent the legate here,
Do in his name religiously demand   140
Why thou against the church, our holy mother,
So wilfully dost spurn, and force perforce
Keep Stephen Langton, chosen archbishop
Of Canterbury, from that holy see ?
This, in our foresaid holy father's name,
Pope Innocent, I do demand of thee
  K John What earthly name to interrogatories
Can task the free breath of a sacred king ?
Thou canst not, cardinal, devise a name
So slight, unworthy and ridiculous,   150
To charge me to an answer, as the pope
Tell him this tale, and from the mouth of England
Add thus much more, that no Italian priest
Shall tithe or toll in our dominions,
But as we, under heaven, are supreme head,
So under Him that great supremacy,
Where we do reign, we will alone uphold,
Without the assistance of a mortal hand
So tell the pope, all reverence set apart
To him and his usurp'd authority   160
  K Phi Brother of England, you blaspheme in this
  K John Though you and all the kings of Christendom
Are led so grossly by this meddling priest,
Dreading the curse that money may buy out,
And by the merit of vile gold, dross, dust,
Purchase corrupted pardon of a man,

Who in that sale sells pardon from himself.
Though you and all the rest so grossly led
This juggling witchcraft with revenue cherish,
Yet I alone, alone do me oppose   170
Against the pope and count his friends my foes.
   Pand Then, by the lawful power that I have,
Thou shalt stand cursed and excommunicate
And blessed shall he be that doth revolt
From his allegiance to an heretic ,
And meritorious shall that hand be call'd,
Canonized and worshipp'd as a saint,
That takes away by any secret course
Thy hateful life.
   Const   O, lawful let it be
That I have room with Rome to curse awhile !   180
Good father cardinal, cry thou amen
To my keen curses , for without my wrong
There is no tongue hath power to curse him right.
   Pand There 's law and warrant, lady, for my curse.
   Const And for mine too   when law can do no right.
Let it be lawful that law bar no wrong
Law cannot give my child his kingdom here,
For he that holds his kingdom holds the law ,
Therefore, since law itself is perfect wrong,
How can the law forbid my tongue to curse?   190
   Pand Philip of France, on peril of a curse,
Let go the hand of that arch-heretic ,
And raise the power of France upon his head,
Unless he do submit himself to Rome
   Eli Look'st thou pale, France? do not let go thy hand
   Const Look to that, devil , lest that France repent,
And by disjoining hands, hell lose a soul
   Aust King Philip, listen to the cardinal
   Bast And hang a calf's-skin on his recreant limbs
   Aust Well, ruffian, I must pocket up these wrongs,   200
Because—

Bast Your breeches best may carry them

K John Philip, what say'st thou to the cardinal?

Const What should he say, but as the cardinal?

Lew Bethink you, father , for the difference·
Is purchase of a heavy curse from Rome,
Or the light loss of England for a friend
Forgo the easier

Blanch   That's the curse of Rome

Const O Lewis, stand fast ! the devil tempts thee here
In likeness of a new-uptrimmed bride

Blanch The Lady Constance speaks not from her faith, 210
But from her need

Const   O, if thou grant my need,
Which only lives but by the death of faith,
That need must needs infer this principle,
That faith would live again by death of need
O then, tread down my need, and faith mounts up ,
Keep my need up, and faith is trodden down !

K John The king is moved, and answers not to this

Const O, be removed from him, and answer well !

Aust Do so, King Philip , hang no more in doubt

Bast Hang nothing but a calf's-skin, most sweet lout 220

K Phi I am perplex'd, and know not what to say

Pand What canst thou say but will perplex thee more,
If thou stand excommunicate and cursed ?

K Phi Good reverend father, make my person yours,
And tell me how you would bestow yourself
This royal hand and mine are newly knit,
And the conjunction of our inward souls
Married in league, coupled and link'd together
With all religious strength of sacred vows ,
The latest breath that gave the sound of words   230
Was deep-sworn faith, peace, amity, true love
Between our kingdoms and our royal selves,
And even before this truce, but new before,
No longer than we well could wash our hands

To clap this royal bargain up of peace,
Heaven knows, they were besmear'd and over-stain'd
With slaughter's pencil, where revenge did paint
The fearful difference of incensed kings.
And shall these hands, so lately purged of blood,   240
So newly join'd in love, so strong in both
Unyoke this seizure and this kind regreet?
Play fast and loose with faith? so jest with heaven,
Make such unconstant children of ourselves,
As now again to snatch our palm from palm,
Unswear faith sworn, and on the marriage-bed
Of smiling peace to march a bloody host,
And make a riot on the gentle brow
Of true sincerity? O, holy sir,
My reverend father, let it not be so!   250
Out of your grace, devise, ordain, impose
Some gentle order, and then we shall be blest
To do your pleasure and continue friends.
    Pand. All form is formless, order orderless,
Save what is opposite to England's love
Therefore to arms! be champion of our church,
Or let the church, our mother, breathe her curse,
A mother's curse, on her revolting son.
France, thou mayst hold a serpent by the tongue,
A chafed lion by the mortal paw,
A fasting tiger safer by the tooth,   260
Than keep in peace that hand which thou dost hold
    K. Phi. I may disjoin my hand, but not my faith.
    Pand. So makest thou faith an enemy to faith.
And like a civil war set'st oath to oath,
Thy tongue against thy tongue O, let thy vow
First made to heaven, first be to heaven perform'd,
That is, to be the champion of our church!
What since thou sworest is sworn against thyself
And may not be performed by thyself,
For that which thou hast sworn to do amiss   270

Is not amiss when it is truly done,
And being not done, where doing tends to ill,
The truth is then most done not doing it
The better act of purposes mistook
Is to mistake again , though indirect,
Yet indirection thereby grows direct,
And falsehood falsehood-cures, as fire cools fire
Within the scorched veins of one new-burn'd
It is religion that doth make vows kept ,
But thou hast sworn against religion,   280
By what thou swear'st against the thing thou swear'st,
And mak'st an oath the surety for thy truth
Against an oath (the truth thou art unsure
To swear, swears only not to be forsworn ,
Else what a mockery should it be to swear !
But thou dost swear only to be forsworn ,)
And most forsworn, to keep what thou dost swear
Therefore thy later vows against thy first
Is in thyself rebellion to thyself ,
And better conquest never canst thou make   290
Than arm thy constant and thy nobler parts
Against these giddy loose suggestions
Upon which better part our prayers come in,
If thou vouchsafe them   But if not, then know
The peril of our curses light on thee
So heavy as thou shalt not shake them off,
But in despair die under their black weight
   Aust Rebellion, flat rebellion !
   Bast   Will't not be ?
Will not a calf's-skin stop that mouth of thine ?
   Lew Father, to arms !
   Blanch   Upon thy wedding-day ?   300
Against the blood that thou hast married ?
What, shall our feast be kept with slaughter'd men ?
Shall braying trumpets and loud churlish drums,
Clamours of hell, be measures to our pomp ?

O husband, how the may, alack, how new
Is husband in my mouth! even for that name,
Which till this time my tongue did ne'er pronounce,
Upon my knee I beg, go not to arms
Against mine uncle.
Const   O, upon my knee,
Made hard with kneeling, I do pray to thee,   310
Thou virtuous Dauphin, alter not the doom
Forethought by heaven!
  Blanch Now shall I see thy love what motive may
Be stronger with thee than the name of wife?
  Const That which upholdeth him that thee upholds,
His honour O, thine honour, Lewis, thine honour!
  Lew I muse your majesty doth seem so cold,
When such profound respects do pull you on.
  Pand I will denounce a curse upon his head.
  K Phi Thou shalt not need England, I will fall from
   thee   320
  Const O fair return of banish'd majesty!
  Eli O foul revolt of French inconstancy!
  K John France, thou shalt rue this hour within this hour.
  Bast Old Time the clock-setter, that bald sexton Time,
Is it as he will? well then, France shall rue
  Blanch The sun's o'ercast with blood fair day, adieu!
Which is the side that I must go withal?
I am with both each army hath a hand,
And in their rage, I having hold of both,
They whirl asunder and dismember me   330
Husband, I cannot pray that thou mayst win,
Uncle, I needs must pray that thou mayst lose,
Father, I may not wish the fortune thine,
Grandam, I will not wish thy wishes thrive
Whoever wins, on that side shall I lose,
Assured loss before the match be play'd
  Lew Lady, with me, with me thy fortune lies.
  Blanch There where my fortune lives, there my life dies

K John Cousin, go draw our puissance together

[*Exit Bastard*

France, I am burn'd up with inflaming wrath ,   340
A rage whose heat hath this condition,
That nothing can allay, nothing but blood,
The blood, and dearest-valued blood, of France
 K Phi Thy rage shall burn thee up, and thou shalt turn
To ashes, ere our blood shall quench that fire
Look to thyself, thou art in jeopardy
  K John. No more than he that threats   To arms let's
   hie !   [*Exeunt*

SCENE II   *The same   Plains near Angiers*

Alarums, excursions   Enter the BASTARD, *with* AUSTRIA'S
head

Bast Now, by my life, this day grows wondrous hot ,
Some airy devil hovers in the sky
And pours down mischief   Austria's head lie there,
While Philip breathes

Enter KING JOHN, ARTHUR, *and* HUBERT

K. John Hubert, keep this boy   Philip, make up
My mother is assailed in our tent,
And ta'en, I fear
 Bast   My lord, I rescued her ,
Her highness is in safety, fear you not
But on, my liege , for very little pains
Will bring this labour to an happy end   [*Exeunt*

SCENE III   *The same*

Alarums, excursions, retreat   *Enter* KING JOHN, ELINOR,
ARTHUR, *the* BASTARD, HUBERT, *and* LORDS

K *John* [*To Elinor*] So shall it be , your grace shall stay
behind
So strongly guarded   [*To Arthur*] Cousin, look not sad
Thy grandam loves thee , and thy uncle will
As dear be to thee as thy father was

Arth O, this will make my mother die with grief !

K John [*To the Bastard*] Cousin, away for England !
haste before
And, ere our coming, see thou shake the bags
Of hoarding abbots , set at liberty
Imprisoned angels   the fat ribs of peace
Must by the hungry now be fed upon   10
Use our commission in his utmost force

Bast Bell, book, and candle shall not drive me back,
When gold and silver becks me to come on
I leave your highness   Grandam, I will pray,
If ever I remember to be holy,
For your fair safety , so, I kiss your hand

Eli Farewell, gentle cousin

K John   Coz, farewell   [*Exit Bastard*

Eli Come hither, little kinsman , hark, a word

K John Come hither, Hubert. O my gentle Hubert,
We owe thee much ! within this wall of flesh   20
There is a soul counts thee her creditor
And with advantage means to pay thy love
And, my good friend, thy voluntary oath
Lives in this bosom, dearly cherished
Give me thy hand   I had a thing to say,
But I will fit it with some better time
By heaven, Hubert, I am almost ashamed
To say what good respect I have of thee

Hub I am much bounden to your majesty

K John Good friend, thou hast no cause to say so yet, 30
But thou shalt have , and creep time ne'er so slow,
Yet it shall come for me to do thee good
I had a thing to say, but let it go
The sun is in the heaven, and the proud day,
Attended with the pleasures of the world,
Is all too wanton and too full of gawds
To give me audience if the midnight bell
Did, with his iron tongue and brazen mouth,
Sound one into the drowsy ear of night ,
If this same were a churchyard where we stand, 40
And thou possessed with a thousand wrongs,
Or if that surly spirit, melancholy,
Had baked thy blood and made it heavy-thick,
Which else runs tickling up and down the veins,
Making that idiot, laughter, keep men's eyes
And strain their cheeks to idle merriment,
A passion hateful to my purposes,
Or if that thou couldst see me without eyes,
Hear me without thine ears, and make reply
Without a tongue, using conceit alone, 50
Without eyes, ears and harmful sound of words ,
Then, in despite of brooded watchful day,
I would into thy bosom pour my thoughts
But, ah, I will not ! yet I love thee well ,
And, by my troth, I think thou lov'st me well

Hub So well, that what you bid me undertake,
Though that my death were adjunct to my act
By heaven, I would do it

K John   Do not I know thou wouldst ?
Good Hubert, Hubert, Hubert, throw thine eye
On yon young boy I 'll tell thee what, my friend, 60
He is a very serpent in my way ,
And wheresoe'er this foot of mine doth tread,
He lies before me dost thou understand me ?

Thou art his keeper.
Hub.   And I'll keep him so,
That he shall not offend your majesty.
   K. John.   Death.

   Hub. My lord?
   K. John.   A grave.
   Hub.   He shall not live.
   K. John.   Enough.
I could be merry now. Hubert, I love thee;
Well, I 'll not say what I intend for thee.
Remember. Madam, fare you well:
I 'll send those powers o'er to your majesty.   70
   Eli. My blessing go with thee!
   K. John.   For England, cousin, go:
Hubert shall be your man, attend on you
With all true duty. On toward Calais, ho!   [*Exeunt*

SCENE IV. *The same. The French King's tent.*

Enter KING PHILIP, LEWIS, PANDULPH *and Attendants.*

   K. Phi. So, by a roaring tempest on the flood,
A whole armado of convicted sail
Is scatter'd and disjoin'd from fellowship.
   Pand. Courage and comfort! all shall yet go well.
   What can go well, when we have run so ill?
Are we not beaten? Is not Angiers lost?
Arthur ta'en prisoner? divers dear friends slain?
And bloody England into England gone,
O'erbearing interruption, spite of France?
   Lew. What he hath won, that hath he fortified: 10
So hot a speed with such advice disposed,
Such temperate order in so fierce a cause,
Doth want example: who hath read or heard
Of any kindred action like to this?

K Phi Well could I bear that England had this praise,
So we could find some pattern of our shame

Enter CONSTANCE

Look, who comes here ! a grave unto a soul ,
Holding the eternal spirit, against her will,
In the vile prison of afflicted breath
I prithee, lady, go away with me   20
   Const Lo, now ! now see the issue of your peace
   K Phi Patience, good lady ! comfort, gentle Constance !
   Const No, I defy all counsel, all redress,
But that which ends all counsel, true redress,
Death, death , O amiable lovely death !
Thou odoriferous stench ! sound rottenness !
Arise forth from the couch of lasting night,
Thou hate and terror to prosperity,
And I will kiss thy detestable bones
And put my eyeballs in thy vaulty brows   30
And ring these fingers with thy household worms
And stop this gap of breath with fulsome dust
And be a carrion monster like thyself
Come, grin on me, and I will think thou smilest
And buss thee as thy wife   Misery's love,
O, come to me !
   K Phi   O fair affliction, peace !
   Const No, no, I will not, having breath to cry
O, that my tongue were in the thunder's mouth !
Then with a passion would I shake the world,
And rouse from sleep that fell anatomy   40
Which cannot hear a lady's feeble voice,
Which scorns a modern invocation
   Pand Lady, you utter madness, and not sorro..
   Const Thou art not holy to belie me so ,
I am not mad   this hair I tear is mine ,
My name is Constance , I was Geffrey's wife ,
Young Arthur is my son, and he is lost

I am not mad I would to heaven I were '
For then, 'tis like I should forget myself
O, if I could what grief should I forget ?   50
Preach some philosophy to make me mad,
And thou shalt be canonized cardinal ,
For being not mad but sensible of grief,
My reasonable part produces reason
How I may be deliver'd of these woes,
And teaches me to kill or hang myself
If I were mad, I should forget my son,
Or madly think a babe of clouts were he
I am not mad , too well, too well I feel
The different plague of each calamity   60
    K Phi Bind up those tresses   O, what love I note
In the fair multitude of those her hairs '
Where but by chance a silver drop hath fallen,
Even to that drop ten thousand wiry friends
Do glue themselves in sociable grief,
Like true, inseparable, faithful loves
Sticking together in calamity
    Const To England, if you will
    K Phi   Bind up your hairs
    Const Yes, that I will , and wherefore will I do it ?
I tore them from their bonds and cried aloud   70
'O that these hands could so redeem my son,
As they have given these hairs their liberty "
But now I envy at their liberty,
And will again commit them to their bonds,
Because my poor child is a prisoner
And, father cardinal, I have heard you say
That we shall see and know our friends in heaven
If that be true, I shall see my boy again ,
For since the birth of Cain, the first male child,
To him that did but yesterday suspire,
There was not such a gracious creature born
But now will canker sorrow eat my bud

And chase the native beauty from his cheek
And he will look as hollow as a ghost,
As dim and meagre as an ague's fit, *as pale*.
And so he 'll die, and, rising so again, *on*,
When I shall meet him in the court of heaven
I shall not know him   therefore never, never
Must I behold my pretty Arthur more
 Pand   You hold too heinous a respect of grief
 Const   He talks to me that never had a son
 K Phi   You are as fond of grief as of your child
 Const   Grief fills the room up of my absent child,
Lies in his bed, walks up and down with me,
Puts on his pretty looks, repeats his words,
Remembers me of all his gracious parts,
Stuffs out his vacant garments with his form ;
Then, have I reason to be fond of grief ?
Fare you well   had you such a loss as I,
I could give better comfort than you do   100
I will not keep this form upon my head,
When there is such disorder in my wit
O Lord ! my boy, my Arthur, my fair son '
My life, my joy, my food, my all the world '
My widow-comfort, and my sorrow's cure !   [*Exit*
 K Phi   I fear some outrage, and I 'll follow her   [*Ernt*
 Lew   There 's nothing in this world can make me joy
Life is as tedious as a twice-told tale
Vexing the dull ear of a drowsy man ,
And bitter shame hath spoil'd the sweet world's taste,   110
That it yields nought but shame and bitterness
 Pand   Before the curing of a strong disease,
Even in the instant of repair and health,
The fit is strongest , evils that take leave,
On their departure most of all show evil
What have you lost by losing of this day ?
 Lew   All days of glory, joy and happiness
 Pand   If you had won it, certainly you had

No, no, when Fortune means to men most good,
She looks upon them with a threatening eye.   120
'Tis strange to think how much King John hath lost
In this which he accounts so clearly won
Are not you grieved that Arthur is his prisoner?
    Lew As heartily as he is glad he hath him.
    Pand Your mind is all as youthful as your blood.
Now hear me speak with a prophetic spirit,
For even the breath of what I mean to speak
Shall blow each dust, each straw, each little rub
Out of the path which shall directly lead
Thy foot to England's throne, and therefore mark.   130
John hath seized Arthur, and it cannot be
That, whiles warm life plays in that infant's veins,
The misplaced John should entertain one hour,
One minute, nay, one quiet breath of rest
A sceptre snatch'd with an unruly hand
Must be as boisterously maintain'd as gain'd,
And he that stands upon a slippery place
Makes nice of no vile hold to stay him up
That John may stand, then Arthur needs must fall.
So be it, for it cannot be but so *in any other way*   140
    Lew But what shall I gain by young Arthur's fall?
    Pand You, in the right of Lady Blanch your wife,
May then make all the claim that Arthur did
    Lew And lose it, life and all, as Arthur did
    Pand How green you are and fresh in this old world!
John lays you plots, the times conspire with you,
For he that steeps his safety in true blood
Shall find but bloody safety and untrue
This act, so evilly borne, shall cool the hearts
Of all his people and freeze up their zeal,   150
That none so small advantage shall step forth
To check his reign, but they will cherish it.
No natural exhalation in the sky,
No scope of nature, no distemper'd day,

'No common wind, no customed event,
But they will pluck away his natural cause
And call them meteors, prodigies and signs,
Abortives, presages and tongues of heaven,
Plainly denouncing vengeance upon John
   Lew. May be he will not touch young Arthur's life,   160
But hold himself safe in his imprisonment
   Pand O, sir, when he shall hear of your approach,
If that young Arthur be not gone already,
Even at that news he dies, and then the hearts
Of all his people shall revolt from him
And kiss the lips of unacquainted change
And pick strong matter of revolt and wrath
Out of the bloody fingers' ends of John
Methinks I see this hurly all on foot
And, O, what better matter breeds for you   170
Than I have named ! The bastard Faulconbridge
Is now in England, ransacking the church,
Offending charity if but a dozen French
Were there in arms, they would be as a call
To train ten thousand English to their side,
Or as a little snow, tumbled about,
Anon becomes a mountain O noble Dauphin,
Go with me to the king 'tis wonderful
What may be wrought out of their discontent,
Now that their souls are topfull of offence   180
For England go I will whet on the king
   Lew Strong reasons make strong actions let us go
If you say ay, the king will not say no   [*Exeunt*

ACT IV

Scene I   A room in a castle

Enter Hubert and Executioners

Hub Heat me these irons hot , and look thou stand
Within the arras   when I strike my foot
Upon the bosom of the ground, rush forth,
And bind the boy you shall find with me
Fast to the chair   be heedful   hence, and watch
    First Exec I hope your warrant will bear out the deed.
    Hub Uncleanly scruples ! fear not you   look to 't
                                        [*Exeunt Executioners*
Young lad, come forth , I have to say with you

Enter Arthur

Arth Good morrow, Hubert
Hub   Good morrow   little prince
Arth As little prince, having so great a title   10
To be more prince, as may be   You are sad
    Hub Indeed, I have been merrier
    Arth   Mercy on me !
Methinks no body should be sad but I
Yet, I remember, when I was in France,
Young gentlemen would be as sad as night,
Only for wantonness   By my christendom,
So I were out of prison and kept sheep,
I should be as merry as the day is long ,
And so I would be here, but that I doubt
My uncle practises more harm to me   20
He is afraid of me and I of him
Is it my fault that I was Geffrey's son ?
No, indeed, is 't not , and I would to heaven
I were your son, so you would love me, Hubert

Hub [*Aside*] If I talk to him, with his innocent prate
He will awake my mercy which lies dead
Therefore I will be sudden and dispatch
  Arth Are you sick, Hubert ? you look pale to day
In sooth, I would you were a little sick,
That I might sit all night and watch with you   30
I warrant I love you more than you do me
  Hub [*Aside*] His words do take possession of my bosom
Read here, young Arthur   [*Showing a paper*
          [*Aside*] How now, foolish rheum !
Turning dispiteous torture out of door !
I must be brief, lest resolution drop
Out at mine eyes in tender womanish tears
Can you not read it ? is it not fair writ ?
  Arth Too fairly, Hubert, for so foul effect
Must you with hot irons burn out both mine eyes ?
  Hub Young boy, I must
  Arth   And will you ?
  Hub   And I will   40
  Arth Have you the heart ?   When your head did but
      ache,
I knit my handkercher about your brows,
The best I had, a princess wrought it me,
And I did never ask it you again ;
And with my hand at midnight held your head,
And like the watchful minutes to the hour,
Still and anon cheer'd up the heavy time,
Saying, ' What lack you ?' and ' Where lies your grief ?'
Or ' What good love may I perform for you ?' .
Many a poor man's son would have lien still   50
And ne'er have spoke a loving word to you ,
But you at your sick service had a prince
Nay, you may think my love was crafty love
And call it cunning   do, an if you will
If heaven be pleased that you must use me ill,
Why then you must ?   Will you put out mine eyes ?

These eyes that never did nor never shall
So much as frown on you
    Hub   I have sworn to do it,
And with hot irons must I burn them out.
    Arth Ah, none but in this iron age would do it!   60
The iron of itself, though heat red-hot,
Approaching near these eyes, would drink my tears
And quench his fiery indignation
Even in the matter of mine innocence,
Nay, after that, consume away in rust,
But for containing fire to harm mine eye.
Are you more stubborn hard than hammer'd iron?
An if an angel should have come to me
And told me Hubert should put out mine eyes,
I would not have believed him,—no tongue but Hubert's 70
    Hub Come forth   [*Stamps*

    Re-enter Executioners, *with a cord, irons, &c.*

Do as I bid you do
    Arth. O, save me, Hubert, save me! my eyes are out
Even with the fierce looks of these bloody men.
    Hub Give me the iron, I say, and bind him here
    Arth Alas, what need you be so boisterous-rough?
I will not struggle, I will stand stone still
For heaven sake, Hubert, let me not be bound!
Nay, hear me, Hubert, drive these men away,
And I will sit as quiet as a lamb,   80
I will not stir, nor wince, nor speak a word,
Nor look upon the iron angerly
Thrust but these men away, and I'll forgive you,
Whatever torment you do put me to
    Hub Go, stand within, let me alone with him
    First Exec I am best pleased to be from such a deed
                           [*Exeunt Executioners*
    Arth Alas, I then have chid away my friend!
He hath a stern look, but a gentle heart

Let him come back that his compassion may
Give life to yours

   Hub   Come, boy, prepare yourself   90
   Arth Is there no remedy ?
   Hub   None, but to lose your eyes
   Arth O heaven, that there were but a mote in yours,
A grain, a dust, a gnat, a wandering hair,
Any annoyance in that precious sense !
Then feeling what small things are boisterous there,
Your vile intent must needs seem horrible

   Hub Is this your promise ? go to, hold your tongue
   Arth Hubert, the utterance of a brace of tongues
Must needs want pleading for a pair of eyes
Let me not hold my tongue, let me not, Hubert,   100
Or, Hubert, if you will, cut out my tongue,
So I may keep mine eyes O, spare mine eyes,
Though to no use but still to look on you '
Lo, by my troth, the instrument is cold
And would not harm me

   Hub   I can heat it, boy
   Arth No, in good sooth , the fire is dead with grief,
Being create for comfort, to be used
In undeserved extremes see else yourself ,
There is no malice in this burning coal ,
The breath of heaven hath blown his spirit out   110
And strew'd repentant ashes on his head

   Hub But with my breath I can revive it, boy
   Arth An if you do, you will but make it blush
And glow with shame of your proceedings, Hubert
Nay, it perchance will sparkle in your eyes ,
And like a dog that is compell'd to fight,
Snatch at his master that doth tarre him on
All things that you should use to do me wrong
Deny their office only you do lack
That mercy which fierce fire and iron extends,   120
Creatures of note for mercy-lacking uses

Hub Well, see to live, I will not touch thine eye
For all the treasure that thine uncle owes.
Yet am I sworn, and I did purpose, boy,
With this same very iron to burn them out

Arth O, now you look like Hubert! all this while
You were disguised

Hub   Peace, no more. Adieu
Your uncle must not know but you are dead;
I'll fill these dogged spies with false reports
And, pretty child, sleep doubtless and secure,   120
That Hubert, for the wealth of all the world,
Will not offend thee

Arth   O heaven! I thank you, Hubert

Hub Silence, no more go closely in with me
Much danger do I undergo for thee   [*Exeunt*

SCENE II   KING JOHN'S *palace*

Enter KING JOHN, PEMBROKE, SALISBURY, *and other* Lords

K John Here once again we sit, once again crown'd,
And looked upon, I hope, with cheerful eyes.

Pem This 'once again,' but that your highness pleased,
Was once superfluous you were crown'd before,
And that high royalty was ne'er pluck'd off,
The faiths of men ne'er stained with revolt,
Fresh expectation troubled not the land
With any long'd for change or better state.

Sal Therefore, to be possess'd with double pomp,
To guard a title that was rich before,   10
To gild refined gold, to paint the lily,
To throw a perfume on the violet,
To smooth the ice, or add another hue
Unto the rainbow, or with taper-light
To seek the beauteous eye of heaven to garnish,
Is wasteful and ridiculous excess

Pem But that your royal pleasure must be done,
This act is as an ancient tale new told,
And in the last repeating troublesome,
Being urged at a time unseasonable   20

Sal In this the antique and well noted face
Of plain old form is much disfigured ,
And, like a shifted wind unto a sail,
It makes the course of thoughts to fetch about,
Startles and frights consideration,
Makes sound opinion sick and truth suspected,
For putting on so new a fashion'd robe

Pem When workmen strive to do better than well,
They do confound their skill in covetousness ,
And oftentimes excusing of a fault   30
Doth make the fault the worse by the excuse,
As patches set upon a little breach
Discredit more in hiding of the fault   *Elenu* ʰⁱ
Than did the fault before it was so patch'd

Sal To this effect, before you were new crown'd,
We breathed our counsel   but it pleased your highness
To overbear it, and we are all well pleased,
Since all and every part of what we would
Doth make a stand at what your highness will

K John Some reasons of this double coronation   40
I have possess'd you with and think them strong ,
And more, more strong, when lesser is my fear,
I shall indue you with   meantime but ask
What you would have reform'd that is not well,
And well shall you perceive how willingly
I will both hear and grant your your requests

Pem Then I, as one that am the tongue of these
To sound the purposes of all their hearts,
Both for myself and them, but, chief of all,
Your safety, for the which myself and them   50
Bend their best studies, heartily request
The enfranchisement of Arthur , whose restraint

Doth move the murmuring lips of discontent
To break into this dangerous argument,—
If what in rest you have in right you hold,
Why then your fears which as they say, attend
The steps of wrong, should move you to mew up
Your tender kinsman and to choke his days
With barbarous ignorance and deny his youth
The rich advantage of good exercise ?   60
That the times enemies may not have this
To grace occasions let it be our suit
That you have bid us ask his liberty ;
Which for our goods we do no further ask
Than whereupon our weal, on you depending.
Counts it your weal he have his liberty

Enter Hubert

K John Let it be so   I do commit his youth
To your direction.   Hubert, what news with you ?
                                  [*Taking him apart*

Pem This is the man should do the bloody deed,
He show'd his warrant to a friend of mine   70
The image of a wicked heinous fault
Lives in his eye , that close aspect of his
Does show the mood of a much troubled breast .
And I do fearfully believe tis done,
What we so fear'd he had a charge to do
  Sal The colour of the king doth come and go
Between his purpose and his conscience,
Like heralds 'twixt two dreadful battles set .
His passion is so ripe, it needs must break

Pem And when it breaks, I fear will issue thence   80
The foul corruption of a sweet childs death

K John We cannot hold mortality's strong hand
Good lords, although my will to give is living,
The suit which you demand is gone and dead
He tells us Arthur is deceased to night

Sal Indeed we fear'd his sickness was past cure
Pem Indeed we heard how near his death he was
Before the child himself felt he was sick
This must be answer'd either here or hence
  K John Why do you bend such solemn brows on me? 90
Think you I bear the shears of destiny?
Have I commandment on the pulse of life?
  Sal It is apparent foul play, and 'tis shame
That greatness should so grossly offer it
So thrive it in your game! and so, farewell
  Pem Stay yet, Lord Salisbury, I'll go with thee,
And find the inheritance of this poor child,
His little kingdom of a forced grave
That blood which owed the breadth of all this isle,
Three foot of it doth hold bad would the while! 100
This must not be thus borne this will break out
To all our sorrows, and ere long I doubt   [*Exeunt Lords*
  K John They burn in indignation I repent
There is no sure foundation set on blood,
No certain life achieved by others' death

Enter a Messenger

A fearful eye thou hast where is that blood
That I have seen inhabit in those cheeks?
So foul a sky clears not without a storm
Pour down thy weather how goes all in France?
  Mess From France to England Never such a power 110
For any foreign preparation
Was levied in the body of a land
The copy of your speed is learn'd by them,
For when you should be told they do prepare,
The tidings comes that they are all arrived
  K John O, where hath our intelligence been drunk?
Where hath it slept? Where is my mother's care,
That such an army could be drawn in France,
And she not hear of it?

Mess.   My liege, her ear
Is stopp'd with dust; the first of April died   120
Your noble mother; and, as I hear, my lord,
The Lady Constance in a frenzy died
Three days before; but this from rumour's tongue
I idly heard, if true or false I know not.
    K. John. Withhold thy speed, dreadful occasion!
O, make a league with me, till I have pleased
My discontented peers! What! mother dead!
How wildly then walks my estate in France!
Under whose conduct came those powers of France
That thou for truth giv'st out are landed here?   130
    Mess. Under the Dauphin.
    K. John.   Thou hast made me giddy
With these ill tidings.

Enter the BASTARD *and* PETER *of Pomfret*

                    Now, what says the world
To your proceedings? do not seek to stuff
My head with more ill news, for it is full.
    Bast. But if you be afeard to hear the worst,
Then let the worst unheard fall on your head.
    K. John. Bear with me, cousin, for I was amazed
Under the tide; but now I breathe again
Aloft the flood, and can give audience
To any tongue, speak it of what it will.   140
    Bast. How I have sped among the clergymen,
The sums I have collected shall express.
But as I travell'd hither through the land
I find the people strangely fantasied;
Possess'd with rumours, full of idle dreams,
Not knowing what they fear, but full of fear:
And here's a prophet, that I brought with me
From forth the streets of Pomfret, whom I found
With many hundreds treading on his heels.

To whom he sung, in rude harsh-sounding rhymes,   150
That, ere the next Ascension-day at noon,
Your highness should deliver up your crown
   K John Thou idle dreamer, wherefore didst thou so ?
   Peter Foreknowing that the truth will fall out so
   K John. Hubert, away with him ; imprison him ,
And on that day at noon, whereon he says
I shall yield up my crown, let him be hang'd
Deliver him to safety , and return,
For I must use thee   [*Exit Hubert with Peter*
                O my gentle cousin,
Hear'st thou the news abroad, who are arrived ?   160
   Bast The French, my lord , men's mouths are full of it
Besides, I met Lord Bigot and Lord Salisbury,
With eyes as red as new-enkindled fire,
And others more, going to seek the grave
Of Arthur, whom they say is kill'd to-night
On your suggestion
   K. John   Gentle kinsman, go,
And thrust thyself into their companies
I have a way to win their loves again ,
Bring them before me
   Bast   I will seek them out
   K John Nay, but make haste , the better foot before   170
O, let me have no subject enemies,
When adverse foreigners affright my towns
With dreadful pomp of stout invasion !
Be Mercury, set feathers to thy heels,
And fly like thought from them to me again
   Bast The spirit of the time shall teach me speed   [*Exit*
   K John Spoke like a sprightful noble gentleman
Go after him , for he perhaps shall need
Some messenger betwixt me and the peers ,
And be thou he
   Mess   With all my heart, my liege ,   [*Exit*   180
   K John My mother dead !

Re enter HUBERT

Hub My lord, they say five moons were seen to-night,
Four fixed, and the fifth did whirl about
The other four in wondrous motion

K John Five moons'

Hub   Old men and beldams in the streets
Do prophesy upon it dangerously
Young Arthur's death is common in their mouths
And when they talk of him, they shake their heads
And whisper one another in the ear,
And he that speaks doth gripe the hearer's wrist,   180
Whilst he that hears makes fearful action,
With wrinkled brows, with nods, with rolling eyes
I saw a smith stand with his hammer, thus,
The whilst his iron did on the anvil cool,
With open mouth swallowing a tailor's news,
Who, with his shears and measure in his hand,
Standing on slippers, which his nimble haste
Had falsely thrust upon contrary feet,
Told of a many thousand warlike French
That were embattailed and rank'd in Kent   200
Another lean unwash'd artificer
Cuts off his tale and talks of Arthur's death

   K John Why seek'st thou to possess me with these fears?
Why urgest thou so oft young Arthur's death?
Thy hand hath murder'd him I had a mighty cause
To wish him dead, but thou hadst none to kill him

  Hub No had, my lord' why, did you not provoke me?

  K John It is the curse of kings to be attended
By slaves that take their humours for a warrant
To break within the <u>bloody</u> house of life,   210
And on the winking of authority
To understand a law, to know the meaning
Of dangerous majesty, when perchance it frowns
More upon humour than advised respect

Hub Here is your hand and seal for what I did

   K John O, when the last account 'twixt heaven and earth
Is to be made, then shall this hand and seal
Witness against us to damnation !
How oft the sight of means to do ill deeds
Make deeds ill done ! Hadst not thou been by,   220
A fellow by the hand of nature mark'd,
Quoted and sign'd to do a deed of shame,
This murder had not come into my mind
But taking note of thy abhorr'd aspect,
Finding thee fit for bloody villany,
Apt, liable to be employ'd in danger,
I faintly broke with thee of Arthur's death
And thou, to be endeared to a king,
Made it no conscience to destroy a prince

   Hub My lord,—   230

   K John Hadst thou but shook thy head or made a pause
When I spake darkly what I purposed,
Or turn'd an eye of doubt upon my face,
As bid me tell my tale in express words,
Deep shame had struck me dumb, made me break off,
And those thy fears might have wrought fears in me
But thou didst understand me by my signs
And didst in signs again parley with sin ,
Yea, without stop, didst let thy heart consent,
And consequently thy rude hand to act   240
The deed, which both our tongues held vile to name.
Out of my sight, and never see me more !
My nobles leave me , and my state is braved,
Even at my gates, with ranks of foreign powers
Nay, in the body of this fleshly land,
This kingdom, this confine of blood and breath,
Hostility and civil tumult reigns
Between my conscience and my cousin's death

   Hub Arm you against your other enemies,
I 'll make a peace between your soul and you   250

Young Arthur is alive   this hand of mine
Is yet a maiden and an innocent hand.
Not painted with the crimson spots of blood
Within this bosom never enter'd yet
The dreadful motion of a murderous thought ~
And you have slander'd nature in my form.
Which, howsoever rude exteriorly,
Is yet the cover of a fairer mind
Than to be butcher of an innocent child

   K John Doth Arthur live ? O haste thee to the peers,   261
Throw this report on their incensed rage,
And make them tame to their obedience !
Forgive the comment that my passion made
Upon thy feature , for my rage was blind,
And foul imaginary eyes of blood
Presented thee more hideous than thou art
O, answer not, but to my closet bring
The angry lords with all expedient haste.
I conjure thee but slowly   run more fast   *Exeunt*

    Scene III   *Before the castle*

    Enter Arthur *on the walls*

   Arth The wall is high, and yet will I leap down .
Good ground, be pitiful and hurt me not !
There's few or none do know me   if they did,
This ship-boy's semblance hath disguised me quite
I am afraid , and yet I'll venture it
If I get down, and do not break my limbs,
I'll find a thousand shifts to get away
As good to die and go, as die and stay   [*Leaps down*
O me ! my uncle's spirit is in these stones
Heaven take my soul, and England keep my bones !   10
       [*Dies*

Enter PEMBROKE, SALISBURY, *and* BIGOT

Sal Lords, I will meet him at Saint Edmundsbury
It is our safety, and we must embrace
This gentle offer of the perilous time
    Pem Who brought that letter from the cardinal ?
    Sal The Count Melun, a noble lord of France ,
Whose private with me of the Dauphin's love
Is much more general than these lines import
    Big To-morrow morning let us meet him then.
    Sal Or rather then set forward , for 'twill be
Two long days' journey, lords, or ere we meet   20

Enter the BASTARD

Bast Once more to-day well met, distemper'd lords '
The king by me requests your presence straight
    Sal The king hath dispossess'd himself of us
We will not line his thin bestained cloak
With our pure honours, nor attend the foot
That leaves the print of blood where'er it walks
Return and tell him so   we know the worst
    Bast Whate'er you think, good words, I think, were best
    Sal. Our griefs, and not our manners, reason now
    Bast But there is little reason in your grief ,   30
Therefore 'twere reason you had manners now
    Pem Sir, sir, impatience hath his privilege
    Bast 'Tis true, to hurt his master, no one else
    Sal This is the prison   What is he lies here ?

                                        [*Seeing Arthur*
    Pem O death, made proud with pure and princely beauty '
The earth had not a hole to hide this deed
    Sal. Murder, as hating what himself hath done,
Doth lay it open to urge on revenge
    Big Or, when he doom'd this beauty to a grave,
Found it too precious-princely for a grave   40
    Sal Sir Richard, what think you ? have you beheld,

Or have you read or heard? or could you think?
Or do you almost think, although you see,
That you do see? could thought, without this object,
Form such another? (This is the very top,
The height, the crest, or crest unto the crest,
Of murder's arms this is the bloodiest shame,
The wildest savagery, the vilest stroke,
That ever wall-eyed wrath or staring rage   50
Presented to the tears of soft remorse)

 Pem All murders past do stand excused in this
And this, so sole and so unmatchable,
Shall give a holiness, a purity,
To the yet unbegotten sin of times,
And prove a deadly bloodshed but a jest,
Exampled by this heinous spectacle

 Bast It is a damned and a bloody work,
The graceless action of a heavy hand,
If that it be the work of any hand

 Sal If that it be the work of any hand?   60
We had a kind of light what would ensue
It is the shameful work of Hubert's hand,
The practice and the purpose of the king.
From whose obedience I forbid my soul,
Kneeling before this ruin of sweet life,
And breathing to his breathless excellence
The incense of a vow, a holy vow,
Never to taste the pleasures of the world,
Never to be infected with delight,
Nor conversant with ease and idleness,   70
Till I have set a glory to this hand,
By giving it the worship of revenge

  Pem. }
  Big   } Our souls religiously confirm thy words.

    Enter HUBERT

 Hub Lords, I am hot with haste in seeking you

Arthur doth live; the king hath sent for you
   Sal O, he is bold and blushes not at death
Avaunt, thou hateful villain, get thee gone '
   Hub I am no villain
   Sal.   Must I rob the law ?

                       [Drawing his sword
   Bast Your sword is bright, sir , put it up again
   Sal Not till I sheathe it in a murderer's skin   80
   Hub Stand back, Lord Salisbury, stand back, I say ,
By heaven, I think my sword 's as sharp as yours
I would not have you, lord, forget yourself,
Nor tempt the danger of my true defence ,
Lest I, by marking of your rage, forget
Your worth, your greatness and nobility
   Big Out, dunghill ' darest thou brave a nobleman ?
   Hub Not for my life but yet I dare defend
My innocent life against an emperor
   Sal Thou art a murderer
   Hub   Do not prove me so ,   90
Yet I am none whose tongue soe'er speaks false,
Not truly speaks , who speaks not truly, lies
   Pem Cut him to pieces
   Bast   Keep the peace, I say
   Sal Stand by, or I shall gall you, Faulconbridge
   Bast Thou wert better gall the devil, Salisbury
If thou but frown on me, or stir thy foot,
Or teach thy hasty spleen to do me shame,
I 'll strike thee dead Put up thy sword betime ,
Or I 'll so maul you and your toasting-iron,
That you shall think the devil is come from hell   100
   Big What wilt thou do, renowned Faulconbridge ?
Second a villain and a murderer ?
   Hub Lord Bigot, I am none
   Big   Who kill'd this prince ?
   Hub 'Tis not an hour since I left him well
I honour'd him, I loved him, and will weep

My date of life out for his sweet life's loss.

Sal. Trust not those cunning waters of his eyes,
For villany is not without such rheum;
And he, long traded in it, makes it seem
Like rivers of remorse and innocency.   110
Away with me, all you whose souls abhor
The uncleanly savours of a slaughter-house;
For I am stifled with this smell of sin.

Big. Away toward Bury, to the Dauphin there!

Pem. There tell the king he may inquire us out.
                                        [*Exeunt Lords.*

Bast. Here's a good world! Knew you of this fair work?
Beyond the infinite and boundless reach
Of mercy, if thou didst this deed of death,
Art thou damn'd, Hubert.

Hub.   Do but hear me, sir.

Bast. Ha! I'll tell thee what;   120
Thou 'rt damn'd as black—nay, nothing is so black;
Thou art more deep damn'd than Prince Lucifer:
There is not yet so ugly a fiend of hell
As thou shalt be, if thou didst kill this child.

Hub. Upon my soul—

Bast.   If thou didst but consent
To this most cruel act, do but despair;
And if thou want'st a cord, the smallest thread
That ever spider twisted from her womb
Will serve to strangle thee, a rush will be a beam
To hang thee on, or wouldst thou drown thyself,   130
Put but a little water in a spoon,
And it shall be as all the ocean,
Enough to stifle such a villain up.
I do suspect thee very grievously.

Hub. If I in act, consent, or sin of thought
Be guilty of the stealing that sweet breath
Which was embounded in this beauteous clay,
Let hell want pains enough to torture me.

I left him well
 Bast Go, bear him in thine arms
I am amazed, methinks, and lose my way   140
Among the thorns and dangers of this world
How easy dost thou take all England up !
From forth this morsel of dead royalty,
The life, the right and truth of all this realm
Is fled to heaven, and England now is left
To tug and scramble and to part by the teeth
The unowed interest of proud-swelling state
Now for the bare-pick'd bone of majesty
Doth dogged war bristle his angry crest
And snarleth in the gentle eyes of peace   150
Now powers from home and discontents at home
Meet in one line, and vast confusion waits,
As doth a raven on a sick-fall'n beast,
The imminent decay of wrested pomp
Now happy he whose cloak and cincture can
Hold out this tempest Bear away that child
And follow me with speed I'll to the king
A thousand businesses are brief in hand,
And heaven itself doth frown upon the land. *[Exeunt*

ACT V

Scene I King John's *palace*

Enter King John, Pandulph, *and* Attendants

K John Thus have I yielded up into your hand
The circle of my glory   *[Giving the crown*
 Pand   Take again
From this my hand, as holding of the pope
Your sovereign greatness and authority
 K John Now keep your holy word go meet the French,

And from his holiness use all your power
To stop their marches 'fore we are inflamed
Our discontented counties do revolt,
Our people quarrel with obedience,
Swearing allegiance and the love of soul   10
To stranger blood, to foreign royalty.
This inundation of mistemper'd humour
Rests by you only to be qualified
Then pause not, for the present time's so sick,
That present medicine must be minister'd,
Or overthrow incurable ensues

   Pand It was my breath that blew this tempest up,
Upon your stubborn usage of the pope,
But since you are a gentle convertite,
My tongue shall hush again this storm of war   20
And make fair weather in your blustering land
On this Ascension day remember well,
Upon your oath of service to the pope,
Go I to make the French lay down their arms

   K John Is this Ascension-day? Did not the prophet
Say that before Ascension day at noon
My crown I should give off? Even so I have
I did suppose it should be on constraint ;
But, heaven be thank'd, it is but voluntary

        Enter the BASTARD

   Bast All Kent hath yielded, nothing there holds out 30
But Dover castle London hath received,
Like a kind host, the Dauphin and his powers
Your nobles will not hear you but are gone
To offer service to your enemy,
And wild amazement hurries up and down
The little number of your doubtful friends

   K John Would not my lords return to me again,
After they heard young Arthur was alive?

   Bast They found him dead and cast into the streets,

An empty casket, where the jewel of life 40
By some damn'd hand was robb'd and ta'en away
  K John That villain Hubert told me he did live
  Bast So, on my soul, he did, for aught he knew
But wherefore do you droop ? why look you sad ?
Be great in act, as you have been in thought ,
Let not the world see fear and sad distrust
Govern the motion of a kingly eye
Be stirring as the time , be fire with fire ,
Threaten the threatener and outface the blow
Of bragging horror so shall inferior eyes, 50
That borrow their behaviours from the great,
Grow great by your example and put on
The dauntless spirit of resolution.
Away, and glister like the god of war,
When he intendeth to become the field
Show boldness and aspiring confidence
What, shall they seek the lion in his den,
And fright him there ? and make him tremble there ?
O, let it not be said forage, and run
To meet displeasure farther from the doors, 60
And grapple with him ere he come so nigh
  K John The legate of the pope hath been with me,
And I have made a happy peace with him ,
And he hath promised to dismiss the powers
Led by the Dauphin
  Bast   O inglorious league !
Shall we, upon the footing of our land,
Send fair-play offers and make compromise,
Insinuation, parley and base truce
To arms invasive ? shall a beardless boy,
A cocker'd silken wanton, brave our fields, 70
And flesh his spirit in a warlike soil,
Mocking the air with colours idly spread,
And find no check ? Let us, my liege, to arms
Perchance the cardinal cannot make your peace ,

Or if he do, let it at least be said
They saw we had a purpose of defence.
    K. John. Have thou the ordering of this present time.
    Bast. Away, then, with good courage! yet, I know,
Our party may well meet a prouder foe.   [*Exe nt.*

SCENE II   *The* DAUPHIN'S *camp at St. Edmundsbury.*

Enter, in arms, LEWIS, SALISBURY, MELUN, PEMBROKE,
    BIGOT, *and Soldiers.*

    Lew. My Lord Melun, let this be copied out,
And keep it safe for our remembrance.
Return the precedent to these lords again,
That, having our fair order written down,
Both they and we, perusing o'er these notes,
May know wherefore we took the sacrament,
And keep our faiths firm and inviolable.
    Sal. Upon our sides it never shall be broken.
And, noble Dauphin, albeit we swear
A voluntary zeal and unurged faith   10
To your proceedings; yet believe me, prince,
I am not glad that such a sore of time
Should seek a plaster by contemn'd revolt,
And heal the inveterate canker of one wound
By making many. O, it grieves my soul,
That I must draw this metal from my side
To be a widow-maker! O, and there
Where honourable rescue and defence
Cries out upon the name of Salisbury!
But such is the infection of the time,   20
That, for the health and physic of our right,
We cannot deal but with the very hand
Of stern injustice and confused wrong.
And is't not pity, O my grieved friends,
That we, the sons and children of this isle,

Were born to see so sad an hour as this ,
Wherein we step after a stranger march
Upon her gentle bosom, and fill up
Her enemies' ranks,—I must withdraw and weep
Upon the spot of this enforced cause,—　　　　30
To grace the gentry of a land remote,
And follow unacquainted colours here ?
What, here ?　O nation, that thou couldst remove !
That Neptune's arms, who clippeth thee about,
Would bear thee from the knowledge of thyself,
And grapple thee unto a pagan shore,
Where these two Christian armies might combine
The blood of malice in a vein of league,
And not to spend it so unneighbourly !

Lew　A noble temper dost thou show in this ,　　　　40
And great affections wrestling in thy bosom
Doth make an earthquake of nobility
O, what a noble combat hast thou fought
Between compulsion and a brave respect !
Let me wipe off this honourable dew,
That silverly doth progress on thy cheeks
My heart hath melted at a lady's tears,
Being an ordinary inundation ,
But this effusion of such manly drops,
This shower, blown up by tempest of the soul,　　　　50
Startles mine eyes, and makes me more amazed
Than had I seen the vaulty top of heaven
Figured quite o'er with burning meteors
Lift up thy brow, renowned Salisbury,
And with a great heart heave away this storm
Commend these waters to those baby eyes
That never saw the giant world enraged ,
Nor met with fortune other than at feasts,
Full of warm blood, of mirth, of gossiping .
Come, come , for thou shalt thrust thy hand as deep　　　　60
Into the pulse of rich prosperity

As Lewis himself so, nobles, shall you all
That knit your sinews to the strength of mine,
And even there, methinks, an angel spake

Enter PANDULPH

Look, where the holy legate comes apace,
To give us warrant from the hand of heaven,
And on our actions set the name of right
With holy breath

   Pand   Hail, noble prince of France!
The next is this, King John hath reconciled
Himself to Rome, his spirit is come in,   70
That so stood out against the holy church
The great metropolis and see of Rome
Therefore thy threatening colours now wind up,
And tame the savage spirit of wild war,
That, like a lion foster'd up at hand,
It may lie gently at the foot of peace,
And be no further harmful than in show

   Lew Your grace shall pardon me, I will not back,
I am too high-born to be propertied,
To be a secondary at control,   80
Or useful serving-man and instrument,
To any sovereign state throughout the world
Your breath first kindled the dead coal of wars
Between this chastised kingdom and myself,
And brought in matter that should feed this fire ;
And now 'tis far too huge to be blown out
With that same weak wind which enkindled it
You taught me how to know the face of right,
Acquainted me with interest to this land,
Yea, thrust this enterprise into my heart.   90
And come ye now to tell me John hath made
His peace with Rome? What is that peace to me?
I, by the honour of my marriage-bed,
After young Arthur, claim this land for mine,

And, now it is half-conquer'd, must I back
Because that John hath made his peace with Rome ?
Am I Rome's slave ?   What penny hath Rome borne,
What men provided, what munition sent,
To underprop this action ?   Is 't not I
That undergo this charge ? who else but I,   100
And such as to my claim are liable,
Sweat in this business and maintain this war ?
Have I not heard these islanders shout out
' Vive le roi ! ' as I have bank'd their towns ?
Have I not here the best cards for the game,
To win this easy match play'd for a crown ?
And shall I now give o'er the yielded set ?
No, no, on my soul, it never shall be said
　　Pand   You look but on the outside of this work
　　Lew   Outside or inside, I will not return   110
Till my attempt so much be glorified
As to my ample hope was promised
Before I drew this gallant head-of-war,
And cull'd these fiery spirits from the world,
To outlook conquest and to win renown
Even in the jaws of danger and of death　　[*Trumpet sounds*
What lusty trumpet thus doth summon us ?

　　　　Enter the BASTARD, *attended*

　　Bast   According to the fair play of the world,
Let me have audience , I am sent to speak
My holy lord of Milan, from the king   120
I come, to learn how you have dealt for him ,
And, as you answer, I do know the scope
And warrant limited unto my tongue
　　Pand   The Dauphin is too wilful-opposite,
And will not temporize with my entreaties ,
He flatly says he 'll not lay down his arms
　　Bast   By all the blood that ever fury breathed,
The youth says well   Now hear our English king ,

For thus his royalty doth speak in me.
He is prepared and reason too he should   130
This apish and unmannerly approach,
This harness'd masque and unadvised revel,
This unhair'd sauciness and boyish troops,
The king doth smile at, and is well prepared
To whip this dwarfish war, these pigmy arms,
From out the circle of his territories
That hand which had the strength, even at your door,
To cudgel you and make you take the hatch,
To dive like buckets in concealed wells,
To crouch in litter of your stable planks,   140
To lie like pawns lock'd up in chests and trunks,
To hug with swine, to seek sweet safety out
In vaults and prisons, and to thrill and shake
Even at the crying of your nation's crow,
Thinking his voice an armed Englishman;
Shall that victorious hand be feebled here,
That in your chambers gave you chastisement?
No: know the gallant monarch is in arms
And like an eagle o'er his aery towers,
To souse annoyance that comes near his nest,   150
And you degenerate, you ingrate revolts,
You bloody Neroes, ripping up the womb
Of your dear mother England, blush for shame:
For your own ladies and pale-visaged maids
Like Amazons come tripping after drums,
Their thimbles into armed gauntlets change,
Their needls to lances, and their gentle hearts
To fierce and bloody inclination

    Lew There end thy brave, and turn thy face in peace
We grant thou canst outscold us fare thee well,   160
We hold our time too precious to be spent
With such a brabbler

    Pand   Give me leave to speak
    Bast. No, I will speak

Lew   We will attend to neither
Strike up the drums , and let the tongue of war
Plead for our interest and our being here
  Bast Indeed, your drums, being beaten, will cry out ,
And so shall you, being beaten   do but start
An echo with the clamour of thy drum,
And even at hand a drum is ready braced
That shall reverberate all as loud as thine ,   170
Sound but another, and another shall
As loud as thine rattle the welkin's ear
And mock the deep-mouth'd thunder   for at hand,
Not trusting to this halting legate here,
Whom he hath used rather for sport than need,
Is warlike John , and in his forehead sits
A bare-ribb'd death, whose office is this day
To feast upon whole thousands of the French
    Lew Strike up our drums, to find this danger out
  Bast And thou shalt find it, Dauphin, do not doubt   180
                                  [Exeunt

          Scene III   *The field of battle*

   Alarums   Enter King John *and* Hubert

  K John How goes the day with us ? O, tell me, Hubert
  Hub Badly, I fear   How fares your majesty ?
  K John This fever, that hath troubled me so long,
Lies heavy on me , O, my heart is sick !

          Enter a Messenger

  Mess My lord, your valiant kinsman, Faulconbridge,
Desires your majesty to leave the field
And send him word by me which way you go
  K John Tell him, toward Swinstead, to the abbey there
  Mess Be of good comfort , for the great supply
That was expected by the Dauphin here,   10

Are wreck'd three nights ago on Goodwin Sands.
This news was brought to Richard but even now :
The French fight coldly, and retire themselves.

K. John. Ay me! This tyrant fever burns me up,
And will not let me welcome this good news.
Set on toward Swinstead : to my litter straight ;
Weakness possesseth me, and I am faint. *[Exeunt.*

Scene IV. *Another part of the field.*

Enter Salisbury, Pembroke, *and* Bigot.

Sal. I did not think the king so stored with friends.
Pem. Up once again ; put spirit in the French,
If they miscarry, we miscarry too.
Sal. That misbegotten devil, Faulconbridge,
In spite of spite, alone upholds the day.
Pem. They say King John sore sick hath left the field.

Enter Melun *wounded.*

Mel. Lead me to the revolts of England here.
Sal. When we were happy we had other names.
Pem. It is the Count Melun.
Sal.   Wounded to death.
Mel. Fly, noble English, you are bought and sold ;   10
Unthread the rude eye of rebellion
And welcome home again discarded faith.
Seek out King John and fall before his feet ;
For if the French be lords of this loud day,
He means to recompense the pains you take
By cutting off your heads : thus hath he sworn
And I with him, and many moe with me,
Upon the altar at Saint Edmundsbury ;
Even on that altar where we swore to you
Dear amity and everlasting love.   20

Sal May this be possible ? may this be true ?
, *Mel* Have I not hideous death within my view,
'Retaining but a quantity of life,
Which bleeds away, even as a form of wax
Resolveth from his figure 'gainst the fire ?
What in the world should make me now deceive,
Since I must lose the use of all deceit ?
Why should I then be false, since it is true
That I must die here and live hence by truth ?
I say again, if Lewis do win the day,   30
He is forsworn, if e'er those eyes of yours
Behold another day break in the east
But even this night, whose black contagious breath
Already smokes about the burning crest
Of the old, feeble, and day-wearied sun,
Even this ill night, your breathing shall expire,
Paying the fine of rated treachery
Even with a treacherous fine of all your lives,
If Lewis by your assistance win the day
Commend me to one Hubert with your king   40
The love of him, and this respect besides,
For that my grandsire was an Englishman,
Awakes my conscience to confess all this
In lieu whereof, I pray you, bear me hence
From forth the noise and rumour of the field,
Where I may think the remnant of my thoughts
In peace, and part this body and my soul
With contemplation and devout desires
   Sal We do believe thee   and beshrew my soul
But I do love the favour and the form   50
Of this most fair occasion, by the which
We will untread the steps of damned flight,
And like a bated and retired flood,
Leaving our rankness and irregular course,
Stoop low within those bounds we have o'erlook'd
And calmly run on in obedience

Even to our ocean, to our great King John
My arm shall give thee help to bear thee hence;
For I do see the cruel pangs of death
Right in thine eye.—Away, my friends! New flight, 65
And happy newness, that intends old right.

                      [Exeunt, leading off Melun.

Scene V. *The French Camp.*

Enter Lewis and his Train.

Lew. The sun of heaven methought was loth to set,
But stay'd and made the western welkin blush,
When the English measur'd backward their own ground
In faint retire. O, bravely came we off,
When with a volley of our needless shot,
After such bloody toil, we bid good night;
And wound our tattering colours clearly up,
Last in the field, and almost lords of it!

Enter a Messenger.

Mess. Where is my prince, the Dauphin?
Lew.   Here: what news?
Mess. The Count Melun is slain; the English lords 10
By his persuasion are again fall'n off,
And your supply, which you have wish'd so long,
Are cast away and sunk on Goodwin Sands.
Lew. Ah, foul shrewd news! beshrew thy very heart!
I did not think to be so sad to night
As this hath made me.—Who was he that said
King John did fly an hour or two before
The stumbling night did part our weary powers?
Mess. Whoever spoke it, it is true, my lord.
Lew. Well; keep good quarter and good care to night: 20
The day shall not be up as soon as I,
To try the fair adventure of to-morrow.

                        [Exeunt.

SCENE VI   *An open place in the neighbourhood of Swinstead Abbey*

Enter the BASTARD *and* HUBERT *severally*

Hub Who's there? speak, ho' speak quickly, or I shoot.
Bast. A friend   What art thou?
Hub   Of the part of England
Bast Whither dost thou go?
Hub What's that to thee? why may not I demand
Of thine affairs, as well as thou of mine?
   Bast Hubert, I think?
Hub   Thou hast a perfect thought
I will upon all hazards well believe
Thou art my friend, that know'st my tongue so well
Who art thou?
   Bast   Who thou wilt and if thou please,
Thou mayst befriend me so much as to think   10
I come one way of the Plantagenets
   Hub Unkind remembrance ! thou and eyeless night
Have done me shame brave soldier, pardon me,
That any accent breaking from thy tongue
Should scape the true acquaintance of mine ear
   Bast Come, come , sans compliment, what news abroad?
   Hub Why, here walk I in the black brow of night,
To find you out
   Bast   Brief, then , and what 's the news?
   Hub O, my sweet sir, news fitting to the night,
Black, fearful, comfortless and horrible   20
   Bast Show me the very wound of this ill news
I am no woman, I'll not swoon at it
   Hub The king, I fear, is poison'd by a monk
I left him almost speechless , and broke out
To acquaint you with this evil, that you might
The better arm you to the sudden time,
Than if you had at leisure known of this

Bast How did he take it ? who did taste to him ?

Hub A monk, I tell you, a resolved villain,   30
Whose bowels suddenly burst out, the king
Yet speaks and peradventure may recover.

Bast Who didst thou leave to tend his majesty ?

Hub Why, know you not ? the lords are all come back,
And brought Prince Henry in their company,
At whose request the king hath pardon'd them,
And they are all about his majesty

Bast Withhold thine indignation, mighty heaven,
And tempt us not to bear above our power !
I'll tell thee, Hubert, half my power this night,   40
Passing these flats, are taken by the tide,
These Lincoln washes have devoured them,
Myself, well mounted, hardly have escaped
Away before conduct me to the king,
I doubt he will be dead or ere I come   *[Exeunt*

SCENE VII   *The orchard in Swinstead Abbey*

Enter PRINCE HENRY, SALISBURY, *and* BIGOT

P Hen It is too late the life of all his blood
Is touch'd corruptibly, and his pure brain,
Which some suppose the soul's frail dwelling house,
Doth by the idle comments that it makes
Foretell the ending of mortality

Enter PEMBROKE.

Pem His highness yet doth speak, and holds belief
That, being brought into the open air,
It would allay the burning quality
Of that fell poison which assaileth him

P Hen Let him be brought into the orchard here   10
Doth he still rage !   *[Exit Bigot*

Pem   He is more patient
Than when you left him, even now he sung
   P Hen O vanity of sickness! fierce extremes
In their continuance will not feel themselves!
Death, having prey'd upon the outward parts,
Leaves them insensible, and his siege is now
Against the mind, the which he pricks and wounds
With many legions of strange fantasies, *army-*
Which, in their throng and press to that last hold,
Confound themselves Tis strange that death should sing
I am the cygnet to this pale faint swan,   21
Who chants a doleful hymn to his own death,
And from the organ-pipe of frailty sings
His soul and body to their lasting rest
   Sal Be of good comfort, prince, for you are born
To set a form upon that indigest
Which he hath left so shapeless and so rude

Enter Attendants, *and* BIGOT, *carrying* KING JOHN *in a*
                     chair

   K John Ay, marry, now my soul hath elbow-room,
It would not out at windows nor at doors
There is so hot a summer in my bosom,   30
That all my bowels crumble up to dust
I am a scribbled form, drawn with a pen
Upon a parchment, and against this fire
Do I shrink up
   P Hen   How fares your majesty?
   K John Poison'd,—ill fare—dead, forsook, cast off
And none of you will bid the winter come
To thrust his icy fingers in my maw,
Nor let my kingdom's rivers take their course
Through my burn'd bosom, nor entreat the north
To make his bleak winds kiss my parched lips   40
And comfort me with cold I do not ask you much,

I beg cold comfort, and you are so strait
And so ungrateful, you deny me that

  P. Hen. O that there were some virtue in my tears,
That might relieve you!

  K. John.   The salt in them is hot
Within me is a hell, and there the poison
Is as a fiend confined to tyrannize —
On unreprievable condemned blood.

     Enter the BASTARD

  Bast. O, I am scalded with my violent motion,
And spleen of speed to see your majesty!   50

  K. John. O cousin, thou art come to set mine eye
The tackle of my heart is crack'd and burn'd,
And all the shrouds wherewith my life should sail
Are turned to one thread, one little hair
My heart hath one poor string to stay it by,
Which holds but till thy news be uttered,
And then all this thou seest is but a clod
And module of confounded royalty

  Bast. The Dauphin is preparing hitherward,
Where heaven He knows how we shall answer him, 60
For in a night the best part of my power,
As I upon advantage did remove,
Were in the Washes all unwarily
Devoured by the unexpected flood   [*The King dies*

  Sal. You breathe these dead news in as dead an ear
My liege! my lord! but now a king, now thus

  P. Hen. Even so must I run on, and even so stop
What surety of the world, what hope, what stay,
When this was now a king, and now is clay?

  Bast. Art thou gone so? I do but stay behind 70
To do the office for thee of revenge,
And then my soul shall wait on thee to heaven,
As it on earth hath been thy servant still

Now, now, you stars that move in your right spheres,
Where be your powers? show now your mended faiths,
And instantly return with me again,
To push destruction and perpetual shame
Out of the weak door of our fainting land
Straight let us seek, or straight we shall be sought,
The Dauphin rages at our very heels   80

   Sal It seems you know not, then, so much as we
The Cardinal Pandulph is within at rest,
Who half an hour since came from the Dauphin,
And brings from him such offers of our peace
As we with honour and respect may take,
With purpose presently to leave this war

   Bast He will the rather do it when he sees
Ourselves well sinewed to our defence

   Sal Nay, it is in a manner done already,
For many carriages he hath dispatch'd   90
To the sea-side, and put his cause and quarrel
To the disposing of the cardinal
With whom yourself, myself and other lords,
If you think meet, this afternoon will post
To consummate this business happily

   Bast Let it be so and you, my noble prince,
With other princes that may best be spared,
Shall wait upon your father's funeral

   P Hen At Worcester must his body be interr'd,
For so he will'd it

   Bast   Thither shall it then   100
And happily may your sweet self put on
The lineal state and glory of the land !
To whom, with all submission, on my knee
I do bequeath my faithful services
And true subjection everlastingly

   Sal And the like tender of our love we make,
To rest without a spot for evermore

   P. Hen I have a kind soul that would give you thanks

And knows not how to do it but with tears.
  Bast. O, let us pay the time but needful woe,   110
Since it hath been beforehand with our griefs.
This England never did, nor never shall,
Lie at the proud foot of a conqueror,
But when it first did help to wound itself
Now these her princes are come home again,
Come the three corners of the world in arms,
And we shall shock them   Nought shall make us rue,
If England to itself do rest but true

NOTES

ACT I SCENE I

1 what ... us? What does the king of France desire with us?
For what purpose are you sent by him to us? The familiar
"France," which in the month of a brother monarch is not out
of place, becomes in the ambassador's mouth the King of
France, as more respectful But kings, in Shakespeare, are
frequently spoken of by the more curt title without any idea of
disrespect, e q *W T* i 1 22, where Camillo says, "*Sicilia* can
not show himself overkind to *Bohemia* "

2 after greeting, the ordinary formal salutations and compliments being supposed to be delivered the *bád tasłimat* of orien-
tal parlance

3 In my behaviour, through me in the character and bearing
which, as his representative, I assume (p below, v 2 129, "For
thus his royalty doth speak in me "

6 the embassy, the message he is commissioned to bring, cp
below 1 22, ii 1 44, and *L L L* ii 1 3, "Consider who the
king your father sends, To whom he sends, and what's his
embassy "

7 in right behalf, in just claim of and as truly represent
ing Arthur, as below, ii 1 153, "England and Ireland, Anjou,
Touraine, Maine, In *right of* Arthur do I claim of thee", and,
in this same scene, 1 34, "Upon the *right* and party of her son "

10 the territories, the territorial dependencies of England,
viz , Ireland, Poictiers, etc

11 Poietiers Maine, the French fiefs which the King of
England claimed by right of descent from Henry II , Earl of
Anjou, etc

13 Which sways titles, by which tenure you wrongfully
hold these possessions several, different, divers

83

16 **disallow of this.** refuse to yield to his demands

17 **The proud   war,** the constraint, compulsion, of war which
shall meet your arrogant refusal with even greater arrogance,
shall chastise your pride with even greater pride. This I think,
is the significance of proud her, just as in the next line, "To
enforce these rights so forcibly withheld," the use of force to
recover that which is held by force alone, is emphasized

19 **Here   blood** you to it, says John, of b'oody war, but
you will find us ready to meet you on your own terms war and
bloodshed are things as much in our way as in yours, and we
shall not shrink from them

22 **The farthest   embassy.** This, the declaration of defiance
from the King of France, is all that he is empowered as ambassador to communicate in case of John's refusal his instructions
preclude his entering into any negotiations, or accepting any
terms but those of complete submission.

21 G **Be thou   heard** Let your speed in conveying my
answer be as the speed of lightning for (other wise) before you
can announce my coming it will be announced by the thunder of
my cannon Johnson objects that the simile "does not suit well
the lightning, indeed, appears before the thunder, but the lightning is destructive, and the thunder is innocent" To which
Monck Mason replies "King John does not allude to the destructive powers either of thunder or lightning; he only means to say
that Chatillon shall appear to the eyes of France like lightning
which shows that the thunder is approaching, and the thunder
he alludes to is that of his cannon Cannon is of course an
anachronism

27 **trumpet of our wrath,** the mouthpiece of our wrath in
trumpet tones

28 **And sullen   decay,** means, says Steevens, "the dismal
passing bell, that announces your own approaching dissolution"
But, though we have in 2 *H IV* i 1 102, "a sullen bell Re-
membered tolling a departed friend,' it is not necessary to see
any allusion to the 'passing bell," which was tolled *after* death,
and while the spirit was supposed to be on its way to its new
abode All that seems to be meant is, 'the gloomy foreteller of
your own (France's) perdition,' in which sense *decay* is often
used by Shakespeare, c q *R II* iii 2 102, "Cry woe destruction, ruin and *decay*", ii *H II* iv 4 66, "Towards fronting
peril and opposed *decay*"

29 **honourable conduct,** such escort, with all marks of respect
and courtesy, as is due to the ambassador of a king. for conduct,
cp *R II* iv 1 157, "I will be his *conduct*"

30 **look to 't,** see that this is done, that he receive proper
escort

31 ever, constantly

32 How that, for 'that' as a conjunctional affix, see Abb § 287

34 Upon   son? in support of the claim, and in the interest, of her son, cp below, ii 1 237

35 8 This   arbitrate   This difficulty, which two kingdoms must now take measures, make preparations, for deciding by a resort to arms, might, if taken in time and in the proper way, have been easily settled by friendly arrangement   For manage, cp *R II* i 4 39, "Expedient *manage* must be made."

39 Our   us, i e are our security, that on which we may rely

42 So much   ear, This much, conscious how poor our right is, I whisper, etc

44 controversy, dispute, quarrel.

48, 9 Our abbeys   charge   John determines to compel by force those contributions from the clergy which, when Henry the Fifth is about to make a similar expedition, are offered by the archbishop in the name of his brethren   see *H V* i 2 130 5

STAGE DIRECTION   Philip   brother   The character of Philip is taken from the old play of "The troublesome raigne of John, King of England," and the name of Faulconbridge is there given to Richard's natural son, who in history is known as Philip, and who, according to Holinshed, avenged his father's death by killing the Viscount of Lymoges

53 honour-giving, it being an especially proud distinction to have this title conferred by so renowned a warrior as Richard

54 knighted in the field, "at the siege of Acon or Acre in the old play, by the title of Sir Robert Fauconbridge of Montbery" (Wright)

58 came not, were not born

61, 2 But for   mother   I *think* we both came of the same father, but only God and my mother *know* for a certainty whether this is so, and to them I refer you on that point

63 Of   doubt, though it is clear that the Bastard had long had his doubts on this point, he does not here mean to emphasize his suspicion, merely saying that, as in the case of all men, there might be a doubt on the subject

64 Out on thee! shame on you '   diffidence, distrust of another, as always in Shakespeare, nowadays the word is used of distrust of oneself, exaggerated modesty

68 The which, see Abb § 270 a', "for *he* we sometimes find in Old English *ha, a* (not confined always to one number or gender

- he, she it they), Marie, Her Ord etc., 177 we also occasion
ally find 'em for there pops me out, quickly turns me out

69 pound for the singular number cp fathers 'five' Temp i
2 39, 'ten miles," M A ii 1 14, "fi teen year," 7 8 lui
ii 115 a thousand pound.' Haml iii 2 9vs; in all such
cases measurement, weight, or value, being looked upon in the
aggregate

71 A good fellow, an honest, plain spoken fellow

73 except land, except with the object of, etc

75 And were him, if he really was the father of us both, as
he was supposed to be, and if this brother of mine was like him,
etc

78 madcap, mad brained fellow ; 'scapegrace' is also still in
use as a term applied to children in fond reproach

79 a trick, a peculiarity of look sometimes of voice, gesture, or
habit cp W T ii 3 106 "The trick of 's frown, i H IV iii
4 416, "a villanous trick of thine eye '

80 affecteth him, takes after him, as though the resemblance
were the result of loving, but unconscious, imitation

81 tokens, evidences of family relationship

82 large composition powerful build ; cp R II, iii 1, 79
"O how that name befits my composition,' where Gaunt is
punning on his own name and his gaunt condition of body

84 And finds Richard And sees that they are Richard
himself, his very image in every respect cp Temp. i 1 29
"his complexion is perfect gallows," i e he has every mark of
being a gallows bird, one destined to be hanged

86 half face, profile, side face as we now call it.

87 With half land together with that resemblance, and
by virtue of it he hopes to get the whole of my land. Theobald
altered half that face to "that half face" but the antithesis
with all my land is more perfect in the old reading, and half that
face may perhaps be regarded as almost a single term

88 A half faced year! The idea, he says, of a fellow like that
inheriting property worth five hundred a year' it is too absurd
Theobald points out that the groats with the face in profile, to
which the Bastard compares his brother's sharp, meagre, countenance, were not coined till 1504, in the reign of Henry VII and
that the earliest groats date no further back than Edward III
For the contemptuous use of 'half faced,' cp ii H IV iii 2
233, "this same half-faced fellow, Shadow "

89 when that, see above, l 32

91 in, on; cp L L L ii 1 135, "For well you know here
comes in embassy The French King's daughter

92 the emperor, Henry VI

93 touching that time, which had reference to those days

94 The advantage, the opportunity afforded by his absence , the ordinary expression is 'took advantage,' not '*the* advantage '

96 I shame to speak, I am ashamed to say

100 this same gentleman, said with a sarcastic emphasis, as frequently in using the phrase ' this same '

102 took it on his death, Staunton is unquestionably right in saying that this means that "he swore, or *took oath, upon his death,* of the truth of his belief " He quotes *M W* ii 2 12, "and when Mistress Bridget lost the handle of her fan, I *took 't upon my honour* thou hadst it not ", 1 *H IV* ii 4 10, " *They take it already upon their salvation,* that though," etc , and Beaumont and Fletcher's *Love's Progress,* v 3, " *Upon thy death I take it* uncompelled That they were guilty " If the words meant, as Steevens interprets them, "when he was dying," they would be no more than a repetition of "upon his death bed," in the line above

103 was none of his, more emphatic than ' was not his,' was one in whom he had no part whatever

105 as was will, according to the terms of my father's will

109, 10 Which fault wives, which transgression is one that all who marry run the risk of having to put up with hazards is here used with reference to stakes in gambling, cp *H V* iii 7 93, " Who will go to *hazard* with me for twenty prisoners ?" and for play false, *Macb* i 5 22, "wouldst *play false* And yet wouldst wrongly win " For Which, with repeated antecedent, see Abb § 269

116 his will, here 'will'=disposition, purpose, design , in 1 130 = testament

117, 8 Whether to enjoy, for the omission and insertion of *to* in the same sentence, see Abb § 350

119 Or the reputed, *i e* or be the reputed, etc , be acknowledged as, etc , with no antithesis between being reputed, and being really, somebody

120 Lord of thy presence, "master of that dignity and grandeur of appearance that may sufficiently distinguish thee from the vulgar, without the help of fortune" (Johnson) cp *M V* iii 2 54, " Now he goes with no less *presence,* but with much more love than young Alcides when," etc

121 an if, if indeed , for an explanation of *an* or *and* in this phrase, see Abb § 105

122 And I him , And if, like him, I had his shape, viz , Sir

Robert's in Sir Robert his we probably have an instance of the old mistaken belief that 'his' represented the inflection of the genitive *eve*, though Rolfe doubts whether this form of the genitive was ever used with the thing possessed 'understood' and not expressed Schmidt considers that in ' Sir Robert's his' (the reading of the folio) we have the 's of the genitive and his combined

123 **riding rods** switches canes used as whips

123, 1 **such** stuff'd, no thicker than eel skin stuffed with straw, etc In 1 *H IV* iii 2 231, Falstaff says of Shallow, "you might have Thrust him and all his apparel into an *eelskin*'

125, 6 **That in mine** goes' That I should be afraid to put a rose in my ear (i e behind my ear) lest I should be compared by passers by to a three farthing piece Queen Elizabeth coined silver three farthing pieces, in many of which she is represented with a rose behind her ear Being of silver, these pieces were necessarily very thin, hence the allusion That roses were worn in the ear by men of fashion is undoubted, but whether those roses were natural, or made of ribbon (what we should now call *rosettes*), or both, has been disputed

127 **And, to** hand and if, in addition to his shape, as a consequence of possessing it, I were heir, etc to, in the sense of addition to, is frequent in Shakespeare see Abb § 185

128, 9 **Would I** face An imprecation upon himself like 'Would I might die if I,' etc , i e I would give it, yes, every foot of it, to be what I am, rather than what he is, in appearance , I swear this, and may I never stir from this place, if I am not swearing the truth

130 **sir Nob,** probably a contemptuous diminutive of 'Robert,' as 'Bob' is used shortly for that name now and as 'Noll' was for 'Oliver' Knight who retains the reading of the first folio, "*It* would not," etc , takes "Nob" for 'head, a cant term which, as he says, was in use in Shakespeare's time, as it is still In that case the meaning would be, 'This face of mine would not under any circumstances consent to be the head of the family "

133 **bound to France,** on the point of setting out for, more commonly nowadays 'bound *for*' a place

136 **Yet sell** dear In spite of its having got you five hundred pounds a year, and therefore in one way being so valuable, any one who should buy it even for five pence, would have a bad bargain

137 **unto the death,** even to death, if need be , for the emphatic the, see Abb § 92

138 **Nay** thither Elinor, playing upon his words, says, 'Nay, I would rather you should precede me thither, i e on the

road to death,' to which the Bastard, keeping up the joke, answers, ' our rustic manners teach us to give precedence to our superiors, it may show but homely breeding in me, still, in accordance with the way I have been brought up, I must desire that your majesty should take precedence of me in that matter as in all other matters '

141 so is   begun, i e that is my first name, my Christian name

145 Plantagenet "was not a family name, but a nick-name, by which a grandson of Geffrey, the first Earl of Anjou, was distinguished, from his wearing a *broom stall* in his bonnet. But this name was never borne either by the first Earl of Anjou, or by King Henry II, the son of that Earl by the Empress Maude, he being always called Henry *Fitz-Empress*, his son, Richard *Cœur-de-Lion*, and the prince who is exhibited in the play before us, John *sans terre*, or *lackland*" (Malone)

146 Brother   side   It is now the turn for the Bastard to patronize his brother, which, however, he does with more good nature than was shown by that brother when he spoke of him as "this same lusty gentleman "

152 Madam   though? Yes, madam, as it so happens, though not in an honest way, and yet what does that matter? What though, a question of appeal, equivalent to ' that does not matter '

154 A landless   squire   A squire, or esquire (lit a shield-bearer, Low Lat *scutarius*) was originally the attendant upon a knight, later a gentleman next in rank to a knight, and, so, commonly a landed proprietor, the modern use of the word Here, a landless knight makes his brother, Robert, a landed squire by resigning his claim to the family property

156 for it   need   For we have already delayed more than enough

157, 8 good   honesty   In allusion to the proverb, "Bastards are born lucky," Faulconbridge says, ' I pray that good fortune may come to you, for you, being legitimate, cannot be so sure of it as bastards, like myself, are, to whom it is the common inheritance '

159 A foot of honour, a step, grade, he being now a grade higher in rank than a plain gentleman   For many a many, in the next line, see Abb § 87

161 make   lady   Any one whom he now marries will, as a consequence, take the title of ' Lady,' the corresponding female title to Knight, any Joan means any woman, however humble her origin, just as ' John ' or ' Jack ' in English, ' Jean ' in French, ' Juan ' in Spanish, are used for any common man, cp *L L L* iii 1 207, "Some men must love my lady, and some

Joan " and v 3 930, "While greasy *Joan* doth keel the pot,"
i e some kitchen wench

162 'Good den follow!' "Faulconbridge is now entertaining
himself with ideas of greatness suggested by his recent knight
hood Good den, Sir Richard, he supposes to be the salutation of
a vassal, God a mercy, fellow, his own supercilious reply to it"
(Stevens) 'Good den' or 'God den,' *i e* good evening. 'God
dig you den,' 'God gi' god den,' and 'God ye god den,' *i e* God
give you good evening, were salutations "used by our ancestors
as soon as noon was past, after which time 'good morrow' or
'good day' was esteemed improper" (Nares, *Gloss*) "God a
mercy," *i e* God have mercy, or perhaps God of mercy

164 6 For conversation for men lately risen to a high posi
tion forget, *i e* pretend to forget, the names of their old associ
ates, to remember them shows too much consideration for their
position, a familiarity too condescending for one who has been
raised to such high rank as yourself Probably in 'your conver
sion' the pronoun is not used specifically but generically =any
man who has been converted, etc.

166, 7 Now your mess now your traveller (your, again
generical) being seated at my table, he and his toothpick,—he
then breaks off and begins his sentence again in another way
my worship's mess, at that part of the table where I as a Knight
shall be placed, *i e* at the upper end of the table "Your wor
ship was the regular address to a knight or esquire, in our
author's time, as your *honour* was to a lord" (Malone) mess
originally a dish of meat, portion of food, from old F *mes* (=Low
Lat *missum*), that which is set or placed, *viz*, on the table, pp
of *mettre*, to place — Low Lat *mittere*, to place, Lat *mittere*, to
send" (Skeat, *Ety Dict*) then a party eating together; and, as
at great dinners the company was usually arranged in fours, a
set of four persons collected together for whatever purpose; cp
L L L iv 3 207, "That you three fools lack'd me fool to
make up the *mess*" Toothpicks were in Shakespeare's day re
garded as among the marks of a travelled man of fashion, and the
references to them as such are frequent in contemporary litera
ture, cp *W T* iv. 4 760, "a great man, I'll warrant; I know
by *the picking on's teeth*"

168 knightly stomach, again dwelling on his newly gained
rank Cp Falstaff's self satisfied reference to his own "portly
belly," *M W* i 3 69

169, 70 Why then countries' why then, ruminating com
fortably over my meal, I proceed to put questions to my fine
fellow who has lately returned from his travels (my generical,
any fellow who happens to be dining with him) picked man of
countries, "travelled fop" (Holt White) Staunton, on *L L L*
v 1, 13, "He is too *picked*, too spruce, too affected, too odd, as

it were too peregrinate, as I may call it," remarks, " *Picked* was applied both to manners and dress   It seems to have meant, *scrupulously nice*   or, as we should now term it, *priggish, foppish* " He compares *Haml* v 1 151, "The age is grown so *picked*," and Chapman's *All Fools*, v 1, "I think he was some barber's son, by the mass, 'Tis such a *picked* fellow, not a hair About his whole bulk, but it stands in point "

171 **leaning**   elbow, in any easy attitude, such as a man of my position may affect

172 **I shall   you,**—I am going to ask you,—at which point he represents himself as being interrupted by his obsequious companion, who is so anxious to answer a man of his rank that he cannot even wait till the question is put

173 **Absey book,** or ABC-book, was a primer which sometimes included a catechism, *i e* a series of questions and answers

174, 5, **'O sir'**   sir, said in ridicule of the extravagance of compliment common in Shakespeare's day

177-81 **And so   conclusion so**   And so, the time being taken up by this exchange of extravagant and prolonged courtesies, and by my companion's boasting of the sights he has seen during his travels, it grows to supper-time without his ever having learnt what it was I wished to ask him

182, 3 **But this   myself,** but such society, however frivolous and worthless, befits a man of my worship's rank and of my soaring mind   In worshipful there is an allusion to "my worship's," in l 190

184, 5 **For he   observation ,** for he is an unworthy product of the age whose manners do not give indication of the experience gained by coming in contact with those of other nations For smack, cp *W T* iv 4 158, "nothing she does or seems, But *smacks* of something greater than herself, Too noble for this place "

186 **And so   no ,** this line is parenthetical   and whether I have these qualifications or not, I am in any case a bastard , I cannot escape being that in a literal sense, however worthy I may show myself of the times in which I live

187-90 **And not   tooth**   the expression is elliptical   And it is not sufficient that he should merely by habit, device, form, and accoutrement, show himself worthy of the time, *he must also be able* of his own ingenuity to make himself agreeable to his contemporaries by administering that kind of flattery which is to their taste   for motion=impulse, cp *T N* ii 4 18, "unstaid and skittish in all *motions* else"; for tooth, cp *T C* iv. 5 293, "But still sweet love is food for fortune's *tooth* "

191, 2 **Which   learn ,** which art, though I will not practise it in order to deceive, yet in order to avoid being deceived myself, I intend to learn

197 strew rising to make surer and cover my path to advancement before the introduction of carpets, it was customary to strew the floors with rushes.

198 That will her That will take the trouble to announce her coming by blowing a horn (as the letter carrier of old days, or his attendant, did), but with an allusion to the old belief that a woman who was unfaithful to her husband caused horns to grow out from his forehead.

200 That holds down? Who pursues my reputation to destroy it, as dogs hunt their quarry from point to point.

202 Colbrand the giant, to whom the Bastard sarcastically likens his brother, was a Danish giant whom Guy of Warwick overcame in combat in the presence of Athelstane.

207 wilt awhile? will you kindly leave us alone together for a time Wright compares *H H*. iii 2 1, "Lords give us leave, the Prince of Wales and I Must have some private conference", and i 3 20 Add in *H VI* iii 2 31, "Ay, good leave have you, for you will have leave '

208 Philip sparrow, the sparrow is called *Philip* from its note, Holt White compares "cry *Phip phip* the sparrowes as they fly," Lyly's *Mother Bombie* and points out that Catullus in imitation of its note formed the verb *pipilare*

209 There's abroad is generally explained 'there are idle rumours or follies abroad,' and in this sense toys is often used by Shakespeare, but the words seem here to mean rather certain trifling incidents have happened, viz, the Bastard's surrender of his property and name, and his consequent knighthood, these of course are not really trifles, though the Bastard makes light of them to Gurney

211, 2 Sir Robert fast, of all the fasts in the Roman Catholic calendar, Good Friday is the most sacred, as being the day on which Christ was crucified, and the Bastard says that Sir Robert might have eaten his part in him without violating that fast, since he really had no part in him, no share in his parentage cp *H T* ii 1 58, "yet you Have too much blood in him."

213 beholding=indebted, the active participle originated in a mistake for 'beholden,' the pass part in the sense of under an obligation, a sense not found in other parts of the verb, though a natural one of *be hold*

214. holp, for instances of the curtailed forms of past participles, see Abb § 343

216 **That honour** You who, if you sought your own advantage, ought to defend my honour by asserting your legitimacy of birth for 'that,' in this vocative sense, see Abb § 201

217 **untoward,** unmannerly in the opposite sense, *toward* is used in *T. S* v. 2 182, " 'Tis a good hearing when children are *toward*,' i e not froward, perverse

218 **Knight Basilisco like** A satirical reference to the old drama of *Soliman and Perseda*, printed in 1599, in which a bragging, cowardly knight, named Basilisco, insists on being addressed by his title, while his servant as persistently calls him "knave, knave"

219 **What! shoulder** Why, I have actually received that honour to dub was primarily to knight, by laying the flat of the sword upon the shoulder of the recipient of that honour from the king, thence to confer any kind of dignity, or new character, name or nickname The derivation of the word is uncertain

222 **Legitimation gone** I have abandoned all pretension to legitimacy of birth, to the name I have hitherto borne, and to the property which went with it

224 **proper,** well-made, fine looking, handsome.

226 **deny the devil,** i e all allegiance to him

220 **dear offence,** heavy offence, Rolfe compares *H V* ii 2 181, "your *dear offences*" Staunton, referring to the fact that the folios read, " *That* art," etc, which was altered by Rowe to "*Thou,*" very ingeniously suggests that the misprint to be corrected is in the preceding line, and that we should read, "Heaven lay not my transgression to *thy* charge That art the issue of my dear offence" He points out that with the ordinary reading we have merely a repetition of what had just been said, "King Richard," etc

231 **by this light,** i e I swear by this light were I again, if my begetting had to be done over again, *and I could chose who should be my begetter, I,* etc

233 **Needs,** the genitive of 'need' used adverbially the use was common in Old English, e g *willes,* willingly, *sothes,* of sooth, truly, etc **dispose,** disposal, for him to dispose of as he pleased

234 **Subjected tribute,** as tribute offered to love, the sovereign, in apposition to heart

235 **unmatched,** matchless, on the passive participle in *ed* used for *-able,* see Abb § 375 Schmidt points out that this word in Shakespeare is accented *unmatched* when trisyllabic, *unmatched* when dissyllabic

270. **The aweless** lion, meaning whom, the lion which usually knows no fear could not conteml "Shakespeare here alludes to the old metrical romance of *Richard Cœur-de-lion*, wherein this once celebrated monarch is related to have acquired his distinguishing appellation by having really, as he was exposed to the fury he is reported to have plucked out a lion's heart having slain him with a blow of his fist. (Percy)

219. **for my father**! for having given out the other father

215. **Ladet** nay, hadst refused to yield to his desires

ACT II   SCENE I

STAGE DIRECTION **King Philip** Mr W W Williams, quoted by Dyce, observes acutely I think, that the prefix *Lewis* to the speech immediately after Arthur, should be "King Philip, not "Lewis". He argues that the words, "At our importance hither to ... [Austria] come, could not be uttered by one so young as Lewis especially in the presence of his father who would be the proper person to welcome the Duke; that Lewis who was about the same age as Arthur, would not would not do thee right", that the first speech given to Philip he had previously spoken and that in the ordinary texts "Well then, to work, etc, implies that King John is founded the corresponding speech is assigned to Philip I have therefore followed Dyce in making the alteration

2 **that great forerunner of thy blood,** your famous ancestor Wright points out Shakespeare's strange carelessness in making Arthur in the direct line of descent from Richard

5 **By this brave** Here, following the old play, Shakespeare is led into two inaccuracies. First, it was at the siege of Chaluz that Richard lost his life long after he had been ransomed from his captivity to Austria secondly, Austria died some years before the commencement of this play.

7 **At our importance,** in answer to our importunate entreaty. *importance* and *important* are frequently used by Shakespeare with this meaning, cp for the subs *M N D* v 1 371 "Murst wrt The letter at Sir Toby's great *importance*", for the adj, *C E* 1 138, "at your *important* letters"

8. **To spread his colours,** to unfold his ensigns of war

9 **to rebuke,** to chastise, the word is chiefly used now of verbal reproach

12 **God shall**, etc "Shakespeare has made Arthur of younger age at this period than historical truth warrants, but he well knew that the truth of tragic story would be more perfectly fulfilled by having a child the subject of injury here The way in which he has drawn the innocent boy throughout is intensely pathetic—a sweet and gentle nature hurled to and fro like a flower amidst tempests bruised, wounded, and finally crushed by the stormy passions and ruthless ambitions of the merciless natures around him That the dramatist has nowise violated natural and characteristic truth, by making the little prince speak with a grace and propriety beyond those generally belonging to children of his age, we have confirmatory evidence in a record made by Froissart in his *Chronicles*, where he describes the conduct of the Princess of France, then 'a yonge childe of eyght yere of age'" (Clarke)

13 **The rather**, for the as the ablative of the demonstrative, see Abb § 94 **his offspring**, Delius points out that not Arthur merely, but the family generally, is here meant, as is shown by the words "their right" in the next line

14 **Shadowing**   war, sheltering as a mother-bird does her young

16 **unstained love**, with a powerless hand, it is true, but at the same time with a love that is sincere and that has no vindictive thoughts on account of Richard's death

18 **Who   right?** who would not desire to obtain for you that which by right is yours? A question of appeal, equivalent to, but more forcibly put than, 'Every one would desire,' etc

20 **As seal   love**, "Indentures were agreements made out in duplicate, of which each party kept one Both were written on the same sheet of paper, or parchment, which was cut in two in a crooked or indented line (whence the name), in order that the fitting of the two parts might prove the genuineness of both in case of dispute" (Note on *Hamlet*, v 1 119, in the *Clarendon Press Series*) The seals of the contracting parties were affixed to these indentures Cp the word 'diploma,' which literally means anything folded double

23 **that pale   shore**, "England is supposed to be called Albion from the white rocks facing France" (Johnson) The chalky cliffs of the southern coast are referred to in *C E* iii 2 129, ii. *H VI* iii 2 101, "As far as I could ken thy *chalky cliffs* "

26 **hedged   main**, cp *Cymb* iii 1 18-20, "your isle, which stands As Neptune's park, ribb'd and pal'd in With rocks unscaleable and roaring waters", and *R II* ii 1 40 63

27, 8 **still   purposes**, ever hitherto secure from foreign attempts at invasion, and confident of so continuing the prepos-

tion from belongs to secure other than confident; purposes
hostile purposes as here, for 'on

29 that utmost west 'Mainland' the largest of the Shet-
land islands, was called '*Ultima Thule*' by the Romans, and the
expression in the text seems a reminiscence of this

31 a more requital, for *more*, used as the comparative of
much, see Abb § 17

37 bent directed, pointed cp. *R. III.* i. 2. 85, "The thigh
thou once didst *bend* against her breast

38 Against town Against the frowning parapets of this
fortified town, cp. below, iii 1 104, "rough *frown* of war"

40 To cull advantages to devise those schemes of attack
which shall be the most advantageous, shall give us the best
chance of forcing our way into the town.

43 But we boy Rather than fail in making it, etc

45 unadvised, rashly, on adjectives used adverbially, see
Abb § 1

46 England, i e the king of England

47 That right war, those rights peacefully conceded which
we are now about to extort by means of war.

49 indirectly, wantonly, wrongfully cp. *H. V* ii iv. 94,
"your crown and kingdom *indirectly* held from him', and in
direction below, iii. 1 276, *J C* iv 3 75, "to wring By any
indirection"

50 Upon thy wish, immediately after, and as though in consequence of, thy wish "The wonder is only that Chatillon
happened to arrive at the moment when Constance mentioned
him, which the French king, according to a superstition which
prevails, more or less, in every mind agitated by great affairs,
turns into a miraculous interposition, or omen of good "
(Johnson)

53. We thee, we tranquilly await the answer which you
bring; refraining, as Constance had advised him, from taking
any steps against the town till John's reply showed whether he
was prepared to surrender his right to it or not For coldly, cp
M A iii 2 132, "hear it *coldly* but till midnight "

55 And stir task. Brace them up to undertake a mightier
task

56 impatient of, refusing to endure, submit to, etc , the
literal sense of the word, and not necessarily implying the idea
of restlessness which it has without the preposition

58 Whose stayed, which compelled me to delay till they
should be pleased to waft me here

59 all as soon, just, quite, as soon

60 His   town, his army is swiftly marching on this place,
for **expedient**, cp *R II* i 4 39, "Now for the rebels that
stand out in Ireland *Expedient* manage must be made "

63 Ate, daughter of Eris, goddess of Discord, was originally
one of the divinities of Olympus, but for her propensity to lead
gods and men into rash acts she was banished by Zeus to the
lower world   In the Greek tragic writers she is represented as
avenging evil deeds and inflicting punishments upon the offenders
and their posterity

64 With her her niece, with her (the queen-mother) has come
her niece

65 of the king's   Steevens would alter this double genitive
into 'of the king,' but the line is (except the word 'with' for
next) taken verbatim from the old play

66 the unsettled   land, all the wild scape graces of the
country, abstract for concrete

67 fiery voluntaries, hot blooded young fellows who have
eagerly plunged into the war of their own accord

68 spleens, fierce tempers, the spleen being regarded, as the
liver was in old days, as the seat of anger, impetuosity, etc

69 Have sold   homes, cp *H V* ii Prol 5, "They sell the
pasture now to buy the horse "

70 Bearing   backs, having expended their patrimony in
buying armour, etc, for this war   Johnson compares *H VIII*
i 1 84, "O, many Have broke their backs with laying manors
on them For this great journey "

71 To make   here hoping by such outlay, by putting down
so rich a stake, to win a fortune at the game of war

72 a braver   spirits, a more choicely picked body of, etc

73 bottoms, vessels, as 'keels' is frequently used   **waft,** i e
wafted, see Abb § 342

75 scath, injury, damage, as in *R III* i 3 317, "To pray
for them that have done *scathe* to us "

76 interruption of, i e interruption caused by, subjective
genitive, **churlish,** ill-mannered in thus interrupting the con
versation

77 circumstance, circumstantial narration

78 To parley   fight, i e the one or the other according as
circumstances may determine

79 expedition, swiftness in appearing here, though Schmidt
takes it for "warlike enterprise," as in i 49, above

81 We must   defence, we must show a corresponding alert-
ness in our preparations to defend ourselves

82. with occasion, mounts step by step, hand in hand, with occasion

87 Let them prepared then let us regard their coming, with something good, since we are prepared to meet it adequately.

83 Our just own, allow us to enter upon possessions justly our own, and that come to us by direct descent.

87, 8 Whiles heaven. While we, acting as God's vice-gerent, punish the proud contempt of His will shown by those who, instead of welcoming peace to earth, angrily drive it back to heaven (twice), etc. whiles, the genitive used adverbially, like nerds, twice, hvile, the substantive being feminine. though Skeat points out that the A. S. genitive is

89 If that, see above, l 22.

93 This toll thine. It should be for you to undertake that on which we are engaged; you should show your love to England by restoring her to it its real owner, viz. Arthur.

91 But thou King, but so far from truly loving England as you ought, you show your hatred to her by undermining, treacherously depriving of his rights, him who is her lawful king. Wright points out that his is here the neuter possessive pronoun.

95. the sequence of posterity, the regular succession from father to son

96, 7 Out-faced crown. Have, by the terror of your acts, caused infant majesty, i.e. "the child that was the legitimate king" (Schmidt) to cower before you, and robbed him, while powerless to resist, of that which is his chief honour, with all the violence of one who ravishes a maiden

101, 2. This little Geffrey, this small form is an epitome of what Geffrey was when he lived, contains in miniature all that Geffrey's form contained in full size, the same idea is repeated in the earlier sonnets, cp also A Y L It 7 191 4, "If that you are the good Sir Rowland's son as mine eye doth his effigies witness Most truly limn'd and living in your face"

102, 3 and the volume, the hand of time shall develop this short writing into an equally large volume; i.e. in time Arthur will grow to the same bulk as his father

106 And this Mason would read 'his' for this. Geffrey's, i.e. heir

107 art king, bear the title of king

108, 9 When o'ermasterest' When there is one living who rightfully owns that crown which you have forcibly seized upon owe = own, the final -n of 'owen' being dropped. For relative pronouns here see Abb §207.

110, 1 From articles' What mi...

you to extort an answer from me to the particular demands you make' From thy articles seems to mean 'by putting forward these demands to compel me to make answer to them', both, articles_and_draw_are_legal_terms   Hanmer reads '*to* thy articles'

112, 3 that stars   authority, who, in the case of anyone possessed of that power which will enable him to carry his ideas into action, prompts good thoughts to inquire into the blemishes by which right is often defaced, to investigate those circumstances which prevent the right from being clearly seen, and so to show that right as it really is   Delius takes the construction as "of strong authority to look", which is possible

116, 7 Under   help, under the authority of that judge I call you to account for the injury done by you, and by the help, etc To 'unpeach' was originally to 'hinder', and thence, as the first thing necessary was to hinder the escape of the accused person, to bring to trial   chastise, accented on the first syllable

119 Excuse, seems to be a translation of the Fr *pardonne*

121. Let me, the preposition being emphatic

122 Thy   king, you intend, or desire, that your bastard should, etc

123 That thou   world   Staunton remarks, "It has been doubted whether Shakespeare, who appears to have had cognizance of nearly every sport and pastime of his age, was acquainted with the ancient game of chess, we believe the present passage may be taken to settle the question decisively   The allusion is obviously to the *Queen* of the chess board, which, in this country, was invested with those remarkable powers that render her by far the most powerful piece in the game, somewhere about the second decade of the 16th century "   Without this allusion the word check loses its full force

127, 8 being   dam, although the resemblance between you is as close as that of rain with water, or, *to use a more fitting comparison*, of the devil with his mother

131 an if, see Abb § 103   The allusion is to Elinor's infidelity to her husband, Lewis the Seventh, when they were in the Holy Land, on account of which he obtained a divorce from her

132 blots, casts dirt upon, befouls his memory

134 Hear the crier   "Alluding to the usual proclamation for *silence*, made by the criers in courts of justice, beginning *Oyez*, corruptly pronounced *O-yes*   Austria had just said Peace !" (Malone)

137, 8 You are   beard   "The proverb alluded to is 'Mortuo leoni et lepores insultant' [even hares insult a dead lion] Erasmi *Adagia*" (Malone)   and there is an allusion to the story that

Austria appropriated the lion's hide worn by Richard after he had plucked out its heart.

139 I'll smoke right; I'll make the hide you wear smoke with blows if I get the chance of finding you alone. Halliwell (*Arch. and Prov. Dict.*) gives 'to beat severely' as the equivalent in the North Country dialect for 'to smoke.'

141, 2. O, well robe. Well worthy was he to wear the lion's skin who himself stripped it from the lion's back, but little does it become him who obtained it only by murdering the lion-slayer

143, 4 It lies ass. It looks as well on his back as the lion's skin worn by Hercules, son of Alcæus, would look on the back of an ass. The old reading was "Alcides shoes," and this it has been attempted to defend by the quotation of numerous passages in which the size of these shoes is referred to. Malone seems to me to make the absurdity complete when he explains "upon an ass" to mean "upon the *hoofs* of an ass." The allusion is of course to the fable of the ass wearing the lion's skin.

146 Or lay crack, i e a weight of blows sufficient to break his back For the omission of the relative see Abb. § 244.

147 this cracker, this boaster, blustering fellow, as often here in Shakespeare; but here with allusion to the last word of the Bastard's speech deafs, deafens.

149 King,—Lewis, determine, etc. The folios read "King Lewis," etc. I have followed Knight in reading King,—Lewis, i e making the appeal apply to both, and leaving the line to Austria. Most modern editors give it to Philip (without the word "King") and the next speech, "Women and fools," etc. to Lewis, this latter, following Theobald and Dyce, I give to Philip For the reasons adduced at the beginning of this scene, it seems altogether improbable that the decision in the matter should be made to rest with Lewis, though Austria might not improperly appeal to both for their opinion. Dyce reads "King Philip determine," etc straight, forthwith

100 it grandam Though it has been shown that *it* was sometimes used for *its* in the dialects of the North Western counties, we probably have here merely an imitation on the part of Constance of the babble of the nursery, in sneering reference to Elinor's address to Arthur, just as in *Lear.* i 4 225, "That it had it head bit off by it young," is merely the Fool's mimicry of similar language

163 Good my mother, for this transposition, see Abb § 13.

105 coil, trouble, commotion, as frequent in Shakespeare, e g *Temp* ii 1 207, "Who was so firm, so constant that this coil Would not infect his reason?"

166 **His mother's shames,** the shames put upon him by his mother

169 **Draws,** for apparent cases of the inflection in *-s*, see Abb § 337

170 **in nature of a fee,** in the way of a fee, as a sort of fee

172 **and . on you,** and to do revenge, take revenge, on you

173 **of heaven and earth,** of heaven by assuming that it will be guilty of the injustice of taking up a wrongful cause, of earth, by imputing to us wrongs which have no existence in reality

174 **of heaven and earth,** by flying in the face of all laws, divine and human

176 **dominations,** sovereign rights, used here only in Shakespeare

178 **Infortunate,** Shakespeare uses this form and '*unfortunate*' indifferently

179 **visited,** sc with chastisement, cp *H V* iv 1 185, "guilty of those impieties for the which they are now *visited*"

180 **The canon him,** referring to the words of the Second Commandment, "visiting the iniquity of the fathers upon the children unto the third and fourth generation of them that hate me", see *Exodus,* xx 5

183 **Bedlam,** lunatic, "a corruption of Bethlehem 'originally the hospital of St Mary of Bethlehem, a royal foundation for the reception of lunatics, incorporated by Henry VIII in 1547' Haydn's *Dict of Dates*" (Skeat, *Ety Dict*)

185 90 **But God her '** The most satisfactory explanation of this passage seems to be that of Mr Roby (quoted in the *Cambridge Shakespeare*), whose punctuation of the text is followed where "God hath made her sin and herself to be a plague to this distant child, who is punished for her and with the punishment belonging to her God has made her sin to be an injury to Arthur, and her injurious deeds to be the executioner to punish her sin, all which (viz, her first sin and her now injurious deeds) are punished in the person of this child Mr Lloyd, who, with the same punctuation, would read, 'her sin, her injury' interprets thus ('Elinor's injuries to Arthur are God's agents to punish him both for the sin of being her grandchild and for the inherited guilt of these very injuries ') Dyce and Singer follow Roderick in reading "plagued for her", and the varieties of punctuation involving varieties of interpretation are numerous in the different editions

191 **unadvised scold,** rash, headstrong, virago

194 **canker'd,** "venomous" (Schmidt), a 'canker' (a doublet

I

of 'cancer') is a worm that eats into flowers, from Lat. *cancer*, a crab. Here Elinor uses will in the sense of 'testament.' Compare *will* in that of 'determination.'

196, 7 It 01 repetitions It is in no way consistent with our royal dignities to encourage these noisy recriminations. To cry aim' was a term used in archery of those who encouraged the archers with their applause, and answered to our 'Well aimed!' 'Bravo!'

198 Some trumpet, *i.e.* trumpeter So, 'standard' for standard bearer, *Temp.* III. 2. 18. "Thou shalt be my lieutenant, monster, or my *standard*"

201 warn'd, summoned us by the sound of the trumpet.

202 for England, in behalf of England

205 parle, parley, conference. F *parler*, to speak.

206 For our advantage, that we might profit by it in first addressing you

207 advanced, moved forward, cp. *L. L. L.* iv. 3. 367, 'Advance your standards, and upon them, lords," Schmidt gives 'waved' as the meaning

208 eye and prospect, this somewhat tautological expression occurs again in *M. A.* iv. 1. 231. "Shall come into the eye and prospect of his soul" possibly it is a hendiadys for 'the eye of your town which is looking out."

209 to your endamagement, with the object, purpose, of inflicting injury upon you

212. Their iron indignation, their angry shower of cannon balls.

215 your winking gates, explanatory of "your city's eyes" "gates hastily closed from an apprehension of danger" (Malone), who compares in *H. IV.* i. 3. 33, "And winking leap'd into destruction" The radical sense of 'to wink' is to move the eyes quickly

216 sleeping stones, carrying on the metaphor of the previous line, as does "beds" in 1. 219

217 doth, if the correct reading, is probably an instance of the old third person pl. in *-th*, see Abb § 334

218 ordinance, cannon, the old spelling of the word which we now write 'ordnance', "it orig. meant the bore or size of the cannon, and was thence transferred to the cannon itself. *Engin de telle ordonnance*, of such a bulk, size, or bore' Cotgrave" (Skeat, *Ety Dict*)

220 dishabited, dislodged, removed from their habitation; for *dis*, used in the sense of *un-* to mean 'without,' see Abb § 430

221 **For bloody   peace,** for your powerful enemies to violate with bloodshed your peaceful town

223 **much expedient,** very expeditious, for ' much ' used as an adverb with positive adjectives, see Abb § 51.

224. **countercheck,** that which, opposed to him, will prevent his approach to batter your walls

229 **folded up in smoke,** whose meaning is obscure, Malone quotes *Lucr* 1027, " This helpless *smoke of words* doth me no right "

230 **To make   ears,** to cause you to listen to, and be misled by, their treacherous proposals

231 **accordingly,** as they deserve, that is, not at all

232 **labour'd spirits,** that have undergone such anxiety

233 **Forwearied,** thoroughly worn out in the effort we have made to arrive in time to succour you, *for-* in forwearied is intensive

236 8 **in whose   holds,** which, by a vow made to God, is pledged to protect the right of him whose hand it clasps '

240 **king o'er him,** i e. *de jure,* though not *de facto*

241 **For this,** in behalf of this

242 **these greens,** these green meadows

243 6 **Being   provokes** Being hostile towards you only so far as we are constrained to be so by that friendly zeal in behalf of this oppressed child which conscience and our vow dictate

248 **owes it,** rightfully owns it

249, 50 **And then   up,** and then our arms, except in point of looks, will have lost all power of injuring you, their mouths being closed like the mouth of a bear with his muzzle on   an allusion to the favourite pastime of bear-baiting, hath may be the old plural or possibly a case of the construction changed by change of thought, as Abbott suggests, § 415, owing to the comparison like to a muzzled bear   the present tense indicates the instantaneous character of the result

251, 2 **Our cannons'   heaven,** i e shall be fired off in the air

253 **unvex'd retire,** unmolested retreat, for the substantive retire, cp 1 136, and *H V* iv 3 85, " that their souls May make a peaceful and a sweet *retire* From off these fields "

256 **to spout,** to pour out in abundance

258 **fondly pass,** foolishly neglect, disregard

259 **roundure,** circle, Fr *rondeur* **old-faced,** looking old and venerable

260 **messengers of war**, cannon balls

261 **these discipline**, these [eights], well disciplined though they be in the arts of war

264 **In that**, it? in that behalf would by, i.e., on those grounds on which we claim the lordship; for the ellipsis in relative sentences, c Abb. § 244

265 **give rage**, cp *J C* III 1 273, "Cry havoc and let slip the dogs of war"

272 **Have world** We have decided to keep our gates closed against all comers

274 **witnesses** if you need evidence to verify our title to the crown, then we have brought thirty thousand each of bravest English mettle ready to spend their lives in proof

278 **as well born bloods**, their equals in birth and courage.

281 **compound**, come to an agreement.

282 **for the worthiest**, in behalf of him who has the best claim

284 G **That King** Who before the fall of evening shall, in the contest to prove who is our kingdom's king, saintly fly to their last home; for feet, cp *Cymb* V 3 25, "To darken those souls that fly backwards"

288 **swinged the dragon**, beat, overcame, but used in a contemptuous sense, a reference to the fight between St George, the patron saint of England, with the dragon, representations of which were, and still are, common as the sign-boards to inns

289 **mine**, general

290 **some fence**, some skill in fighting

292 **I would you** I would make a cuckold of you, alluding to the old belief explained in note on I 1 219, cp *Oth* IV 1 63, "A horned man's a monster and a beast"

295, 6 **where regiments** Where we will make the most skilful disposition of our forces

297 **to take field**. To take up the most advantageous positions

299 **the rest**, i.e. the French army · **God right**, may God and the justice of our cause fight on our side!

STAGE DIRECTION In many editions the beginning of a new scene is marked here · excursions are marchings across the stage of troops representing the two armies

302 **by the France**, through the instrumentality of the French forces

306 **Coldly earth**, i.e. instead of warmly embracing their wives

307 **with little loss**, with small expenditure of blood

308 **dancing**, proudly waving as in triumph

309 **triumphantly display'd**, drawn up in all their pride and pomp after this victory

314 **Commander day** victorious in the hotly contested battle just over, for **malicious**, cp *A C* iii 13 179, "I will be treble sinew'd, hearted, breath'd, And fight *maliciously*"

316 **Hither blood**, cp *Macb* ii 3 118, "Here lay Duncan, His *silver skin* lac'd with his *golden blood*"

317 **crest**, helmet

318 **staff**, i e shaft of a lance, and so the lance itself, no Englishman of any rank has been struck down by a French weapon

321 **And, like huntsmen**, Johnson believes that it was "one of the savage practices of the chase, for all to stain their hands in the blood of the deer, as a trophy" Knight, comparing *J C* ii 1 26, refers to the old English custom of "taking assay of the deer," by cutting a slit along its brisket, which however would hardly involve the wholesale empurpling indicated here and in *Julius Cæsar*

323 **Dyed foes** a pun upon the words *dye* and *die*

324 **give way**, allow them entrance

325 **might behold**, were able to behold

327 **whose equality censured**, though the thought is obscurely expressed, the meaning is, 'and we cannot, carefully as we have tried to do so, determine which of you is superior to the other'

328 **censured**, estimated

STAGE DIRECTION **powers**, forces, as frequently in Shakespeare **severally**, separately, from two different points

335 **Say, on?** Do you intend, now that you have had such evidence of our power, freely to allow our claim?

336-40 **Whose ocean.** In plain language, For if you seek any longer to bar that claim, the result will be that your country will be plunged into a conflict which will devastate it from one end to the other **thy impediment**, the hindrances offered by you to its free course **native channel**, that channel in which, if not hindered by impediments, it would naturally flow **with course disturb'd**, in a turbulent and muddy volume, as opposed to its natural clearness

342 **We of France**, we who belong to France, we Frenchmen

344 **'climate**, "is used here strictly in accordance with its

primary sense,—the slope of the celestial sphere, relatively to a particular region of the earth" (Singer).

347　Or add　dead, or add ourself to the number of the dead; cp *H. V.* iv. 8. 106, "Here was a royal fellowship of death."

348　scroll, the list of killed and wounded; cp *H. V.* iv. 8. 79, "Here is the number of the slaughter'd French" (showing a paper)

349　with　kings. With the record of the slaughter of kings; though the plural is used, the king refers to himself only.

352　O, now　steel; Death prepares himself for the feast which is at hand, providing himself with sharp teeth, *i.e.* the swords of soldiers, wherewith to masticate his food; chaps, a doublet of 'chops,' jaws, used in the plural only.

354　mousing, eagerly tearing, as a cat tears a dead mouse. Malone quotes Dekker's *Wonderful Year*, "Whilst Troy was swilling sack and sugar, and mousing fat venison."

355　undetermined differences, doubtful quarrels; 'difference' in this sense is frequent in Shakespeare, indicating disputes much more serious in character than those to which the word is now applied

356　these royal fronts, these kings with frowning looks; amazed, not knowing what to do, bewildered; see below, v. 2. 51.

357　havoc, A.S. *havoc*, destruction; used as a verb also by Shakespeare and Massinger. Cp *J. C.* iii. 1. 273, "Cry 'Havoc' and let slip the dogs of war"; according to Blackstone, the signal in war that no quarter was to be given.

358　You equal potents, equally powerful ones; for the plural of participles or adjectives used as substantives, see Abb. § 433.

359, 60　Then let　peace. Fight until the defeat of one of you shall leave the other to the peaceful enjoyment of that which he claims.

361　yet, so far, up to the present time.

363　In us　deputy, in us who represent ourself and need no other representative.

366, 7　And bear　you. And, unlike Philip, who pretends to represent the King of England, do here come in the person itself of the King of England, master of that personality and of you. Somewhat similar is the expression in *H. I.* ii. 4. 137, "Between the promise of his greener days And these he *masters* now," *i.e.* those over which he has complete mastery.

338　A greater　this. Tollet thought that a greater power might mean the Lord of Hosts who had not yet decided the superiority of either army; but, surely, the greater power is their *fears*.

369, 70 **And till   gates,** and until the matter in dispute be clearly settled one way or other, we are determined to maintain as before our position of doubt by keeping our gates firmly closed.

371, 2 **King'd   deposed.** The reading King'd is Tyrwhitt's emendation for "Kings," and the sense will be 'Owing allegiance to our fears, recognizing them only as the masters we must obey, until those masters are deposed, those fears resolved, by one or other of you proving himself our King', of for 'by' is freq in Shakespeare   Staunton, who retains "Kings," explains, "we shall trust to our strong-barred gates as the protectors or Kings of our fear"   Delius, also retaining "Kings," takes it as a vocative, and regards "our strong-barr'd gates of our fear" as = "our gates strong-barr'd of our fear"   Dyce compares *H V* ii 4 26, "For, my good liege, she [? e England] is so idly *king'd*"

373 **scroyles,** Fr *escrouelle,* a scabby fellow   **flout,** treat with contempt, mock

374 **securely,** without any anxiety for themselves

375, 6 **whence   death**   Whence they look down, grinning and mockingly pointing at the contest as it rages below , in scenes and acts there is of course an allusion to the divisions of a play , to these citizens the contest is something as diverting as a play, though so toilsome to the actors engaged in it

377 **Your royal presences,** your Majesties here present

378 **mutines,** mutineers , the same form of the word is used in *Haml* v 2 6, "worse than the *mutines* in the bilboes"   The reference is said to be to a "History of the latter Times of the Jewes Common-Weale," etc , written in Hebrew by Joseph ben Gorion and translated into English by Peter Morwyn, of which Malone met with a copy printed in 1715 ∫In this History it is related how, when Jerusalem was besieged by Titus, the three factions within the walls combined, on a certain occasion, in a sally against the Roman army⌡

379 **Be friends.** Craik, on *J C* iii 1 200, writes, "'This grammatical impropriety,' Henley very well remarks, 'is still so prevalent, as that the omission of the anomalous *s* would give some uncouthness to the sound of an otherwise familiar expression'   We could not, indeed, say '*Friend* am I with you all'; we should have to turn the expression some other way   In *T C* ii 4 72, however, we have 'And I'll grow *friend* with danger' Nor does the pluralism of *friends* depend upon that of *you all* , 'I am friends' is equally the phrase in addressing a single person *I with you am* is felt to be equivalent to *I and you are*", conjointly   **town   together,** direct your attention with fiercest energy against this town

382 **charged mouths**, up to their mouths, loaded with more than their usual charge, of powder and ball

383 **soul fearing**, soul terrifying, as Shakespeare writes... 'to fear' for 'to terrify' **brawl'd down** brought to the ground by the noisy discharge of the... cannon

384 **flinty ribs** the stone walls, which by John had been called the 'cheeks' of the city

385 **I'd**, I would, if I were in your place, **play**, ... with the artillery **jades**, properly a term for a worn out, broken down horse, thence contemptuously applied to both men and women

386, 7 **Even air** Till the moment when, stripped of all defence, they shall be as open to your attack as the air around us **vulgar**, common to all

390 **point to point**, Delius compares *Mach* 1 2 56, "Point against point rebellious, arm gainst arm"

391 **call forth** ... for minion, ... darling, a favourite, cp *Mach* 1 2 19 "Like valour's minion"

394 **And victory**, her...

395 **states**, princes, representatives of a body politic

396 **smacks** policy? Does it not relish of good policy, the well known and much vaunted policy for the emphatic the, see Abb § 92

398 **it**, *sc* the suggestion **knit our powers**, combine our forces

399 **even**, level

401 **An if**, see Abb § 107 **mettle** the same word as metal the former form being used metaphorically, the latter, literally

402 **peevish**, this word, which is used by Shakespeare in a variety of senses, seems here to mean 'foolishly obstinate'

404 **saucy walls**, walls that so impudently deny us entrance, the epithet being transferred from the defenders to the walls themselves

406 **Why then defy**, i e let us defy **pell mell**, with ding dong energy, from "O F *pesle mesle* (mod F *pele mele*), 'pell mell, confusedly' Cot The literal sense is 'stirred up with a shovel'—F *pelle*, a shovel, fire shovel which is from Lat *pala*, a spade, peel, shovel, and O F *mesler*, to mix, from Low Lat *misculare*, extended from *miscere*, to mix" (Skeat, *Ety Dict*)

407 **Make ourselves**, spend our blows upon each other, Delius compares *Macb* ii 1 64, "for it is a knell That summons thee to heaven or to hell "

412 **their drift**, then shower, that which is driven by the thundering cannon

413 O discipline ! O wise arrangement !

417 fair-faced league, smiling-friendship

419, 20 Rescue field Save those who have come here prepared to offer up their lives in battle, to die peacefully in their beds

421 Persever not, do not obstinately persevere in your purpose of first battering down this town, and of then fighting among yourselves, perséver, with the accent on the penultimate

422 with favour, i e assured that we will listen graciously

424 niece "The Lady Blanch was daughter to Alphonso the Ninth, King of Castile, and was niece to King John by his sister Elianor' (Steevens)

427 Where Blanch ? He could not find it in greater perfection than in Blanch

428 zealous, is explained by Johnson as "pious or influenced by motives of religion," in contradistinction to "lusty love," love which has its origin in the senses, cp "zealous kiss," in 1 19 above, i e holy kiss, as ratifying a vow

431 bound richer blood, confine, enclose, blood of nobler origin, cp T C iv 5 129, "my mother's blood Runs on the dexter cheek, and this sinister Bounds in my father's "

434 If not complete, O, say, etc All that can be said is that, etc , that is the only want of completion, the only imperfection in him Many editors retain the old reading "complete of," and explain it to mean "complete in such beauty, virtue," etc , but Shakespeare nowhere else has 'complete of,' though he twice has 'complete in,' viz , H VIII iii 2 49, "She is a gallant creature, and complete In mind and feature", T G ii 4 73, "He is complete in feature and in mind " The correction in the text is Hanmer's

435 to name want, that can be called 'want '

436 If want he unless the fact that she is not he may be called want

438 such as she, such as she is , many editors adopt Thirlby's conjecture "such a she "

439 a fair excellence, a piece of excellence only half made up (cp "scarce half made up," R III i 1 21), and left to be completed by union with him

443, 4 And two kings, and you, kings, shall be two shores such as I have described (i e banks glorified by the silver currents) to two streams such as I have mentioned (i e two silver currents) when they have been united and become a single stream, yea, you shall be boundaries controlling the stream

447 if you them, if you unite them in marriage

146 battery, the act of battering

148 spleen "Our author uses *spleen* for any violent hurry, or tumult of speed. So, in *V. N. D.* [I. 1. 146] he applies *spleen* to *lightning*. I am loth to think that Shakespeare meant to play with the double of *watch* for repaid, and the *watch* of a gun." (Johnson) I am afraid there can be no doubt that Shakespeare intended the pun

152 Lions more confident, *i.e.* are not more resolute

154 peremptory, sternly resolved, the 1st, meaning of the word is 'destructive, Lat *peremptorius*

455 Here a a stay, an obstacle, *check*, *i.e.* in the resolute determination of the citizen. For stay, editors have suggested 'say,' *i.e.* bray, boast, and 'flaw,' *i.e.* gust of passion, blast of menace

456 7. That shakes   rage.   Which makes old Death so furious with rage, at having the career of carnage interrupted, that he almost bursts his tattered clothes. His rottenness makes him all the more easily shaken. So far from stay being inappropriate here, as it is contended, it seems to me peculiarly appropriate. Death would not be alarmed by either a boast or a menace, but his terrible agitation is natural at the thought of being disappointed of the feast that was 'toward,' provided that the kings were not dissuaded by the Citizen from their first intention. It is to be noticed that the remainder of the speech, which deals with the boastful character of the Citizen's declaration, has reference to the effect which the Bastard humorously pretends it has had upon the hearers, but no reference to the effect produced upon Death

457 large, literally and metaphorically.

461 lusty blood, braggart spirit

462 He speaks , bounce.   His words are nothing less terrible than fire and smoke and brag for speaks plain fire, cp *H. 1 i. 2.* 156, " I speak to thee *plain* soldier '; *T. N. i. 5.* 115, " He speaks nothing but *madman* "

463 bastinado, a sound beating , Span. *bastonada*, a beating with a stick , Span *baston*, a stick, staff

465 But buffets, that does not buffet

466 Zounds, for 'God's wounds' as ''s blood ' for 'God's blood,' ''a life,' for 'God a life ', all petty forms of oath

467 my   father, him whom till lately he had supposed to be his own father also

468 conjunction, the proposed agreement

470, 1 by this   crown, by tying this knot of marriage, you shall at the same time make so fast, secure, that title to the crown

which otherwise you may, and probably will, have much trouble
in establishing

472, 3 **That you   fruit** That Arthur shall receive no such en-
couragement from his allies as will enable him to realize the hope
he now has of gaining the throne of England ; green, youthful,
inexperienced, as in *A C* 1 5 73, "my salad days when I was
green in judgment "

474 **a yielding,** an inclination to yield

476 **Are .   ambition,** are in a state to appreciate, susceptible of,
this desire

477, 9 **Lest zeal   was Zeal,** eagerness in Arthur's behalf
Knight follows Hanmer in inserting a comma after melted, and
remarks, "The 'zeal' of the King of France and of Lewis is 'now
melted '—whether that melting represent metal in a state of
fusion [as Steevens explains] or dissolving ice [Johnson's view],
it has lost its compactness, its cohesion, but 'the windy breath'
of soft petitions,'—the pleading of Constance and Arthur,—the
pity and remorse of Philip for their lot,—may 'cool and congeal'
it 'again to what it was'—may make it again solid and entire "
In support of this explanation it may be urged that there had as
yet been no **windy breath,** etc to melt the *zeal*, the yielding,
which Elinor believes she detects, being due only to considerations of policy as urged by the Citizen , on the other hand, the
words **Of soft   remorse** are more applicable to a wind that melts
than to a wind that congeals

481 **This   town** This agreement which we, though threatened so fiercely by you, propose in so friendly a spirit

482, 3 **that hath   city** referring to John's having seized
the opportunity, and interrupted France in the words, "For our
advantage," etc , ll 206, *et seqq*

485 **this book of beauty,** this beautiful face of the Lady
Blanch , Malone compares *Per* 1 1 15, "Her face the *book of
praises* " , Rolfe, *R J* 1 3 87, "This precious *book of love,* this
unbound lover "

490 **Find   dignity,** hold to be subject to my high office as
King of England, and inheritor of the French fiefs for liable, cp
J C 11 2 104, "And reason to my love is *liable* "

494 **Holds hand with,** goes hand-in-hand with, is the equal of,
etc

498 **shadow,** reflection , cp *R II* 1v 1 293, "The shadow of
your sorrow hath destroy'd The *shadow* of your face" (1 e seen
in the mirror brought to him), *J C* 1 2 58, "And it is very
much lamented, Brutus, That you have no such mirrors as will
turn Your hidden worthiness into your eye That you might see
your *shadow* "

500) and makes shadow; or I makes ... no better than a shadow in comparison with the glorious held in her eye

503 Drawn eye There pictured on the surface of her eye ball its colours all too flattering, for table at this rate, cp. d H 1 1 106 "to sit and draw His arched brows, his hawking eye, his curls, In our heart's table'

504 7 Drawn traitor the Bastard alludes to the old sentence passed upon those guilty of high treason, that they should be drawn on a hurdle to the place of execution, there hung by the neck till they were dead, and then cut up into four quarters—their heads, as a rule, being stuck upon spikes on the top of Temple Bar 'The same quibble occurs in M. W. H. I. 213; M. A. n. 2 22.

509 In such as he That so poor a creature as this should be in love with one so matchless in her person as Blanch is

512, 3. That will, that thing, whatever it may be that inclines him to like you I can easily bring myself to like, I may make regard, making his liking my own Cp M H i. 3 53 "He hath studied her will and translated her will out of honesty into English '

511 more properly, more modestly with reference to the 'ease' with which she had said she could bring herself to like him

515 I will love I will force it upon my love (though I shall not have much difficulty in doing so, though the force I shall have to employ will be no great force), compel my heart to give it entrance. Of course the distinction which she pretends to draw is merely a playful one

517. worthy love, deserving love, the omission of the prep 'of' after worthy is frequent in Shakespeare

519 Though judge, even though I should judge you with the harshest thoughts that I am capable of

522, 3 That she say That she (your niece, or I) is ever bound to act in accordance with whatever your wisdom may dictate

525 Nay, ask me, etc Your question should not be whether I can bring myself to do so, but rather whether I can refrain from doing so

527 Volquessen "This is the ancient name for the country now called The Vexin in Latin, Pagus Velocassinus That part of it called the Norman Vexin was in dispute between Philip and John' (Steevens)

530 marks the old English 'mark' was worth thirteen shillings and fourpence

531 **withal**, herewith, with the terms I offer

532 **daughter**, i e her who is to be your daughter in-law So, in *M A* iv. 1 24, Claudio, before the marriage has taken place, calls Leonato 'father,' and Leonato him 'son'

533 **It likes us**, on the abundance of unpersonal verbs in Early and Elizabethan English, see Abb § 297 **close your hands**, for references in Shakespeare to the ceremony of joining hands at betrothal in evidence of the contract, and of the exchange of a formal kiss between the contracted parties, see *W T* i 2 103, 4, *Temp* iii 1 89, *H V* v 2 133

535 **assured**, affianced, as in *C E* iii 2 145, "this drudge swore I was *assured* to her" Walker, offended by the jingle, though such jingles are very common in Shakespeare, would read 'affied'

537 **that amity**, those whom your suggestion has made friends; abstract for concrete

538 **presently**, at once, as generally in Shakespeare **St Mary's chapel.** "This is said to be the so called Church of Roncevay, dedicated to St Mary the Virgin in 1028 and re-dedicated in 1119 by Pope Calixtus II It is now used as a chapel for the students of the School of Arts" (Rolfe)

540 **troop**, assemblage

541, 2 **for this** much for, had she been present, she would have done all in her power to prevent this contract which has now been made up

543 **tell me, who knows**, let whoever knows tell me

544 **passionate**, given up to grief, cp *T G* i 2 124, "Poor forlorn Proteus, *passionate* Proteus"

547 **content**, satisfy

548 50 **In her vantage** It was in her behalf, to uphold the right of her son, that we came hither, and that right we are conscious of having abandoned in order to secure our own advantage we therefore owe her some reparation

550 **heal up all**, set everything straight, make all whole; **up**, intensive

552 **Earl of Richmond**, the title borne by Arthur's grandfather

554 **repair**, in this sense of resort to, come to, has no connection with 'repair'=restore, but is ultimately derived from the Lat *repatriare*, to return to one's own country

555 **our solemnity**, the marriage ceremony about to be solemnized

558 **her exclamation**, the loud reproaches that may be expected of her unless we stop her mouth by making her some acceptable offer

563 departed part, vanished, given up, a part. To 'part' and to 'depart' were formerly synonymous, like 'merit' and 'demerit,' et.... Staunton refers to *I. I. L.* ii. 1 147, "Which we much rather had *depart* withal"

566 rounded in the ear, whispered with "The name Rune was so called from the term which was used by our barbarian ancestors to designate the mystery of alphabetic writing. This word Run resembled mystery or secret; and a verb of this root was in use down to a comparatively recent date in English literature as an equivalent for the verb to whisper. In Chaucer's *Friar's Tale*, 7152, the Sompnour is described as drawing near to his travelling companion, 'Ful prively, and rouned in his ere,' i.e. quite confidentially, and whispered in his ear. It was used also of any kind of discourse, but mostly of private or privileged communication in council or conference. This root became round and round, on the principle of s attracting n to follow it. As in *The Faery Queene*, iii 10 30 — 'And in his eare him rounded close behinde'" (Earle, *The Philology of the English Tongue*, §§ 93 4)

568 That broker, though in l 582, and in Shakespeare generally, 'broker' is 'go between,' 'procurer,' yet it here seems rather to mean a cheating agent in matters of trade, one who, no matter whom he has dealings with, manages to drive an unfair bargain ep Bacon, *Essays*, xxxiii, "But the games of bargains are of a more doubtful nature, when men shall wait upon others' necessity, *broke* by servants and instruments to draw them on, and the like practices, which are crafty and naughty" To 'broke' is from the A S *brucan*, Ger *brauchen*, to use, manage, hence, to do business, and has no connection with to 'break' that still faith, who ever strikes a fatal blow at honesty.

569 he that, on 'he' for 'him,' see Abb \k 216

571, 2 Who, having that, a confusion of construction between 'who having nothing else to lose but their good name, are by him cheated of that,' and 'who, they having nothing else to lose,' etc cheats them of that, in the former case 'who' will refer to maids, in the latter to commodity For the idea, cp *Oth* iii 3 159, "he that filches from me my good name Robs me of that which not enriches him, And makes me poor indeed"

573 That gentleman, that bland looking, insinuating fellow, cp *Oth* i 3 403, "He hath a person and a *smooth* dispose To be suspected". tickling, flattering, cajoling, cp *Cymb* i 1 85, "How fine this tyrant Can *tickle* where she wounds" Commodity, self interest

574 the bias of the world, who gives that inclination to the world that the bias gives to the bowl in the game of bowls, to

which pastime, so favourite a one in his day, Shakespeare makes frequent reference   The bias, or inclination given to the bowl by a weight inside it (which weight was itself called the bias) enabled it to reach the 'jack,' the mark at which it was aimed, by an indirect, circuitous path, when, if it had been aimed straight, it would have been stopped by other bowls previously bowled and lying near the 'jack' Henderson quotes *Cupid's Whirligig*, 1607, "O the world is like a *byas* bowle, and it runs all on the rich mens sides "

575 **who**   **well**, which naturally is well poised, balanced, for who, referring to itself, see Abb § 228, and on who, = though it, §§ 263, 4   **peised**, balanced

576 **Made**   **ground**, made to run directly upon level ground, i e which, if circumstances did not prevent it, would naturally act in a fair way

578 **This**   **motion**, this force which diverts out of the straight line things in motion

579 **Makes**   **indifferency**, causes it to head away, to turn off, from anything like straightforwardness, impartiality   Cp *indifferent* = impartial, *R II* ii 3 116, and *indifferently* = impartially, *T A* i 1 240   Schmidt explains 'head' as 'free scope, licence,' and derives the metaphor from horsemanship   But though we speak of giving a horse his head, i e letting him go unchecked, we do not speak of his taking his head, or taking head

580 **From**   **intent** i e from anything definite and direct

582 **this broker**, see note on 1 568, above   **this   word**, which can distort everything at its will, cause everyone to change from one purpose to its opposite

583 **Clapp'd   France**, suddenly forcing itself upon the attention of fickle France   "A continuation of the well-sustained metaphor derived from the game of bowls   The aperture on one side which contains the *bias* or weight that inclines the bowl in running from a direct course, was sometimes called the eye " (Staunton)   Or rather, the small plug of wood let into the bowl at the aperture made to insert the weight

584 **his own   aid**, the aid which he had come determined to give to Arthur's cause   Mason, who has been followed by some modern editors, altered aid into 'aim', but the following line, "From a resolved and honourable war," is evidently exegetical of the words determined aid, and own, to which Mason objects, indicates his original intention as contrasted with the intention into which he has been seduced

588 **But for bécause** is tautological, either 'but for the reason,' or 'but because,' would be sufficient to the sense

589, 90 Not that   prise Not that I pretend to have sufficient virtue to refuse bribes in angels (f re... upon the coins called, worth ten shillings, and f's be named bounds. John compares M 1 n 7 5. "Ibs I e... In In deed A man that bears the lustre of an angel" salutes to be read with a doubt meaning an 'Inn' in R. J r. O II, "this fran d powder Which as they face consume" an I elsewhere clutch shut tight

591 But for, but be was unattempted wh h was as white I was not yet by its favonte enhancnng I to bribe

592 ralleth on, alas a, of course ille se plea not prose It Is used of a hand but my hand bear in reality revise "I," and the case is also often ted by the parenthesis, "Like a poor beggar"

597 being rich, when I am rich my virtue be, my virtue shall consist in, shall show itself by, etc

597 upon, for the sale of advantage, see Abb, § 191

598 be my lord, be thou my protector

Act III. Scene I

1 to swear a peace, to confirm by the vows taken in the marriage ceremony that peace to which they have bound themselves, cp J C h 1 113, "And let us swear our resolution"

2 false   join'd, Lewis be ng false an having assented to the agreement, Blanch, as belonging to the party of John, who had deprived Arthur of the crown

4 thou hast   misheard   you have not told your message aright, you must have mistaken the message given you to deliver

5 Be   advised, be careful in what you say, in a matter of such importance weigh well your words that you may not give a false impression

6 dost but say, i e you cannot really mean it

7 I trust   thee, I firmly hope that I have no good reason for believing your statement it being but the empty breath of an ordinary man (in opposition to a "king s oath" in 1 10)

9 Believe   thee, be assured that I do not feel any assurance as to what you say

10 to the contrary, in support of the contrary

12 capable of fears, susceptible of fears, as above, n 1 476, "*capable* of this ambition" She is, she says, ill in body beaten down by wrongs, a widow with no one to protect her, and finally a woman; all of which circumstances combine to make her greatly subject to fears　For the repetition of the word fears, Delius compares a similar repetition of the word 'ring' in *M V* v 1 199-202　In reality she was not a widow at this time, but "married to a third husband, Guido, brother to the Viscount of Touars　She had been divorced from her second husband, Ranulph, Earl of Chester" (Malone)

16 8 And though　day. And even if you should now confess that you were jesting with me in what you said, so harassed have my nerves been that I shall not be able to make peace with them so as to prevent their quaking and trembling the whole day long, confess, subjunctive mood　But **they will quake**=as that they will not quake　For **take a truce**, in this sense, Staunton compares *R J* III 1 162, "Could not *take truce* with the unruly spleen of Tybalt, deaf to peace", and Delius, Beaumont and Fletcher's *Coxcomb*, "*Take truce* awhile with these immoderate mournings"

19 by shaking of thy head, we should now say either 'by shaking thy head,' or 'by the shaking of thy head', on 'of,' with the verbal used substantively, see Abb § 178

21 What means　thine? What do you mean by laying your hand upon your breast with that gesture of sorrow? For of **thine,** cp below, l 209, where there is no conception of one out of a class, and see Abb § 239

22, 3 why holds　bounds? why do the tears well up in your eyes and threaten to fall, like a river so swollen that it appears about to overflow its banks　For **rheum** = tears, cp below, iv 1 33, *Cor* v 6 46, "a few drops of women's *rheum*"　**Proud,** in the sense of 'swollen,' occurs again in *M N D* II 1 91, "fogs, which falling in the land Have every pelting river made so *proud* That they have overborne their continents"　**peering o'er,** as 'overpeering' in *Haml* iv 5 99, "The ocean, *overpeering* of his list", though there the ocean actually does what the river here only threatens

24 sad signs, signs of sadness, his shaking of his head, etc

27, 8 As true　true. As true as I believe you think those false who give you good reason to believe the truth of my story (sc John, Philip, Lewis, etc)

29 if thou teach, if your purpose is to teach, etc , **teach,** subjunctive

31 encounter so, meet in such conflict

33 Which, of such kind that, see Abb § 268

34 Lewis　thou? Is it settled that Lewis shall marry Blanch? if so, what a condition is yours, my son!

35 **France** ... **me'** If France has made friends with England, then, etc.

36 **brook, endure**, "M. E. *bruke*, which almost invariably had the sense of 'to use' or 'to enjoy'" (Skeat, *Ety. Dict.*).

39 **But spoke ... done**, except that I have put into words the deeds of others.

40 **heinous**, lit. hateful, Fr. *haine*, hate

41 **harmful, injurious**, almost = hateful

42 **be content**, restrain your passionate grief: cp. *M. A.* v. 67, "*Content yourself* ... God knows I loved my niece"

44 **slanderous ... womb**, a disgrace, in your appearance, to her who bore you

45 **Full of ... stains**, full of unpleasing blemishes and unsightly marks, such as she particularizes in the next line but one.

46 **swart, swarthy ... prodigious**, "so deformed as to be taken for a foretoken of evil" (Johnson). Compare Richard's description of himself in *R. III* i. 1. 18 *sqq*

47 **Patch'd, disfigured**, covered all over

50 **Become, suit, adorn**

52. **Nature ... great** cp. *Tamburlaine*, ii. 1. 33, 4, "Nature doth strive with Fortune and his stars To make him famous in accomplished worth"

53, 4 **Of Nature's ... rose** In the gifts of Nature you may claim to rival the lily in its fairness, and the half blown rose in its delicate pink tints, the force of **half-blown** lies in the fact that as the rose becomes full blown and is more exposed to the sun, its tints deepen

55 **won from thee**, enticed away from your side

57 **golden hand**, hand which holds in it the means to bribe, in this case not material gold, but the golden opportunity offered to France of benefitting himself by the alliance into which he had just entered.

58 **To tread ... sovereignty**, to trample beneath his feet all regard for kingly dignity

59 **And made ... theirs** And made the majesty of France a band to that of Fortune and King John, used France as a means of satisfying their desires

62 **thou fellow**, here, and to the end of her speech, she is addressing Salisbury

63 **Envenom ... words**, speak of him in words that have all the malignant bitterness of poison ... **get thee gone**, be off ... a contemptuous form of dismissal

64 **And leave ... alone**, do not concern yourself with, etc

65 **to under-bear,** to bear up against as best I may

66 **I may not   kings** I am forbidden to go back without taking you with me

68-74 **I will   to it** The reasoning here seems to be as follows —I will teach my sorrows to be proud, for, bowed down as I am by grief, which humiliates those subject to it, bowed down by such a weight of grief that no supporter but the huge firm earth can sustain it, yet, in company with that grief, I proudly summon kings to assemble before me and it, proudly bid kings bow down in their turn before a throne occupied by myself and sorrows. It is the association with proud grief (to which she herself bows) that gives her pride sufficient to summon kings to do homage in **state** there seems an allusion to the word in the sense of a chair of state, as in *Cor* v 4 22, *Macb* iii 4 5, and in **supporter** the same image is kept up, the allusion being to the props that held up the canopy over the state For **stoop**, Hanmer gives *stout*, and is followed by Johnson, Dyce, and Staunton

75 **fair daughter,** see note on ii. 1 532

76 **festival,** an adjective, as in *R J* iv 5 84, "All things that we ordained *festival* "

77. **To solemnize,** in order to give especial solemnity to, etc

78 **Stays in his course,** lingers in his course, perhaps with an allusion to *Joshua*, x 12, "Then spake Joshua to the Lord in the day when the Lord delivered up the Amorites before the children of Israel, and he said in the sight of Israel, Sun, stand thou still upon Gideon, and thou moon in the valley of Ajalon." **plays the alchemist,** Malone compares Sonnet xxxiii 4, "*Gilding* pale streams with heavenly *alchemy* " in **precious** there is an allusion to the pretended transmutation, by the philosopher's stone, of the commoner metals into the precious ones

80 **The meagre   earth.** In *M V* iii 2 104, ' *meagre* lead,' the colour of which is much the same as that of earth, is mentioned in connection with ' gaudy gold ', but the meaning of ' meagre ' is ' scanty,' ' barren,' and both there and here the contrast is rather between poverty and richness, than between the dulness and brightness of colour **cloddy,** made up of shapeless lumps

81, 2 **The yearly   holiday** This day, as it returns in its annual course, shall always be observed as a holiday

85 **in   golden letters,** in letters of gold to mark the honour in which it is held Is there here any allusion to the Sunday Letter and the Golden Number of the Prayer Book, by which the festival of Easter is determined ?

86 **high tides,** " solemn seasons, times to be observed above

others (Steevens) "the usual sense" of tide "is 'season' or hour, hence the time between the flux and reflux of the sea, and, finally the flux and reflux itself—A.S. *tid*, time, hour ... (Skeat, *Ety. Dict.*) There is perh. an allusion to the fact that it is common in calendars to mark the times of the high and low tides.]

87 **Nay, week.** "In allusion to Job, in 3, 'Let the day perish,' etc., and v. 6, 'Let it not be joined to the days of the year, let it not come into the number of the months'" (Malone)

89 **stand still,** still be left in the calendar

90 **that their ... day,** that they may not be delivered of a child on that day; apparently another scriptural allusion, cp. *Matthew*, xxiv. 19, "And woe unto them that are with child, and to them that give suck in those days', though 'else' there is meant'three'.'

91 **prodigiously be cross'd,** be disappointed by the production of a prodigy, a monster ... "So, in *M.N.D.* [v.l. 420] 'Nor mark *prodigious*, such as are Despised in nativity'" (Steevens)

92 **But on this day,** except on this day; for but, in this exceptive sense, see Abb § 124.

93 **No bargains made.** 'In the ancient almanacks, the days supposed to be favourable or unfavourable to bargains, are distinguished among a number of other particulars of the like importance. This circumstance is alluded to in Webster's *Dutchess of Malfy*, 1523 'By the almanack, I think To choose good days and shun the critical ... Again, in the *Elder Brother* of Beaumont and Fletcher '—an almanack Which thou art duly poring in, to pick out Days of Iniquity to cozen fools in'" (Steevens)

94 **all things ... end,** i.e. may all things, etc

98 **pawn'd ... majesty'** pledged you my word, as king, to endow your son with ample possessions

99 **beguiled, deceived.** **a counterfeit,** i.e. a false coin ... "A *counterfeit* formerly signified also a portrait. A representation of the king being usually impressed on his coin, the word seems to be here used equivocally" (Malone)

100 **being ... tried,** being subjected to the usual test of the touchstone for ascertaining whether the coin was a genuine one, the touchstone, "or Lydian stone used for testing any metal which had the appearance of gold" (Tawney, on *R. III* ii. 2 8)

102, 3 **You came ... yours** Johnson points out the double sense in which "arms" is used here, as=(1) in war, (2) in embraces. **strengthen it with yours,** i.e. by the alliance you have entered into with John

104, 5 **The grappling ... peace** Just as the warmth with which foes grapple one another in mortal strife is, by contrast, represented as having grown cold in the peaceful arrangement that has been made, so the rough frown of war has given wry to a peace which is likened to the face of those women who make up their beauty by the help of rouge and pigments Shakespeare's plays abound in allusions to this practice

106 And our league It is by wronging us that you have been able to make this alliance our used objectively, the oppression of us

108 be husband heavens! Stand forth as my champion, as my husband would if he were alive '

110 Wear peace, complete the day without war breaking out ' a prayer which is almost immediately fulfilled by the interposition of Pandulph

112 peace! be still , a word which Constance immediately takes up in another sense

114 O, Lymoges! O, Austria! Steevens points out that Shakespeare following the old play, in which Austria is called "Lymoges, the Austrich duke," has conjoined the two well known enemies of Richard, Leopold, Duke of Austria, who threw him into prison, and Vidomai, Viscount of Limoges, in besieging whose castle of Chaluz he was fatally wounded Lymoges must be read as a trisyllable , see Abb § 489

115 That bloody spoil the lion's hide, already referred to

116 little, an adverb , some editors hyphen the word with valiant

117 Thou ever side ' You who always throw your weight, such as it is, on the stronger side , you who ever fight 'on the side of the stronger battalions,' as Napoleon said Providence did

119, 20 But when safety ' except when Fortune, that capricious dame, is by your side to show you where you may most safely take up your position, which cause you may most safely espouse

121 soothest up greatness Flatterest those who are in power, who have the upper hand This use of up to give the sense of completion is very frequent in Shakespeare

122 ramping, "properly to climb, scramble, rear" (Skeat, *Ety Dict*), thence to bound, leap , a term especially used, in the heraldic form 'rampant,' of the lion, and here particularly pointed, Austria, who wore the skin, and wished to play the part, of the lion, being spoken of as a ramping fool, instead of a 'ramping lion '

123 Upon my party, in my behalf, in support of my cause

125 Been sworn my soldier, devoted yourself to be my champion

126 **thy stars**, the good fortune promised you by the stars which preside over your birth

127 **fall over**, fall away from me, and go over to my foes

128 **Thou hide?** The idea of your wearing a lion's hide! It is too preposterous? Off it for shame, let shame constrain you to put it off, doff = do off, as doff = do on, don't = do on, dup = do up.

129 **And hang limbs** Allusion is here supposed by some editors to the calf-skin in which Court Fools were commonly dressed; but, though Constance calls Austria a fool, it is his cowardice that she is especially emphasizing here, and, doing so, she tells him that the hide of a timorous animal like the calf is much more fitted for his wear than that of a lion **recreant** cowardly, apostate

130 **O, that... to me!** ...so that I might take that revenge on him that I cannot take upon a woman

132 **for thy life**, at any price, even if your life were at stake

131 **We like thyself** John thinks it incumbent upon him to rebuke the Bastard, and tells him that he does not remember his own position and the superior rank of the Duke

135 **legate**, commissioner, ambassador, deputy, from Lat. *legare*, to appoint send

136 **anointed deputies**, kings were spoken of as "the Lord's anointed," i.e. as receiving, when crowned and anointed with the holy oil, a commission to act as God's vicegerents on earth

137 **errand** mission, though the original meaning and derivation seem uncertain

138 **Pandulph.** "Pandulphus de Masca a native of Pisa, was made 'Cardinal of the Twelve Apostles' in 1182. He was appointed one of the guardians of Henry III, who rewarded his services in obtaining peace with the French by the bishopric of Norwich, to which he was elected in 1218; he died in 1226" (French, *Shakespeareana Genealogica*, p 17)

140 **religiously demand**, in accordance with the dictates of our holy religion

142 **spurn**, we now say 'spurn' a thing, or 'kick against' a thing, but not 'spurn against' it **force perforce**, this expression, which is frequent in Shakespeare, is merely a strengthened form of the word 'perforce,' a compound of Lat *per*, through, and L *force*, from Lat *fortis*, strong, brave

143 **Stephen Langton.** In 1205, upon the death of Hubert Walter, archbishop of Canterbury, John de Gray, bishop of Norwich, was, at the bidding of John, elected to the vacancy by the monks of Canterbury, and enthroned as Primate, though these monks had previously chosen their sub-prior, Reginald, as

170 alone   oppose, do set myself alone in opposition...

172 lawful power, the power with which I was lately entrusted...

174 excommunicate, on the omission of ... in participles ending in *-ed* and *-ate*, see Abb. J. 42.

177 Canonized, with the accent on the second syllable, entered in the canon or list of saints: that hand, i.e. the owner of it.

179, 80 O lawful   awhile! As you have said that by lawful power you excommunicate him, so let it be lawful for me too to join for awhile with Pope in cursing him. To join: you Rome and room, which occurs elsewhere in S., is here strongly out of place at so solemn a time ... Rome was pronounced like 'room' not quite in S.'s time...

182, 3 for without   right. For because her champion is both the wrong, and he who upholds and on ... the extent of her cursing the wrongs I have suffered, with a play upon the words right and wrong...

187, 8 what law   wrong. Here again Constance is seen to be doing wrong in a double way; (1) when it is unlawful to repair that harm to enforce justice, let it be considered ... truly in accordance with the spirit of law ... to wrong (injury) from redressing it. If, at least if I render not wrong (... ...) it cannot be called a wrong ... ...

189, 90 Therefore   curse! Therefore, since Law in this case as it is in itself the highest injustice (you ... it cannot have the right to forbid my doing what is wrong: cursing John, it cannot be so illogical as to forbid my following Romish example.

191 And raise   head, summon the whole power of your kingdom to chastise him.

196, 7 Look   soul. That is your business, Sovereign, it is for you to take care that France does not repent, for, if he does, you will lose a soul which evidently ought to be yours.

200. pocket up   put up with. Shakespeare is fond of this phrase with a quibble, see i. *H. IV.* iii. 3. 164, *H. V.* iii. 2. 51.

203 What   cardinal? What can he possibly say except to echo the cardinal's words? Who can expect to find any newness in a character like his?

204 Bethink you, father; consider the importance of the matter.

204-7 for the   easier. For the difference between the two courses set before you is that in the one case you bring down upon yourself a new curse from Rome, in the other you merely sacrifice the slight advantage of friendship with England, therefore relinquish that the consequence of which is of less import

ance   purchase, acquisition, Kitchin (*Gloss*) on the *Faery Queene*, 1 3 16, says, "Fr *pourchasser*, It *procacciare*, to hunt after, *chase*, thence to catch (the same word save that *chase* is from Fr *chasser*, and *catch* from It *cacciare*), to seize, rob, thence to obtain, thence to buy,   connected with Lat *capio*, *capio*", Forgo, commonly, but wrongly, spelt 'forego,' the prefix *for* being intensive, as in 'forbid,' 'forswear,' etc.

207 That's   Rome   That is, the curse of Rome is easier, lighter to bear, than the loss of England's friendship

208, 9 the devil   bride   The devil tempts you to keep faith with England, and so to break faith with me, by offering you the Lady Blanch in marriage   For '*untrimmed*,' the old reading, Dyce reads '*uptrimmed*,' and supports the conjecture by *R. J* iv 4 24, "Go, waken Juliet, go and *trim* her *up*", and Marlowe, *Ovid's Elegies*, "But by her glass disdainful pride she learns, Nor she herself, but first *trimm'd up*, discerns " Delius follows Dyce Staunton thinks the old reading may be defended by the custom in former times of the bride at her wedding wearing her hair un-braided, and hanging loose over her shoulders   The strongest objection to '*untrimmed*' is, I think, to be found in the word new, which seems here to be used as an adverb, 'newly decked out ' The allusion to the temptation of St Anthony seems to me as apt whether Blanch was '*untrimmed*' or '*uptrimmed*,' and the objection that "there was no time to trim Blanch up" is almost puerile

210 from her faith, out of her belief, in accordance with what she believes

211 6 O, if   down!   O, if you admit my need, which need would have no existence if faith had been kept with me, that need necessarily infers this consequence, that if my need were put an end to, faith would once more be a living one   O then, if you tread my need under foot (*i e* take away the causes of it), faith necessarily mounts up, while if you maintain my need (*i e* the causes of it), you are, by doing so, treading faith under foot   Only and but in l 212 are tautological

218 O, be   well!   Constance, playing on John's remark that Philip is moved (*i e* shaken in his resolution) and does not answer, says, addressing Philip, 'if you are moved, let your movement be away from him, forsake your alliance with him, and, so doing, answer in a way that becomes you '

220 most sweet lout! my precious oaf, bumpkin !

222, 3 What canst   cursed?   It is impossible for you to say anything that will not lead to worse perplexity, if the outcome of what you say is that you incur the penalty of excommunication and the curse of Rome

224 make   yours, put yourself in my place

225 **bestow yourself**, act, &c.

227 9 **And the ... vows**. It seems doubtful whether the construction here is 'the conjunction of our souls is married in league,' the words 'coupled ... vows' being an amplification of 'married in league', or, 'the conjunction of our souls being married in league is "coupled," etc. In either case there is tautology, for the meaning is nothing more than, 'the inward union of our souls is outwardly ratified by the solemn compact we have made with formal exchange of vows.'

233 5 **but now ... peace**, only just before, in fact so recently that we have since had only time enough to wash hour hands in order hastily to arrange this peace between us by the union of Lewis and Blanch to clap up. cp. *1 S ii. 1 337*, "was ever match *clapped* up so suddenly?" See note on it *1 CLL.*

237, 8. **where ... kings** using which (*i.e.* the pencil of slaughter), revenge depicted, etc

240. **so strong in both**, has been variously explained at (1) these hands so strong in hatred (as shown by bloodshed) and in love, (2) so newly joined in love which in both is so strong. The former explanation seems to me the better one, as completing a climax, the degrees of which are, 'so lately purged,' 'so newly joined,' 'so strong, etc

241. **this ... regreet**, this renewal of friendly feeling; the substantive seems to have the full force of *re-* in composition, as the verb has in *R II i 1 132*, though Steevens explains it by "an interchange of salutation," and Schmidt by "greeting."

242 **Play ... faith** Juggle with good faith fast and loose, "a term to signify a cheating game, of which the following is a description. A leathern belt is made up into a number of intricate folds, and placed edgewise upon a table. One of the folds is made to resemble the middle of the girdle, so that whoever should thrust a skewer into it would think he held it fast to the table, whereas, when he had so done, the person with whom he plays may take hold of both ends, and draw it away. The trick is now known to the common people by the name of *pricking at the belt or girdle*, and perhaps was practised by the gypsies in the time of Shakespeare" (Sir J. Hawkins, quoted by Dyce, *Gloss.*) Nares points out that the drift of the game was to "encourage wagers whether the belt was fast or loose, which the juggler could easily make it at his option." The phrase is again used in *A C iv. 12 28*, and *L L L i 2 162, iii. 1. 104*, and is common in modern parlance.

244 **to snatch**, *i.e.* with haste.

245 8 **and on ... sincerity** to desecrate with bloodshed the consummation of peace, and disturb the smiling looks of good faith

by fierce discord' ι e are peace and good faith to be made the battle-field of fierce passions'

250 Out   grace, by your good favour

251   order, arrangement, rather than command, as l 253 shows
blest, happy

253, 4 All   love   No form or method, except such as debars you from all amity with England, is worthy of the name of form or method

257 A mother's curse, the curse of a parent having special weight   France has always claimed to be the 'Eldest Son of the Church'

258 the tongue, "in which the poison of serpents was supposed to dwell" (Wright)

259 A chafed lion, the old reading was 'cased', the emendation is due to Theobald, and is supported by Dyce from *H VIII* III. 2 206, "so looks the *chafed lion* Upon the daring huntsman," etc, and from two passages in Beaumont and Fletcher   **mortal,** deadly

261 Than   peace, than continue to hold with feelings of friendship, etc

264 set'st   oath, set oath against oath, in conflict

268, 9 What   thyself, the oath which you have since taken is an oath against yourself, prejudicial to yourself, and, being so, is one which you may not keep

270, 1 For that   done, for that which you have sworn to do wrongly, ceases to be wrong when done in the truest sense, ι e not done at all, left undone   Ritson compares *L L L* iv 3 363, "It is religion to be thus forsworn"

272, 3 And being   doing it   And if one abstains from doing an act in cases where the doing is likely to produce evil, the essence of the promise is secured by that abstention

274, 5 The better   again, the best thing that a man can do when he has formed a mistaken project, is to make another mistake, the mistake of not doing what he intended   For the form of the participle **mistook,** see Abb § 343

275, 6 though   direct, though the line of conduct be in this way not a straightforward line, yet by its crookedness in not doing what it had engaged to do, because the doing would be a sin, it regains its former straightforwardness

277, 8 as fire   new-burn'd   As the application of a heated substance drives out the fire from the veins of one who has just burnt himself, cp *Cor* iv 7 54, "One fire drives out one fire, one nail, one nail," though there is no reference to the homœopathic effect here spoken of

270-81 It is ... swear'st, it is by religion that oaths are made binding, but the oath which you have now taken against that by which your oaths are made binding is an oath against religion. ellipses of the preposition similar to that of 'the thing thou swearest, or by,' are frequent in Shakespeare.

282, 3 And mak'st ... oath, and employ an oath as a guarantee of your good faith in violating an oath.

284 6 the truth ... forsworn, the essential part in that truthfulness to which you bind you to bind yourself by an oath, is that it should not forswear itself, but the essential point in what you swear is that you should be forsworn ... the line Else ... swear! is parenthetical.

287 And most ... swear, and then most deeply forsworn when you keep the oath you have sworn

288, 9 Therefore ... thyself, so that your later vows, if kept, being contradictory of your earlier vows, are an act of rebellion against yourself. thy later vows Is, ellipse of for 'the taking of thy later vows is,' etc

290 2. And better ... suggestions And no nobler victory can you ever win than by arming your better parts against such vain and immoral temptations. 'suggestion' and 'suggest,' in this sense, are frequent in Shakespeare

293, 4 Upon which ... them In and or support of which better side of your nature you will have our prayers, if you permit them, are willing to accept them. vouchsafe, "to vouch or warrant safe, sanction or allow without danger, condescend to grant (F. —L.) Merely due to the phrase vouch safe, i e vouch or warrant is safe, guarantee, grant 'The two words were run together into one" (Skeat, Ety Dict)

295 The peril ... light, for this confusion of proximity, causing a plural verb, see Abb § 412

296 as thou, as that thou, etc

297 black weight, hideous, dismal In this speech, purposely made obscure in order to represent the casuistical rhetoric of the priestly mind, I have given what seems on the whole the most satisfactory text, and such explanations as it appears to bear To quote all the many varieties of reading, and their consequent varieties of interpretation, would be out of place in an edition of this kind

298 Rebellion ... rebellion! This seems to mean that, in Austria's opinion, for the legate to threaten a king in such terms is nothing else but plain rebellion Will 't not be? i e that you will hold your tongue Possibly we should read 'wilt not be?', i e will you not keep quiet?

299 **Will not   thine'** Shall we have to get a calf's skin to muzzle you with' For of thine, see Abb § 239

301 **Against   married'** Against the family with which you have allied yourself by marriage'

302 **our feast,** *i e* marriage feast **with slaughter'd men,** with the slaughter of men, with that as an accompaniment

303 **braying,** a word particularly applied to express the harsh sound of the trumpet, another word specially used of the trumpet is 'blare'

304 **Clamours of hell,** in apposition to trumpets and drums, *i e* which are suited to hell   **measures   pomp,** the music which accompanies our bridal ceremonies   Delius quotes the corresponding line from the old play, "Drums shall be music to our wedding day"   The ordinary meaning of 'measure' is a 'grave and solemn dance,' and so Fleay, quoted by Rolfe, takes it here

305 **alack,** alas, according to Skeat, probably from M F *lak,* loss, failure, etc, and so signifying 'ah' failure,' or 'ah' a loss'

306 **Is husband,** *i e* the word 'husband', even   **name,** for the sake of that name, or in behalf of that name

308 **go not   uncle,** do not make war upon my uncle

312 **Forethought,** already designed

313 **may,** can

315, 6 **That   honour,** that by which he who supports you is himself supported, namely his honour, can be more powerful with him than the name of wife   The words recall Lovelace's lines to Lucasta, on going to the wars, "I could not love thee, dear, so much Lov'd I not honour more"

316 **O, thine   honour'** bethink you of your honour, your honour, I say, that precious possession' Cp *Oth* ii 3 262-5, "Reputation, reputation, reputation' O, I have lost my reputation' I have lost the immortal part of myself, and what remains is bestial   My reputation, Iago, my reputation'"

317 **I muse,** I wonder

318 **When   on.** When considerations of such deep importance urge you to a decision   **respects,** considerations

320 **fall from thee,** fall off from you, abandon your alliance, cp above, iii 1 127, "*fall over* to my foes"

321 **O fair   majesty'** Now have you nobly resumed that kingly dignity which you seemed to have laid aside   The image is that of an exile who has returned to his own country, the exile being Philip's kingly dignity

322 **O foul   inconstancy!** Delius quotes 1 *H IV.* iii 3 55,
"Done like a Frenchman, turn and turn again !"

323 **within this hour,** before this hour is past.

324 **the clock-setter,** who regulates the clock, points its hands
as they should be, i e measures the life of man, and brings him
to his grave, as the sexton does. **sexton.** a corruption of
'sacristan,' originally one who had charge of the sacred vest-
ments, then a grave-digger

325 **Is it   true?** Is he to decide how things shall go? well
then, if that is the case, France certainly shall pay the penalty
of his treachery. Of course there is no logical connection
between the two things, in fact the humour consists in their
irrelevancy.

326. **The sun's   blood** In *Haml* 1 1 117, 9, we have, "stars
with trains of fire and dews of *blood*, Disasters in the sun," but
here the idea rather is that everything is so imbued in bloodshed that the very sun is hidden by it.

327 **withal,** with, as the word always means in Shakespeare
when at the end of a sentence.

330 **They   me** Alluding, according to Steevens, to the well
known Roman punishment by which criminals were tied to the
legs of horses, and, these being driven in different directions,
torn limb from limb

333 **the fortune,** the good fortune.

334 **wish   thrive,** wish that your desires may prosper

336 **Assured   play'd.** To me it is certain that the result
will be loss, certain even before the contest is begun. **in match**
the allusion is to some game, probably tennis, to which Shakespeare has many references.

338 **lives,** Fleay, quoted by Rolfe, prints *lies*, and remarks,
"*Lives* was often pronounced *lees*, as here, so that *lie* and *live*
had the same sound   The letter *v* could be omitted between
any two vowels "

339 **puissance,** a trisyllable, as in *H V* ii 2 190, ii *H IV*
i 3 77

342 **allay.** Capell inserts *'t,* and Dyce follows him   but the
pronoun can be supplied in thought.

343 **The blood   blood,** the blood, and that too the highest-
valued blood, etc.

346 **jeopardy,** "hazard, peril, danger (F,—L.). The original
sense was a game in which the chances are even, a game of
hazard, hence hazard or chance   —O F *jeu parti,* lit. a divided
game "   (Skeat, *Ety Dict*)

Scene II

2 Some airy devil. "Shakespeare here probably alludes to
the distinctions and divisions of some of the demonologists, so
much regarded in his time   They distributed the devils into
different tribes and classes, each of which had its peculiar
qualities, attributes, etc   These are described at length in
Burton's *Anatomie of Melancholy*, Pt 1 sect 11 p 45, 1632
'Aerial spirits or divells are such as keep quarter for the most
part in the aire, cause many tempests, thunder and lightnings,
teare oakes, fire steeples, houses, strike men and beasts, make it
raine stones,' etc " (Percy)

4 While   breathes, until I have slain Philip   Delius explains
"while Philip (i e he himself) takes breath," i e with a view to
renewing the combat   But though we have the word elsewhere
in this sense, e q 1 *H IV* 1 3 102, 11 4 275, v 3 46, it
seems more in the character of the Bastard to determine upon
Philip's death as well as that of Austria

5 Philip, make up, come up quickly with help 1 *H IV* v
4 5, cp **Philip, a slip** for 'Richard,' which Theobald would
read

6 My mother, etc   Steevens points out that Shakespeare has
here disregarded history, as the Queen-Mother, whom John had
made Regent in Anjou, was at this time safe in the castle of
Mirabeau in that province

9, 10 But on   end, go on, go forward with the battle which
a very little more exertion on your part will turn into a complete victory

Scene III

1 behind, i e in France, while John returns to England

2 strongly guarded, with a sufficient force to ensure her
safety

5 O, this, i e his being in John's power

7 bags, money bags

8, 9 set at liberty Imprisoned angels , I have not hesitated to
follow Dyce and Grant White in adopting Walker's transposition here   by the old reading the rhythm of both lines is
destroyed   **angels,** with the same pun as in 11 1 590

10 now, Warburton would read 'war', Hanmer, 'maw',
Malone at first thought of 'hungry *soldiers*,' but afterwards was
of opinion that this was implied in the text   Hungry is used by

John generally, but probably also with a special reference to himself is short of money.

12 Bell ... candle. Knight shows that Chaucer was acquainted with this form of excommunication, and quotes a minutely detailed account of the ceremony given by Fox, in which we have "the bishops, and clergy, and all the several sorts of friars in the cathedral,—the cross borne before them with three wax tapers lighted, and the rest of the people assembled. A priest, all in white, mounts the pulpit, and then begins the denunciation. The climax of the cursing was when each taper was extinguished, with the pious prayer that the souls of the 'malefactors and schismatics' might be given 'over utterly to the power of the fiend, as this candle is now quenched and put out.'"

13 bucks, beckons. As in M. W. L. 3. 90, 7, gold and silver, as equivalent to 'money,' have the singular verb. "Or if your gold and silver ewes and rams."

17 cousin, of which "coz" in the next line is an abbreviation, was a term formerly used to signify various degrees of relationship, and not merely, as now, the child of a parent's brother or sister; much the same as 'kinsman' or 'kinswoman,' from "O. F. cosin, cousin—Low Lat. cosinus. A contraction of Lat. consobrinus, the child of a mother's sister, a cousin, relation". (Skeat, Ety. Dict.)

22 with advantage, with interest, with something to boot. The word is used in the literal sense of interest upon money in M. V. 1. 3. 71, 1 H. IV. ii. 1. 599.

23 voluntary oath, the oath to serve me in any way in your power which you took without its being asked by me.

26 fit ... time, will keep it for a time better suited for the discussion of such a matter. The reading of the folios is 'tune,' which Pope, who has been followed by most modern editors, altered to time. Delius, Staunton, and Knight retain 'tune,' the last of them remarking, " We are by no means sure that the change [made by Pope] was called for. The 'tune' with which John expresses his willingness to 'fit' the thing he had to say is a bribe,—he only now gives flattery and a promise. 'The tune' for saying 'the thing' is discussed in the subsequent portion of John's speech." Staunton doubts the necessity of the change because " these words were often used, of old, as synonymous."

29 much bounden, obliged, as we say now, greatly your debtor for such an expression of your good will; for other instances of irregular participial formations, see Abb § 344.

31, 2 and creep ... good. And however slowly time may creep on, the hour will come, sooner or later, when I shall be able to give proof by deeds of the professions I now make   For never, where we should use 'ever,' see Abb § 52

33 let it go, let it pass unsaid for the present

35 Attended   world, it is the being attended by these pleasures as a retinue that makes the day so proud.

36 all too, entirely too   gawds, show ornaments, Lat *gaudium*, gladness, joy; Shakespeare uses the word both literally and metaphorically

37. to give me audience, to allow of that which I have to say being listened to as it ought to be

38. brazen, seems to be used with a sub reference to its metaphorical sense of shameless, unabashed

39. Sound one   ear of night, 'one' is Theobald's correction of 'on', 'ear,' for 'race,' occurred to Dyce, Staunton, and Collier Staunton remarks, "It has been suggested that the 'midnight bell' might mean the bell which summoned the monks to prayer at that time, and that the 'sound on' referred to repeated strokes rather than to the hour of one proclaimed by the clock, but is there not something infinitely more awful and impressive in the idea of the solemn, single, boom of a church clock, knelling the death of time, and startling the hushed and drowsy ear of Night, than in the clangour of a whole peal of bells?" Steevens thought so too and referred to *Haml* i 1 39, "The bell then beating *one*" Delius, who retains 'on' and 'race,' explains the former word by reference to the repeated strokes of the bell, and 'race' by 'course' Though drowsy belongs more properly to night than to 'race,' if that reading is retained, it seems to me unlikely that Shakespeare should have closely coupled two words so antagonistic in sense

41. possessed, wholly taken up with, wholly under the influence of; with an allusion to the 'possession' of a man by an evil spirit frequently referred to in Shakespeare

43 baked, hardened, congealed

44 O which   merriment, which under other circumstances courses through the veins with a pleasant titillation, causing that idiot, laughter, to hold possession of men's eyes, and to constrain their cheeks to shake with foolish merriment in support of keep, Staunton, who at one time thought the word might be a misprint for 'peep,' quotes *L L L* iv 3 324, "Other slow arts entirely *keep* the brain"

47 A passion   purposes, the whole line is in apposition to laughter.

48 if that, see Abb § 287.

50 conceit, conception, literally 'that which is conceived,' and since the conception of a man by himself is so often unduly

favourable, the word now days means vanity, or over estimation of oneself

51 harmful, such things as are in his mind not being fit subjects for open speech

52 brooded, i.e. having a brood to plant, sitting on brood; the word being here not a participle, but an adjective formed from the noun 'brood.' Steevens quotes Milton, L'Allegro, 6, "Find out some uncouth cell where brooding Darkness spreads his jealous wings", "plainly alluding to the custody of one of fowls while they are sitting," i.e. upon their eggs

55 troth, faith, a doublet of 'truth'

57 Though that ... act, even though my deeds were a necessary consequence to my act

61 He is ... way he is like a serpent ... take in my path, deterring me from my course and threatening to put his fangs into me. Wright compares Gen. xlix. 17, "Dan shall be a serpent by the way"

63 lies ... me, seems ever present to arrest my steps

64 Thou ... keeper you are his appointed guardian

65 offend, prove a stumbling block to.

66 My lord. The full stop put a full stop, which by most modern editors has been altered into a note of interrogation or of admiration. This alteration seems to us a mistake, for Hubert's answer is rather one of acquiescence, than of inquiry, or surprise.

67 I could ... now You have entirely anticipated the current of my thoughts

68 Well ... thee He pauses, pretending that he was reluctant to say in what manner he meant to show his love, but that it was better not to put his intentions into words.

70 these powers, i.e. the forces he had promised in l. 2 of this scene

71 cousin, addressed to Arthur Malone remarks, "King John, after he had taken Arthur prisoner, sent him to the town of Falaise, in Normandy, under the care of Hubert his Chamberlain, from whence he was afterwards removed to Rouen, and delivered to the custody of Robert de Vespont. Here he was secretly put to death."

72. your man, your servant, as frequently in Shakespeare.

SCENE IV

1 the flood, the ocean

2. A whole ... sail. Warburton and Delius see an allusion to the defeat, in 1588, of the Spanish Armado, or Armada, as it is

now generally called, though 'armado' is the Spanish word for a war fleet   convicted, is explained by Malone to mean "over-powered, baffled, destroyed." He quotes Minsheu's *Dict*, 1617, "To *convict*, or convince, a Lat *convictus*, overcome" Pope altered the word to 'collected', Malone, who is followed by Delius, conjectured 'connected'; Mason, 'converted', Dyce, 'convected', Spedding, 'combined'

5 what can   ill ? How can anything turn out well, when we have fared so badly ? *i. e.* it is impossible that anything, etc

7 divers, various, many

8 bloody England, *i. e.* John

9 O'erbearing interruption, setting at naught our endeavour to stop him   spite of, in spite of; cp *Lear*, ii 4 33, "Deliver'd letters, *spite of* intermission"

11 So hot   disposed, so fierce a haste, regulated with such prudence, in so orderly a manner; advice, for deliberation, is frequent in Shakespeare

12 Such   cause, such moderation and precision of action in an undertaking of such heat, excitement. 'Course' is Theobald's alteration of cause, and by Staunton is taken to mean "the *carrière* of a horse, or a *charge*, in a passage of arms"

13 Doth   example · is without previous example. who read, *i e* no one has ever before read of, etc

14. kindred   like, is tautological.

15 had, should have

16 So, provided that   pattern, example of a king who had been put to such shame.

17 a grave   soul, one who can hardly be called the living residence of a soul.

18 her will, the will of the spirit

19 In the   breath. Mason explains this as "the same vile prison in which the breath is confined; that is, the body" Malone, "'The vile prison of afflicted breath,' is the body, the prison in which *the distressed* soul is confined" He compares in *H VI* ii 1 74, "Now my *soul's* palace is become her prison", and *Lucr* 1725, "That blow did bail it [*sc* the soul] from the deep unrest Of that polluted *prison* where it *breathed*" The former explanation seems to me the better one

23 defy, reject, renounce, as frequently in Shakespeare

24 But that, except that.

26 odoriferous   rottenness ! an instance of what the grammarians call the figure 'oxymoron,' *i e.* a witty saying, the more pointed from being paradoxical.

27 lasting, enduring, perpetual.

28. prosperity, prosperous men, abstract for concrete. "These, David, are the things that make death terrible," was Johnson's remark after going over Garrick's handsomely furnished house.

29 detestable, with the accent on the first syllable.

30 vaulty brows, the empty sockets of the eyes over which the brows are arched.

31 And ring worms, and wear as rings on my fingers the worms that form part of your household.

32. gap of breath, "is the mouth, the outlet from which the breath issues" (Malone) fulsome, nauseous, disgusting: lit. superabundant, cloying, from *full* with the suffix *some.*

33. carrion monster, a monster that feeds on putrefying bodies; for carrion, in an adjectival sense, cp. *M V* ii. 7. 63, "A carrion Death "

35. buss wife, as though I were your wife, or as your wife would do. buss had hardly in Shakespeare's day the familiar and somewhat comic sense it now has. Tennyson seems to have had this passage in his mind when in his *Vision of Sin* the skeleton is addressed in the words, "Buss me, thou rough sketch of man, Far too naked to be shamed." Misery's love, thou with whom the wretched fall in love.

36 affliction, afflicted lady, as though she were the personification of affliction. cp. "excellent falsehood!", said of Cleopatra, *A C.* i. 1 40.

37. having breath, so long as I have breath

38 the mouth, the thunder which we hear so often, know so well

39. a passion, an outburst of wrath

40 that anatomy, that dread skeleton, Death.

42. modern, ordinary ; as always in Shakespeare.

44. not holy, 'not' is omitted in the three first folios, in serted in the fourth. Dyce and Delius adopt Steevens' conjecture, 'unholy '

48. to heaven, on 'to,' in such phrases as this, see Abb. § 190.

49. like, likely, probable.

50 what grief, how great grief.

51 Preach mad, do not use your philosophical arguments to teach me resignation, but preach some philosophy which will teach me to be mad, as the only way of escaping my grief.

52. canonized, as above, iii. 1 177, accented on the second syllable

53 **sensible of grief,** sensitive to, etc

54 **produces,** brings forward, adduces

55 **How I   woes,** showing in what way, etc   for of = out of, from, see Abb § 166

58 **a babe of clouts,** a doll made up of rags , "clout—W clout, Corn clut, a piece, patch " (Skeat, Ely Dict)

60 **The   plague,** each individual stroke of calamity

63 5 **Where   grief,** where merely by accident a drop has fallen which has turned to silver a golden thread of hair, unnumerable other threads of hair in firm friendship have assumed the same hue of grief   The idea is of a corroding acid falling upon, and taking the colour out of, some substance , here calamity having whitened one of her hairs, all those in its neighbourhood show their love by voluntarily turning white also   **wiry,** strong, and with a reference to the likeness between hair and wire

68. **To England   will   **"It has been conjectured that the unhappy Constance, in her despair, addressed the absent King John —'Take my son to England, if you will ' Does she not rather apostrophize her hair, as she madly tears it from its bonds ?" (Staunton)

71 **so redeem,** i e could as easily free him from his bonds as they have freed my hairs from their bonds

73 **envy at,** grudge

75 **Because   prisoner,** for nothing deserves to be at liberty while he is in confinement

80 **but yesterday suspire,** was born only yesterday, breathed for the first time , **suspire,** properly only to breathe

81. **There was not,** there has never been   **gracious,** well favoured, comely, as frequently in Shakespeare

82 **canker sorrow,** sorrow which eats into beauty as the canker worm eats into the buds of flowers

85 **As dim   fit,** as pale and wasted as one who has had an attack of ague; Lettsom compares R II iii 2 190, "This ague-fit of fears "

86 **And so,** in that wasted condition   **and rising,** and he rising

88, 9 **never Must I,** I am destined never, etc

90 **You hold   grief   **You allow grief to subdue you too completely, and so are guilty of sin   "The Cardinal," says Delius, "speaks as a priest, and as such Constance answers him," priests of the Catholic Church being forbidden to marry   For **respect,** cp. M V i 1 74 "You have too much respect upon the world "

91 **He talks   son.** Steevens compares Macb iv 3 216, "He

has no children," said by Macduff when, Ross having brought tidings of the murder of his wife and children. Malcolm tries to comfort him. So, *H. J. d 2 1*, "He jests at scars that never felt a wound."

93 **Grief fills,** etc. To Philip's rebuke, "You are as fond of grief as of your child," Constance replies, 'If I am, it is because grief assumes the likeness and ways of that child.'

96 **Remembers,** reminds; gracious parts, i.e. winning gifts, personal and moral.

97 **stuffs** form, fills out his garments with an image of himself.

98. **Then, have** grief? We should now say, "Then have I not," etc.

101 **this form,** this orderly arrangement of joy; but; the hands which confined her locks in an orderly way.

102. **When wit.** When the state of my mind presents such a contrast to the state of my hair.

104 **my all the world,** to be regarded as a single many-worded term.

106 **some outrage,** done upon herself.

107 **joy,** a verb.

108. **Life tale.** Malone believes that Shakespeare here had in mind the words of the 90th Psalm, "For when thou art angry, all our days are gone, we bring our years to an end as it were a *tale that is told*." He also quotes, *Macb. v. 5 26, 7*, "Life's but a walking shadow ... it is a tale 'Told by an idiot, full of sound and fury, Signifying nothing."

110 **And bitter taste.** Perhaps with a special reference to the joy which, as a newly married man, he ought to be feeling, but is not. The folios have 'sweet word's,' which Malone endeavours to defend by explaining that the 'sweet word' is 'life.'

111 **That,** so that.

114, 5 **evils** evil, clearly, I think, an allusion to the miracle of Christ in casting out a devil from a man possessed, *Mark i 26*, "And when the unclean spirit *had torn him*, and cried with a loud voice, he came out of him."

116 **by losing of,** see note on ii 1 19. this day, i.e. the battle, though the Dauphin takes the word in its ordinary sense.

118 **If you had,** certainly you would have lost "all days of glory," etc.

122 **In this won,** in this which he regards as a victory.

125 **Your blood.** Then, if you are grieved at this, you show yourself as 'green in judgment' as you are young in years.

127-30 For even   throne, for the breath of the words I am about to speak will be sufficient to remove every obstacle, even the smallest, from the path by which you shall march straight to the throne of England , that is, if you will listen to me, you will see plainly what the steps are that you will have to take, and how your path will be smoothed, in making your effort to get possession of the English throne   **each dust**, each particle of dust , cp iv 1 93, and *R II* ii 3 ,91, "Dared once to touch *a dust* of England's ground "   **rub**, that which causes friction, an impediment , often used in Shakespeare in reference to the 'rubbing' of bowls one against another

132 whiles, see note on ii 1 87

133 misplaced John, John who has no right to the place, usurping John

135 unruly, a hand that is guided by no rule, unscrupulous Delius compares *Macb* iii 1 63, "put a barren sceptre in my gripe Thence to be wrench'd by an unlineal hand "

136 as boisterously, by the same forcible means

137 And he   up, and he whose position is a slippery one, does not hesitate to make use of any support, however vile, to keep himself from falling

138 him, reflexive

139 That John, in order that, etc

140 but so, in any other way

143 all the claim, claim to everything that Arthur claimed

145 How green   world ! How simple-minded you are though living in a world so worn and jaded ! Possibly also with the idea of its familiarity with stratagems such as those of which the Dauphin is so innocent

146 you, for you , *i e.* that will serve your purpose, on *me, thee, him*, etc , representing the old dative case, see Abb § 220

147 in true blood, "the blood of him that has the just claim" (Johnson)

148 Shall find   untrue Shall find no other safety than that to be obtained by bloodshed, a safety with a treacherous foundation

149 so evilly borne, so discontentedly endured , the folios have *born*, which some edd retain, with the meaning, I suppose, of 'which had such an evil origin' Dyce, Staunton, Delius and Rolfe read *borne*

151, 2 That none   it, that no opportunity shall offer itself for limiting his power that they will not eagerly seize upon

153 exhalation, meteor , cp i *H IV* ii 4 352, "My lord, do you see these meteors ? do you behold these *exhalations?*"

Milton, *P. L.* v. 186, show us the word is all this to raise, that which is sucked up from the earth by the sun, "Vapours and exhalations, that now rise from hill or steaming lake."

154 scope, which has been diverted into a new track of nature, "may," according to Schmidt and Dyce, "is everything which lies within the limits of Nature's power." Rolfe, who gives "free play, operation" as the meaning, see, justly remarks that *scope* "could refer only to a prodigy or something in the ordinary course of nature, as if the context considered only common and customary phenomena which the people ascribe to be prodigies and signs." *distemper'd day, stormy day.*

156 But they cause, which they will not dissociate from its natural cause

157 Abortives, monstrous births prosages, omens: tongues of heaven, indications of heaven's will

160 May be, it may be, possibly

161 But Imprisonment. But considers himself to see in the fact of Arthur's being confined in prison

163 If that already, if it be that he has not already been made away with, on the other 'that' to 'if,' see Abb. § 287.

164 Even news, the very moment the news of your approach shall be noised abroad

166 And kiss change, and gladly welcome that change to which they are such strangers, having so long groaned under his tyrannical rule

167, 8 And pick John. And find strong pretext for fierce revolt in the bloody deeds of John's hands. This not very delicate metaphor is indicative of an age in which men were less careful than now of personal cleanliness.

169 hurly, what in *Macb.* i. 1. 4, is called 'hurly-burly,' confusion, tumult, from Fr. *hurler*, to howl, yell on foot, in motion, started, an expression commonly used in sporting, cf. *1 H. IV.* i. 3. 278, "Before the game is afoot, thou still let'st slip", *H. V.* iii. 1. 32.

170, 1 And, named' And, O, a proceeding still more actively working in your behalf than anything I have yet mentioned'

172, 3 ransacking charity, plundering the Church, and so turning into ill will any good feeling the people might have for John Schmidt explains Offending charity as sinning against piety'

174 they call, "An allusion to the reed, or pipe, termed a *bird call*, or to the practice of bird catchers, who, in laying their nets, place a caged bird over them, which they term the

call-bird or bird-*call*, to lure the wild birds to the snare   Thus
in Beaumont and Fletcher's play of *The Bloody Brother*, iv 2,
Pippean, the scout or decoy of the Astrologers, tells them —
'—but it is I that bring you in your rents for 'em, 'tis Pippean
That is your *bird-call* " (Staunton)

175   to train, to allure

176, 7 Or as   mountain   Bacon, in his History of Henry
VII speaking of Simnel's march, observes that " their *snow-ball*
did not gather as it went " (Johnson)   tumbled about, being
rolled about   Anon, " immediately   —A S *on an*, lit in one
moment   —A S *on*   often used with the sense of *in*   and A S
an, the old form of *one* " (Skeat, *Ety Dict*)

178, 9 'tis   discontent, i e   there is no saying how their discontent may not be turned to your profit

180   topfull, full to the brim, completely, cp *Macb* 1 5 43,
" from the crown to the toe *top-full* Of direst cruelty "

181   whet on, stimulate, sharpen to the action

ACT IV   SCENE I

STAGE DIRECTION   a castle   In many editions the locality is
given as Northampton, but Malone points out that there is no
reason for this beyond the fact that in the first Act John seems
to have been in that town   Arthur was in reality put to death,
or died, in Rouen, but there is no certainty even as to the
manner of his death

1   Heat me, i e   for me , see Abb § 220

2   arras, tapestry hangings, so named from Arras, in Provence,
where they were most commonly made   Shakespeare frequently
notes the use that was made of them as places of concealment
For words similarly derived see Trench, *The Study of Words*,
pp 153 *et seqq.*

3   bosom, Delius compares *R II* iii. 2 147, " Write sorrow
on the *bosom* of the earth "

4   which, for ' which,' used interchangeably with ' who,' see
Abb § 265

6   I hope   deed, I hope the warrant you have received will
justify the deed

7   Uncleanly, foul, unbecoming, scruples

8   to say with, to speak with

10, 1 As little   be   As small, insignificant, a prince as one
can possibly be who has such just claim as I have to be more
of a prince

12 I   **merrier** There have been times in my life when I was merrier

16 **Only** wantonness, only out of perversity. Steevens, in illustration of this association, quotes, among other passages, Lyly's *Midas*, 1592, "*Melancholy*, is *melancholy* a word for a barber's mouth? Thou shouldst say heavy, dull, and doltish, *melancholy* is the crest of courtiers, and now every base companion, etc., says he is in *melancholy*." **By my christendom**, by my faith as a Christian. The word was also used for christening, and for baptismal name

17 **So I were**, provided I were

19, 20 **but   me** If it were not that I suspect my uncle is plotting worse injuries to me **practices = plots**, frequent in Shakespeare

21 **so you would**, if only you would, etc.

25 **prate**, used of the language of children as well as for such a chattering

27 **sudden**, swift

30 **watch with you**, keep watch by your bedside, nurse you

33, 4 **How now   door!** What is the meaning of your demeaning yourselves, you foolish tears, that drive away the pride of cruelty which should possess my heart? **dispiteous**, stronger than 'unpitying', as positive instead of negative. **out of door**, we should now use the substantive in the plural, as Shakespeare does generally

35 **resolution**, unbending sternness of purpose

37 **fair writ**, plainly written, for the part see former etc. Abb. § 342.

38 **Too fairly   effect** Arthur, using the word fairly in its ordinary sense, answers, "Yes, too fairly, considering; its total purport"

41 **the heart**, such hardness of heart.

42 I   **handkercher**, I bound my handkerchief; 'kerchief' is lit. *couvre chef*, that which covers the head, and 'handkerchief', a cloth of a like nature used by the hand, handkercher being merely a shortened colloquial form, as in *H. V.* iii. 2. 54, "as familiar with men's pockets as their gloves or their handkerchers."

43 **wrought it me**, worked, embroidered, it for me,

44 **And   again**, and precious as it was, I never asked you to return it to me

45 **held   head**, laid my hand upon your head to cool it, or to soothe the pain by pressure

46, 7 **And   time** And with the same watchfulness with which the minutes keep count of the passing hour, I contrived from minute to minute to cheer you up as best I could, **the watchful minutes to the hour is a** transposition for 'the minutes watchful to the hour' Schmidt explains to the hour as = till the hour is full,' a sense which I do not think the words will bear

47 **Still and anon**, continually, literally 'ever and at once.'

48. **grief**, bodily pain

49 **What good love**, what office of love can I perform? What token of my affection can I show?

50 **lien**, another form of 'lain,' found in the quartos in *Haml* v 1 190, *Per* iii 2 85

52 **sick service**, at your service when sick, Delius hyphens the two words, and compares 'sick-bed'

56 **Why   must** Why, then, it cannot be helped

57 **nor never**, the emphatic double negative

58 **So much as**, even

59 **And with   out** And not only must I put them out, but I must do so, as I have sworn, by burning with hot irons.

60 **iron age**, cruel age

61 **heat**, for the omission of the termination *-ed* after *d* and *t*, see Abb § 342

63 **his fiery indignation**, its; Steevens says the phrase is from *Hebrews*, x 27, "a certain fearful looking-for of judgment, and *fiery indignation*", of course in the text fiery is used literally

64 **the matter**, Dyce adopts Lettsom's conjecture, 'water,' comparing iv 3 107 110, "Trust not those cunning *waters* of his eyes," and "Like *rivers* of remorse and *innocency*" if matter is retained the sense will be the same, viz, my tears

66 **But   eye** Merely in consequence of, out of remorse for, having at one time been guilty of containing fire intended for such a cruel purpose

67 **hammer'd iron**, iron beaten into strongest consistency by the hammer

69 **should**, was intending, the conjunctive of 'shall', see Abb § 326

70 **no   Hubert's**, I would not have believed any tongue except Hubert's Steevens reads, "I would not have believed no tongue, but Hubert's," and justifies the double negative by quoting from *A Y L* iii. 5 27, "*Nor*, I am sure, there is *no* force in eyes That can do hurt" Knight, adopting a conjecture of Steevens', marks an aposiopesis, "No tongue but Hubert's,"— i e would have convinced me

72. **as I bid you**, i e as I *bade* you, see above, l 4.

73, 1 **my eyes** men. The mere look of the cruel men has been enough in it. If to put my eyes out, to blind &c.

77 **stone still**, as motionless as a stone; cp. 'stone blind,' 'stone deaf'

82 **Nor look angerly** nor even look angerly at &c. for angerly see Abb § 447, and cp. *M* *of* *ur* 5 1, "Why, how now, He ate! you look angerly"

81 **let me alone** leave me to deal with &c in deal with alone, *M* E *of* (*v* ill) and &c

84 **I am deed, I am only** so glad to be away from, to have nothing to do with, as is a deed out 'from' see by trans with out a verb of action, see Abb § 158

87 **child** see Abb § 417

89, 90 **that his yours** That his feeling of pity may grow new life to kindle again, yours

92 **mote** in the folios, 'moth,' which is only an other spelling of mote; cp *Haml* i 1 112, "A mote it is to trouble the mind's eye"

93 **a dust**, a particle of dust, see in 1 128

94 **Any sense'** Anything that can as pain to an organ so exquisite and so delicately sensitive

95 **Then feeling if you felt . boisterous**, "The word (formerly intractable, violent) has come to be restricted to 'loud weather' (*H* *I* iii 3 11) and like any discontentment" (Rolfe) here it means 'causing so much of annoying, irritation.'

97 **Is promise'** Is this the way you keep your promise' referring to l 81 go to here in exclamation of impatience or rebuke, sometimes of exhortation

98 9 **the utterance eyes**, even a brace of tongues would be insufficient to plead for the preservation of a pair of eyes, want pleading, lack eloquence in pleading Must needs, see note on 1 1 203

100 **Let me tongue**, do not compel me to be silent

102 **So I may**, provided I may

103. **Though you'** If for no other occupation but, etc.

104. **the instrument**, the burning iron.

105 **would not**, is unwilling

106 8 **with grief extremes**, from grief at the thought of being so undeservedly used for such measures of cruelty, it being created to give comfort The burning iron I is been spoken of as having feelings of its own, and now the same tenderness is predicated of the fire see else yourself, if you do not believe what I have said, look at the coal

109 There is   coal Grey would alter this to " There is no malice burning in this coal ", but this burning coal probably means nothing more than this coal which had been lighted, though the fire in it was now almost extinct   for malice, cp ii 1 231, " Our cannons' *malice* "

111 And strew'd   head The ashes which remain on the top of a partially burnt out coal are likened to the ashes which penitents heaped on their heads to express their contrition , To repent in ashes and sackcloth, or ashes and dust, is a phrase common in the Bible   Cp *R II* v 1 50, 1, " And some (i e of the logs of wood) will mourn in ashes, some coal black, For the deposing of a rightful king "

114 shame of, shame at

115 sparkle, shoot up in sparks into your eye

117 Snatch at, snap at, make a bite at, endeavour to bite , at indicates the effort   tarre, urge, set him on , cp *Haml* ii 2 370, " and the nation holds it no sin to *tarre* them to controversy ", an old English word from A S *tyrgan,* to irritate , used by Wiclif in his translation of the Psalms, " They have *tarrid* thee to ire," which in the authorized version reads, " they provoked him to anger "

118 should use, conj of ' shall ', all things that you may intend to use "

119 Deny   office, renounce their proper function

120 which   extends, which fierce fire and iron go out of their way to show , fire and iron being regarded as one idea have the singular verb

121 Creatures   uses Creatures well known for employment in deeds of cruelty   Craik, *Eng of Shakespeare,* § 181, remarks, " We have come in the language of the present day to understand *creature* almost exclusively in the sense of a living creature, although it was formerly used freely for everything created,—as when Bacon says (Essay, Of Truth), ' The first creature of God, in the works of the days was the light of the sense '   or (*Adv of Learning,* Bk 1), ' The wit and mind of man, if its work upon matter, which is the contemplation of the creatures of God '   or as it is written in our authorized version of the Scriptures (1 *Tim* iv 4), ' Every creature of God (πᾶν κτίσμα Θεοῦ) is good ' "

Cp *Temp* iii 3 74, " Incensed the seas and shores, yea, all the *creatures*," i e everything created, the winds, thunders, etc

122 Well, see to live, " well, live, and live with the means of seeing , that is, with your eyes uninjured " (Malone)

123 For   treasure, even if by so doing I could gain all, etc owes, possesses, as commonly in Elizabethan English

124 am I sworn, am under the bond of an oath

125 same very, tautological; Rolfe compares *R. III.* in. 2. 19, "That this same very day your enemies cannot die at Pomfret."

126 Your dead, your uncle must not know anything, except that you are dead, he must be led to suppose that you are dead

129 dogged, hard hearted, inhuman.

130 2 and secure thee, and secure in the belief that not to win all the wealth in the world would I injure you; 'doubtless, free from fear, cf. 1 *Hen IV* in. 2. 20). 'I am do I know I can purge Myself,' etc." (Rolfe)

132 offend, injure

134 closely, secretly, privately

134 undergo, subject myself to, render myself liable to, etc.

SCENE II

3, 4 This superfluous This once more, except that it so pleased you, and, so far, cannot be regarded as superfluous, was once more than was necessary Steevens points out that this was really John's fourth coronation, Malone that his second coronation was at Canterbury in 1201, his third also at the same place, in 1202 after the murder of his nephew, "probably with a view of confirming his title to the throne, his competitors no longer standing in his way"

5, 6 And revolt, and since then nothing has occurred to deprive you of the dignity with which you were invested, nor has the loyalty then pledged to you been stained by revolt.

7, 8 Fresh state. 'No newly excited craving disturbed the minds of your subjects with a desire for change and for improvement of condition. There is a superfluity here of expectation, and a sort of confusion between, 'Expectation of change or improvement of condition did not agitate the land,' and, 'Change or improvement of condition was not longed for by the land, so as to disturb it.'

10 To guard before, to ornament more richly a title that was already richly adorned; 'guards' were fringes or trimmings with which garments were ornamented, as in *M. A.* i. 1. 289, "The body of your discourse is sometime guarded with fragments, and the guards are but slightly basted on neither", *L L L* iv. 3 58

15 eye of heaven, the sun, to garnish, to trick out, the word seems to have here a belittling sense, cp *M. V* iii. 5. 71, "A many fools, that stand in better place, Garnish'd like him", and *L L L* ii. 1 78

17 But   done, if it were not that it is of course necessary for us to do whatever you, in your royal pleasure, may think fit to order   Both here and in his former speech, Pembroke's words have a considerable flavour of suppressed sarcasm

18, 9 This   troublesome, almost a repetition of Lewis' words, iii 4 108, 9.

20 Being   unseasonable, especially as being insisted upon at an unfortunate time, urged seems to me to refer to act not to tale

21. well noted, familiar and, so, beloved

23, 4. And, like   about, and as a wind veering from one side of a sail to the other, changes the course of a vessel, so this veering about of your purposes causes men's thoughts to turn from one point to another, prevents their being steady, to 'fetch about,' is a nautical term signifying to tack, to turn to the wind

25 consideration, deliberate thought, reflection

26, 7 Makes   robe, makes healthy opinion appear diseased, and truth to be doubted, when they are seen dressed out in so new fashioned a garb, cp "dressed in an opinion," M V i 1 91, "attired in wonder," M A iv 1 146   For the transposition of new a, see Abb § 432, new, adverb

29 They do   covetousness, they only mar their skill by their anxiety to improve what cannot by any skill be improved upon, Cp Lear, i 4 369, "Striving to better, oft we mar what's well", and Sonnet, ciii 9 10

30 excusing of   On 'of' after a verbal noun, see Abb § 178, and on the omission of 'the' before a noun already defined by another noun, § 89

32 breach, rent

33 in hiding, see Abb § 164   fault, blemish

38, 9 Since   will, since all our wishes, and every particular of them, halt, arrest themselves, when your highness wishes something contrary, there is a play upon would and will.

41 possess'd you with, acquainted you with, as frequently in Shakespeare   and think, i e and I think

42 And more   strong, and more reasons of even greater weight I shall communicate to you, when my fears are less than they now are, for when, Tyrwhitt's conjecture, the folios read 'then' for the double comparative, lesser, see Abb § 11   indue, probably for 'endue,' an older spelling of 'endow'

44 would   reform'd, desire to see reformed

48 To sound, to proclaim

50 Your safety, i e for your safety   the which, on 'the' used where there is more than one possible antecedent from

which selection must be made, see Abb. § 279. Here 'you' has
placed in your is the other antecedent; them, for 'they,' seem
to be due to the words in the previous line which he is using
almost as a quotation

51 Bend   studies, direct their best endeavours, have as the
principal object of their efforts

52 enfranchisement, the setting at liberty; old F. *franchir*, to
free, deliver

53 discontent, abstract for concrete, the contented people

54 To break into   to break out into

55 If what   hold, if you hold by the tenure of right that
of which you have undisturbed possession, see the cross L

56-60 Why then   exercise?   Why then, should your fears,
which, it is commonly said, accompany the steps of injustice
only, incite you to keep in continual your kinsman, to allow the
weed, ignorance, to choke up all better growth in the soil of his
mind, and to deny him while young the advantage of engaging in
manly exercises, referring especially to those martial exercises
which in former times were so large a portion of a prince's education   Pope transposed then and should, and is followed by Dyce
Lettsom suggests, "Why then so fears   should," etc., and a
full stop at exercise   Possibly the construction was intended
to be, 'Why then your fears should move you, we cannot see,'
and that, in his expansion of the idea, Shake. is too forgot how
he had begun   Instances of equal carelessness in regard to con
struction occur in his plays   To mew up, "properly a term in
falconry   *Mew* is the place, whither it be abroad or in the
house, in which the Hawk is put during the time she casts, or
doth change her feathers'   R. Holme's *Academy of Armory and
Blazon* "   (Dyce, *Gloss.*)   In to choke, there may be an allu
sion to the parable of the sower, some of whose seeds, when sown,
"fell among thorns, and the thorns sprung up and choked
them," *Matthew*, xiii. 7   Cp *0th* i. 3. 322, where the body is
spoken of as a garden which we may have either "sterile with
idleness, or manured with industry "

61, 2 That   occasions, in order that those who are hostile to
things as they now are may not have this argument wherewith to
adorn their rhetoric on occasions for holding forth against you,
such, for instance, as are described in ll 187, etc   Schmidt takes
occasions as = "matters which they may urge against you "

62, 3 let it be   liberty, let the concession which you have
promised us (see ll 15, 6, above) be his liberty; it is superfluous   There seems to be a confusion between, 'let it be our suit
(which you have bid us make) to ask his liberty,' and 'let his
liberty be the suit which you have bid us make '

64-6 Which   liberty In asking for which liberty we are consulting our own interest so far only as to us, whose well-being depends on you and your well-being, it appears to be for your good that he should be released   Our well-being depends upon yours ; yours, in our opinion, depends upon his being released , and so, in asking that release, we, while primarily consulting your welfare, are in a secondary degree, but only in a secondary degree, consulting our own welfare   **our goods,** the good of us severally

68 To your direction, for you to give him such an education as may seem best fitted for his years

69 should, who should , who, if he did his commission, would do, etc   For the omission of the relative, see Abb § 244

71, 2 The image   eye , in the look of his eye you may see a hateful crime reflected   **close aspect,** appearance of sullen reserve

73 Does show   breast , indicates a mind burdened with the consciousness of some terrible crime

74, 5 And I   do   And I greatly fear that what we so feared he had been commissioned to do, has already been done , 'tis, is really superfluous , on 'what' used relatively, here after an unemphatic antecedent 't (in 'tis), see Abb § 252

76, 7 The colour   conscience, he becomes pale, or his natural colour returns to his cheek, according as determination to have his nephew murdered, or remorse at that idea, is uppermost in his mind.

78 Like   set   Like heralds going and coming between two armies drawn up in battle array   Theobald, who laughed at the idea of heralds being set between two hosts, altered set to 'sent', and Dyce, without good reason, as it seems to me, scoffs at the suggestion of set being joined to battles

79 His passion   break. A metaphor from a tumour, ep *Haml* iv 4 27, "This is the imposthume of much wealth and peace, That inward breaks "

81 The foul   death   The foul murder of a sweet child , foul corruption merely carries on the metaphor of the tumour

82 We   hand. Powerful as we are, we cannot restrain death's hand

83 living, full of life, strong , used for the sake of the pun

84 The suit   dead   Your suit for Arthur's liberty has come to an end with his death

85 to-night, last night, as in ll 165, 182

86-8 Indeed .   sick   These lines are of course spoken with stern irony.

89 This hence Either in this world or the next, John will have to render an account for Arthur's death; up. v. ii. 22.

91 the shears of destiny, an allusion to the Fates, of whom Clotho held the distaff, Lachis wove the web, and Atropos cut the thread, of life.

92 Have I life? Is it for me to say how long the pulse of life shall continue to beat, and when it shall stop?

93 apparent, evident, manifest

94 That greatness It that any one, however high his position, should attempt that foul play with such unabashed audacity, cp. 2 H. IV. iii. 2. 168

95 So speed! May you, in the measure you are playing, succeed according to your deserts; see not succeed at all

96 Stay yet, or till I can accompany you

97, 8 And find grave And walk out with you the inheritance upon which this poor child has entered, the possession of a grave which has been ruthlessly forced upon him, this poor child who was heir to so mighty an inheritance, this poor child whose sway should have extended over all this land

99, 100 That blood hold, three foot of his country's soil is now sufficient space for him who by right of descent was lord of its length and breadth For foot in the sing. see note on i. 1. 69 We still use 'foot,' 'stone,' 'pound' in the same way bad world the while! "A bad world now a-days" Cf. 1 H. IV. ii. 1 116. 'God help the while' a bad world, I say', and Rich. III iii. 6 10, 'Here's a good world the while'" (Rolfe.)

102 To all, 'to' marking the result, consequence and doubt, and not only will break out, but will break out soon

104 There blood, power founded on blood had has but a slippery basis

106 fearful eye, terrified look

107 inhabit cheeks, we say 'inhabit,' or 'dwell in,' but not 'inhabit in.'

108, 9 So foul weather so heavy a sky can only be cleared by the bursting of a tempest, therefore hasten to get rid of the stormy elements with which you are evidently charged: i.e. quickly tell your news, however bad it may be: for weather, = storm, cp. W. T. iii 3 104. "both roaring louder than the sea or weather"

110 From England. John's question, "how goes all in France," means 'how do matters fare in France?' But the messenger, taking the words literally, answers, 'all in France are on their way to England' power, force

111 **For any preparation,** got together for any foreign expedition

112 **in the land.** Throughout the length and breadth of a country

113 **The copy them** the example which you set them by your sudden invasion of their country has been learnt by them, the lesson you taught them has been laid to heart.

114 **For prepare,** for when you might expect to hear that preparations are being made, etc

115 **The tidings comes,** Shakespeare frequently uses the word with a verb in the sing , as though it were on the same footing with 'news' 'Tidings' are "things that happen, usually, information about things that happen" (Skeat, *Ety Dict*)

116, 7 **O, where slept?** Steevens quotes *Macb* 1 7 35, "Was the hope *drunk* wherein you dress'd yourself? hath it *slept* since?" **intelligence,** spies, abstract for concrete, as in 1 *H IV* iv 3 98, "Sought to entrap me by *intelligence* "

117 **Where- . care,** it is doubtful whether in the first folio the word is 'care' or 'care,' in the three others it is 'care,' which gives a good sense, viz., 'How has my mother shown that care which might be expected of her, in not obtaining, and sending me, information of this preparation,' i e she has not shown that care, etc

118 **drawn,** assembled, gathered together

119 **And she it,** without her hearing of it

120-2 **The first died.** Constance died in 1201 at Nantes, Elinor in 1204 at Fontevreaux

123, 4 **but heard,** but this I heard only as an idle rumour

125 **occasion ,** "the course of events which were following each other in rapid succession Cp 11 *H IV* iv 1 72, "And are enforced from one most quiet there, By the rough torrent of occasion " (Wright)

·126 **pleased,** satisfied, brought into good humour again

127 **What , dead ,** What ! is my mother really dead !

128. **How France ,** If so, then my affairs in France are in a bad way, my possessions in great danger of being torn from me **walks** here= 'fares,' the lit meaning of which is to 'go '

129 **conduct,** lead, generalship

130 **That here?** which you speak of with such certainty as having already landed, about which at all events you have no such doubts as about Constance's death

131 **giddy,** dizzy with amazement

132 **the world,** people in general who were aware of his pro-

cealings, those with whom he had to remonstrate while wringing
the money out of the clergy

143 to stuff, to cram

135, 6 But if   head. There was to be a suppressed climax
here, as it were, ' I was about to tell you bad news, but if you
shrink from hearing it,' etc.

117 Bear with me, be patient with me, do not be angry at my
having greeted you so roughly.   amazed, bewildered, the word
formerly had a stronger sense than it has now

145 Under the tide, under the weight' and flood of evil
tidings

139 Aloft the flood, my head which for a moment sank under
it, is now also out again.   i.e. I have now entirely recovered my
fortitude   Balfe points out 'aloft' is nowhere else used by
Shakespeare as a preposition

140 speak   will   However evil its tidings may be

141 How   sped how I have succeeded, 'success' being the
older meaning of 'speed'

144 I find   fantasied, I found the minds of the people
occupied with strange fancies, I did, the historic present, but
somewhat strange in such close connection with the past travell'd;
fantasy the fuller and older form of 'fancy'

146 Not   fear   Delius compares Macb. iv 2 20, "But cruel
are the times   when we hold rumour From what we fear, but
know not what we fear"

147 a prophet. "This man [Peter of Pomfret] was a hermit in
great repute with the common people   Notwithstanding the
event it said to have fallen out as he had prophesied, the poor
fellow was inhumanly dragged at horses' tails in the streets of
Warham, and, together with his son, who appears to have been
more innocent than his father, hanged afterwards on a gibbet   "
(Douce)

148 From forth, out from, see Abb. § 156, and for whom in connection with that, which generally comes nearer the antecedent,
§ 260   Pomfret, a contraction of Pontefract, a town in Yorkshire.

149 treading   heels, closely following him

151 Ascension day, the anniversary of the day on which Christ
ascended to heaven, otherwise called 'Holy Thursday', see Mark,
xvi. 19

158 Deliver . safety.   Make him over to safe keeping

159 I must use thee   I have work for you to do

163 With eyes   fire, i e flaming with rage

165 Of Arthur, whom, a confusion of construction between,

'Of Arthur, who they say is dead,' and, 'Of Arthur, whom they say your agent has put to death' See Abb § 410

166 On your suggestion, at your prompting

167 into   companies, into the company of these men

170 Nay, but   before   Aye, seek them out, but do it swiftly, putting your best foot foremost (as we say), i e with all the speed of which you are capable

171 no   enemies, no subjects as enemies, subject is here an adjective

172 adverse, hostile

173 With   invasion ! With all the pomp of that resolute invasion which must needs strike terror into their souls

174 Be   heels, an allusion to the winged Mercury, the messenger of the gods, as he is shown in paintings and statues, the wings being attached to his ankles

175 like thought, with all the speed of thought

176 The spirit   time, the state, condition, of the time so full of commotion and hurry

177 sprightful, sprightly, instruct with alacrity Spoke, on the curtailed form of the past participles, see Abb § 343

178 Go   him, said to the Messenger

182 they say   to-night This incident, which is mentioned in the old play, and by some historians, seems to be seriously believed by certain of the commentators Cp J C ii 2 17-24, Haml i 1 113-20, for similar portents to night, see above, 1 85

185 beldams, crones, old hags, "ironically used for *beldame*, i e fair lady, in which sense it occurs in Spenser, *F Q* iii. 2 43" (Skeat, *Ety Dict*)

186 Do prophesy   dangerously, comment upon the phenomenon in dangerous anticipation of the coming events it indicates

187 is common, is a common subject of conversation

188 shake   heads, to express their gloomy thoughts

189 whisper   another, on the omission of the preposition see Abb § 200

190 doth   wrist, in the excitement of telling the story, or, possibly, in pantomimic representation of the manner of Arthur's death

191 makes   action, shows his horror by his gestures

193 thus, Hubert here imitates the smith's attentive attitude, his mouth agape with terror

195. swallowing, eagerly taking in.

196 treasure, yard i come

197, 8 which feet, which, in his haste to run out and listen to the story, he had put on wrongly, the right shoe on the left foot and vice versa; falsely carelessly, by mistake. Johnson, not knowing that in old days, as now, shoes were made to fit the right and left foot severally, here censures Shakespeare's ignorance.

199 a man, no. Abb. 187

200 That Kent that were drawn up in battle array

201 unwash'd artificer, dirty artisan: in *J C* 1. 2. 240, etc, and in *Cor* 11. 3. 60, etc., the dirt of the common people is emphasized. It seems unlikely that in the word artificer Shakespeare intended that humorous euphemism for hand craftsman which Delius sees.

202 Cuts off, suddenly interrupts.

203 possess fears, to fill up fill of, to flood my mind with, etc

207 No had. Rowe reads "Had none", Knight, "No had"; but Arrowsmith (*Notes and Queries* vol vii p. 251, First Series), quoted by Dyce and Staunton, adduces from our older writers numerous instances of this phraseology, e.g. 'no did,' 'no had,' 'no will'

208. It is the curse of kings etc. Malone thinks it "extremely probable that our author meant to pay court to Elizabeth by this covert apology for her conduct to Mary". But surely Elizabeth could not even pretend to pretend that Mary's execution was not a deliberate act on her part

209, 10 By slaves life By subservient wretches who construe the ill tempers of monarchs as a sufficient warrant for committing murder on their behalf. bloody, which becomes bloody by their action; a proleptic use, cp *Haml* 1. 5. 90. "And 'gins to pale his *ineffectual fire*," i.e. the fire which thus becomes ineffectual. Delius compares *Macb* 11. 3. 72-4, "Most sacrilegious murder hath broke ope The Lord's anointed temple, and stole thence The life of the building"

211 And on authority, and on the slightest sign being given by those in power, etc.

212-4 To understand respect. To take that sign for a command, and to interpret for themselves the secret wishes of kings in cases when probably their anger is due rather to a sudden freak of caprice than to any settled purpose; dangerous seems here to mean 'when in a state of fury' advised, deliberate, as 'advice' often = deliberation

215 **Here is   did**   For this and the following speeches, compare the dialogue between Bolingbroke and Exton, *R II* v 6 34 52

216, 7 **O, when   made,** ι e the Day of Judgment, when men will have to render their account to God

218 **to damnation,** with the result of condemning us to perdition

220 **Make   done** ᵗ make is an instance of confusion of proximity due to the intervening plural nouns , Dyce and Knight transpose deeds and ill, Dyce because in such passages the order of the words which are emphatically repeated is rarely, if ever, changed , Knight, because the old reading "might apply to good deeds unskilfully performed"   **by, at hand**

222 **Quoted,** "noted , from the notes or marks in the side (*coté*) or margin of a book   See *L L L* ii 1 246," "His face's own margent did *quote* such amazes " (Wright)   sign'd, stamped , but further carrying on the figure in Quoted, nature having set her signature to her handwriting

226 **Apt, fit and ready   liable,** has much the same sense here as apt , literally 'allied with the being employed,' ι e one who in another's mind is associated with such an idea, "From F *her* to tie   —Lat *ligare*, to tie, bind " (Skeat, *Ety Dict*)   in danger, in a matter dangerous not in its undertaking, but in its results

227 **faintly   thee,** in ambiguous language hinted at the subject of Arthur's death , cp *M A* ii 1 310, "I have *broke* with her father, and his good will obtained "

228 **to be endeared,** in order that you might win the favour

229 **Made   conscience,** treated it as a matter about which you need have no scruples of conscience

233 **Or turn'd   doubt,** or looked upon me in a way that showed doubt as to my real meaning, whether I could really mean anything of so hideous a nature

234 **As bid me,** such as would bid me

238 **in signs again,** with corresponding, reciprocative signs , for sin Lettsom would read 'signs', but parley with sin seems to me particularly forcible, as indicating the tentative character of his communion with crime

239 **Yea,** without stop, not only readily parleyed with sin, but at once came to terms with it

240 **consequently,** pursuantly, thereafter , cp *R II*. i 1 102, "That he did plot the Duke of Gloucester's death   And *consequently*   Sluiced out his innocent soul through streams of

blood', P.V. m. 4.7) to act... d, but he thy hand to it,
for 'to a attention the fore in... d. it... quantity is usual in the
latter of two classes, see Ab. § 420.

213 my   braved, my regal dignity insulted

215 ... Nay   death. her and even... say on, I picture this
is civil war between my... idea and the desire for my
nephew's death, up what Salisbury says above, II 76, 7. this
deadly land, for the sake of that gain from civil war   this con
ano   breath the body which best tenants the soul is this the up
n II 31 is 1 11s, etc   where the escape, is more fully
worked out. Johnson spares the S.C. in L.O.I. '... the state
of men. Like to a little kingdom... suffers then the nature of an
insurrection,' see where the... emotions, the spirit of man, is in con
flict with the moral instruments, the bodily organs.

211 Arm you, the imperative, is almost equal it t... d
you are a sorry figure than I... what you have to do is to
arm yourself against your external enemies, leave it to me to
make, etc

252 a maiden, so as indeed he... a maiden had

254, 5 Within   thought this of course is untrue, as we
have seen in the first Scene of this Act   woman, impulse, idea

256 And   form, and in slandering my personal appearance
(see above, II. 221, 5), you have slandered my nature.

257 O Which   child. For though it they have it is outwardly
so rough, it yet inclines a soul too tender to contemplate the
murder of, etc   For the ellipsis in fairer than to be, see Ab.
§ 280

261 Throw   rage like water upon... r

262 And   obedience! And bring them humbly back to that
obedience which is due from them

263 Forgive   made, forgive the uncomplimentary terms in
which my anger, not I, spoke of, etc

264 feature, form, person in general: we now speak of 'the
features' of the face, but the 'make' of the body; Shakespeare
uses 'feature' more widely, and more in accordance with its
derivation, fr. factura, fashion, make.

265 foul   blood, eyes which in imagination beheld you
stained with blood, made you appear to be, etc.

267 closet, private apartment.

268. with   haste, as quickly as circumstances will possibly
permit, there seems to be the idea of convenience to the lords
as well as of haste on the part of Hubert

269 I conjure   fast. My words of adjuration to you are but
slow, do not in your going imitate their tardiness

SCENE III

1 **The wall**, etc "Our author has here followed the old play
In what manner Arthur was deprived of his life is not ascer-
tained Matthew Paris, relating the event, uses the word
evanuit [i e disappeared], and indeed, as King Philip afterwards
publickly accused King John of putting his nephew to death,
without either mentioning the manner of it, or his accomplices, we
may conclude that it was conducted with impenetrable secrecy
The French historians, however, say that John coming in a boat,
during the night-time, to the castle of Rouen, where the young
prince was confined, ordered him to be brought forth, and having
stabbed him, while supplicating for mercy, the King fastened a
stone to the dead body, and threw it into the Seine, in order to
give some colour to a report, which he afterwards caused to be
spread, that the prince attempting to escape out of a window of the
tower of the castle, fell into the river, and was drowned "
(Malone)

3 **There 's**, for the inflection in *s* preceding a plural subject, see
Abb § 335

4 **semblance**, appearance, the dress he had assumed

5 **venture it**, *i e* to jump down , but it is used indefinitely,
see Abb § 226

6 **If I limbs**, if I get down *without breaking my limbs*, the
getting down is certain, the getting down *in safety*, problem
atical

7 **shifts**, contrivances, ways

8 **as die and stay**, as to remain here to meet that death which
is certain to befall me

11 **him**, the Dauphin **St Edmundsbury**, or Bury St Edmunds,
the capital of Suffolk

12, 3 **It is time** It is the only safe course for us to take,
and we must gladly accept so friendly an offer made to us in a
time of so much peril.

16, 7 **Whose import** Whose private communication to me
of the friendly feeling in which I am held by the Dauphin, is of
a much ampler nature than would be gathered from these lines ,
for **private**, an adjective used as a substantive in the singular,
see Abb § 5, where the word is quoted as used in a similar way
by B Jonson, *Sejanus*, iii 1

19 **set forward**, set out on our journey.

20 **or ere**, for this reduplication for the sake of emphasis, see
Abb § 131

21. **distemper'd**, angry, ruffled in temper , the word is used by

Shakespeare in a variety of cases, to indicate payment for want of assonant. In Once more well met, there is a reference as Fabian points out to the same thing in iv. 2. 162, where the Bastard speaks of their rage against the king.

22 by me, as his agent 's' stands, stands, always, as ever

23 Lath us, I am by his strictness driven to seek blows to

24, 5 We will honours, we will not hold if our honour to add warmth to that cloak, appearance, of dignity which he wears, a cloak now nearly come to ——, and furthermore be besmirched with blood, in ii. 1 ——, we have ——, and besmirched with steel," but there, as in Mac. v. 2 113, "dishise the rebel with hidden help" the ob. is that of adding ——; here, of adding warmth, i.e. to assist it, him with our friendship, we whose honour is so pure, while his is so besmeared with guilt

27 the worst, i.e Arthur's death

28, 9 Whatso'er think. Whatever you may imagine, it would be better for you to return a courteous answer

29 Our now It is our sorrows, and not our characters, that make us answer in this way, cp above, v. 2. 263, 4, and li. 2. v 1 75. "My poverty, but not my will, consents." It thus takes griefs for 'grievances' but, if so, the Bastard purposely mistakes the meaning reason, speak, as often in Shakespeare.

30, 1 But there now But you have little reason for your grief, therefore it would be only reasonable that you should behave with courtesy

32 impatience privilege If we are wanting in courtesy, allowance is to be made for our anger

33 'Tis else Yes, replies the Bastard, so much allowance that it (anger) may be allowed to annoy its master, if it likes, though it ought not to be allowed to annoy any one else

34 What here? Who can it be that has here? What, with less definiteness, I think, than 'who'

35 O death, beauty' O death, that hast been beautified in the person of this pure souled and princely boy! that hast reason to be proud of the form thou hast assumed!

36 The earth deed The earth refused to conceal his murder, cp Alonzo's speech, Temp iii 3. 96, etc, where the sea, the winds, the thunder, proclaim his sin

37, 8 Murder revenge Murder, remorseful for his deed, exposed the body, so as to stimulate those who found it to take revenge Murder, personified

39, 10 Or, when, grave Or, when he (Murder) doomed so much beauty to die, found that it was too precious and too noble to be consigned to the grave, there to moulder and be eaten of worms -

41-5 have you   another? Have you before beheld such a spectacle? or have you even read or heard of such a one? or could you imagine one such, if you tried? or do you, although you see it, imagine, without feeling sure, that you see it? could imagination, unless it had this object before it, create such another?

46, 7 crest   arms   this is the crest to the armorial bearings that murder boasts, or, rather, a crest over and above that crest, a double crest, as it were, crest, literally, the comb or tuft on a bird's head, then the 'cognizance' worn on the top of the helmet to distinguish the wearer

48 The wildest savagery, the most extravagant piece of savage butchery

49 wall-eyed, glaring, literally, having a beam in the eye Cp *T A* v 1 44, "Say, *wall eyed* slave"

50 Presented   remorse   Offered as an object to call forth the tears of tender pity, remorse, pity, as most usually in Shakespeare

51 in this, in the presence of this, when compared with this this murder is sufficient to excuse all murders of former times

52 sole, unique; cp *Sonn* xxxvi. 7, "love's *sole* effect"

54 To the   times   The folio has 'sinne of times,' which Pope altered to 'sins of time,' a reading adopted by Dyce   Delius points out that sin is used collectively, and that unbegotten goes with times   For times, in the sense of past times, cp *H V* II. 4 83, "By custom and the ordinance of *times*"

55 a   bloodshed, an act of deadly, etc

56 Exampled   spectacle   When it can quote this as a precedent

58 heavy, brutal.

59 If that   hand.   If it really be the work of any hand, which I can hardly believe   ・

60 If that   hand !   Salisbury, indignantly repeating the Bastard's words, asks, 'Do you mean to say that you doubt its being the work of any hand?'

61 we had   ensue   we had a presentiment of what was to happen

62, 3 It is   king   The work is the work of Hubert's hand, the planning and the intention belong to John, practice, = contrivance, plot, is frequent in Shakespeare.

64, 5 From whose   life, from rendering obedience to whom, I, as I kneel before this dead body, forbid my soul, with a curse upon it if it refuses or fails to obey; perhaps with an allusion to the papal interdict, for ruin of a dead body, cp. *Cymb.* IV. 2. 351, "He came up the churchyard. It was a sorting building," said of Cloten's corpse.

66 his excellence. Delius points out that his refers to ruin of sweet life, i.e. the excellence of Prince's dead body; breathing, speaking, breathless, that hast a breath in it.

67 The incense vow, a vow offered up before the shrine of his soul, as incense is offered up before the altar in churches.

68 to taste, perhaps persons are not used to taste, still I use to eat freely of it. "There is copy of the vows made in the ages of superstition and chivalry" (Johnson).

69 to be infected, as though delight in such carnal pleasures would be a disease, something that would pollute him.

71, 2 Till I revenge Till I have made this hand glorious by the noble act of revenge for Arthur's death Farmer would read 'head' for hand referring it to the head of princes, and interpreting a glory as the aureole commonly seen in pictures round the heads of saints. Malone compares "I will not return, Till my attempt so much be glorified, As to my ample hope was promised," cp. 2 III also *P. C.* v. 1. 27, "Jove, let Caesar live, If to my sword his fate be not the glory."

73 religiously, i.e. binding themselves by a like vow

76 O, he is death. He is so utterly without shame that he does not blush, even though knowing himself a murderer

77 Avaunt, away from our sight, "shortened form from the F. phrase *en avant*, forward' on' march' The F. *avant* is from the Lat. *ab ante*" (Skeat, *Ety. Dict.*)

78 Must law? Will you by staying here compel me to kill you, and so to rob the hangman of his due?

79 Your again. Sheathe your sword, and do not defile it by shedding this man's blood, cp. *Oth.* 1. 2. 59, "Keep up your bright swords, for the dew will rust them," and with similar contempt

83 forgot yourself, show yourself forgetful of your rank by attacking me

84 Nor defence Nor run upon the danger of a combat with me in defence of my innocence, true, which consciousness of my innocence makes rightful.

85, 6 Lest I nobility Lest I, heeding only your passion, be led to forget that respect which is due to a man of your personal worth and high position

87 dunghill! filthy beast. Wright points out that the full form is 'dunghill cur,' as in *2 H. IV.* v. 3. 108 brave, defy.

88, 9 **Not   life** not for any consideration would I defy a nobleman, but in defence of my life, knowing myself to be innocent, I dare fight even with one much higher in rank than a nobleman, even with an emperor   For innocent life, Dyce, comparing *Macb* iii 1 79, would read "innocent *self*," but the jingle seems to me quite after the fashion of this play

90 **Do   so** do not, by compelling me to kill you, make me one

91, 2 **Yet I   lies** So far, I am no murderer, though you may force me to be one, if you attack me   **whose   lies**, an indirect and apologetic way of calling Salisbury a liar

94 **Stand   you**, stand aside; and do not interfere in our quarrel, or I shall be provoked into doing you an injury

95 **Thou   better**, for the construction due to a feeling that the old impersonal construction is ungrammatical, see Abb § 352

97 **Or teach   shame**, or allow yourself in your outburst of passion to insult me by a blow, **spleen**, see note on ii 1 68

98 **betime**, i e by time, in good time, quickly, more commonly 'betimes'

99 **Or I'll   toasting-iron**, or I will so hack you and your miserable weapon, **toasting-iron**, a contemptuous phrase for a sword, cp *H V* ii 1 8, 9, "I dare not fight, but I will wink and hold out mine *iron*   it is a simple one, but what though' it will *toast* cheese, and," etc

106. **My   life**, so much of life as it is given me to live, the allotted period of my life

108 **For   rheum**, for villains are ready enough with their tears, if occasion demands them, **rheum**, see note on iii 1 22

109, 10 **And he   innocency**, and he, having so long practised, dealt in, such display of tears, has learnt the art of making them appear as though they were the outflow of pity and innocence, for traded, cp *T C* ii. 2 64, "Two *traded* pilots 'twixt the dangerous shores of will and judgement"

112 **The   slaughter-house** this noisome atmosphere of butchery

114 **Bury**, see above, iv 3 11.

115 **he may   out**, if he is so anxious to see us, as you say, let him seek us out at Bury, and he will find us there

116 **Here's   world!** Here is a pretty state of things! **fair work**, ironically

117, 8 **Beyond   mercy**, infinite and boundless as God's mercy is, it cannot reach you and save you from damnation, if, etc Cp *W T* iii 2 208-13

121 **nay, black nay,** in comparison it is possible, your guilt is beyond all parallel. Staunton thinks that "Shakespeare had here probably in his mind the old religious plays of Coventry, some of which in his boyhood he may have seen, where the damned souls had their faces all blackened."

123, **I so ugly**, to see a fiend of hell as hideous as you, etc.

125 **Upon my soul** his protestation of innocence is interrupted by Faulconbridge. If thou ... consent, if, without actually having done the deed yourself, you were even a consenting party to it.

126 **do but despair,** you have only to despair, and I'll, etc. Delius points out the reference to Judas Iscariot's hanging himself after betraying Christ; see Matthew, xxvii. 5.

129 **a rush beam,** even so frail and feeble a thing as a rush will serve as a beam from which to hang yourself.

132, 3 **And it up.** And it and all have fully authorised as the whole ocean itself to drown you up, I deem.

135 **sin of thought,** sinful thought.

136 **of the breath,** we should now say either 'the stealing of that,' or 'stealing that'; cp. Abb. § 178.

137 **which clay,** cp. above, i. 2. 246, "this clay of blood and breath."

138 **want pains,** be lacking in pains, not have enough wherewith to, etc.

140 **amazed,** as in a maze, bewildered.

142 **all England,** i.e. in the person of its rightful king; cp. A. C. ii. 7. 947, "Eno. There's a strong fellow, Menas. Men. Why? A. o. A' bears the third part of the world, man," i.e. Lepidus, who, with Cæsar and Antony, shared the government of the world between them.

143 **this royalty,** literally, this mouthful, small piece, i.e. the body of the youthful Arthur.

144 **The life realm,** the life and, with it, all rightful claim to the throne, of this realm.

146 **scamble,** scramble, struggle for; cp. H. V. i. 1. 4, "the scambling and unquiet time", and v. 2. 215. according to Skeat, scamble is put for scample, from scamp, Ital. scampare, to escape, from Lat. ex, out, and campus, a field, especially a field of battle.

part **teeth,** tear in pieces, as dogs, etc., fighting over prey.

147 **The state** "That is, the interest which is not at this moment legally possessed by anyone, however rightfully entitled to it. On the death of Arthur the right to the English crown devolved to his sister, Eleanor" (Malone). **proud swelling state,** monarchy with its grandeur.

149 **dogged,** like a sullen dog.

150 snarleth in, fiercely faces and snails at

151 Now   home, invading forces and discontented people of
the country come together in one line, join together in attack,
for discontents = malcontents, cp 1 *H IV* v 1 76, "of fickle
changelings and poor *discontents*"

152, 4 and vast   pomp And utter confusion is only waiting
for the death of usurped authority to tear it in pieces, just as
the raven hovers over a dying animal, waiting for the moment
when its death shall allow it (the raven) to begin its feast, in
plain language, men are only waiting for John's dethronement to
plunge the country into a state of anarchy

155 cincture, that with which his cloak is girdled, kept close
to his body

156. Hold   tempest. Hold out *against* this, etc., endure
this, etc

158 are   hand, require to be quickly attended to

ACT V   SCENE I

2 The   glory, cp *Macb* 1 5 30, "All that impedes thee
from *the golden round*, Which fate and metaphysical aid doth
seem To have thee crown'd withal", and 11 *H IV* iv 5 36,
"This is a sleep That from the *golden rigol* hath divorced So
many English kings"

3 as holding, as a tenure derived from the Pope

5 holy word, as being the word of a holy man

6 his holiness, i e the Pope, so in *A C* i 2 20, "Vex not
his *prescience*," a title jestingly given to the Soothsayer, unless
his holiness = its holiness, i e of your word from, i e derived
from

7 'fore   inflamed Mason objects to 'fore on the ground
that the nation was already inflamed, and that John had said so
But inflamed means 'in a general blaze of insurrection,' which
John has hardly admitted to be the case

8 counties, it is doubtful whether this means here the division
of the kingdom so called, or the nobility, as in *M A* 11 1 195,
M V 1 2 49, and elsewhere, the words Our people in the next
line look as if the two classes, the nobility and the common
people, were meant

10 the love of soul, heartfelt love

11 stranger, an adjective

12, 3 This   qualified this torrent of ill will can be checked
by you alone

15 **That minister'd**, that medicine must be properly administered

18 **Upon**, as a consequence of

19 **convertite**, here, 'one who has returned to the true faith,' a convert from his own heresy

21 **make weather**, cause, bring about, fair weather.

23 **Upon your oath**, you having made oath or asseveration to, etc.

27 **give off**, "take off and give up" (Wright)

29 **I did constraint** I understood him to mean that I should do so upon compulsion

31 **Dover castle** "Hubert de Burgh, with a hundred and forty soldiers, defended it for four months" (French, *Shakespeareana Genealogica*)

35, 6. **And wild friends** And among your friends, who are but few, and those by no means assured, the greatest perplexity prevails   **amazement** is just omitted and represented as going to an excited way up and down the ranks of John's friends, as if to tamper with their faith, up and down is probably a preposition, as in in 3 11, *J C* i 4 25, "who swore they saw Men all in fire walk up and down the streets."

10, 1 **An empty awry** The mere case, or setting, from which the precious stone has been stolen, Malone compares *R II* i 1 180, "A jewel in a ten times barr'd up chest Is a bold spirit in a loyal breast."

13 **for know**, for anything he knew to the contrary, so far as he knew

16 **sad**, gloomy

17 **Govern eye** regulate your looks,

48 **Be time** show yourself as full of activity as the time itself is

49, 50 **outface horror**, bear down with your stern looks the boastful men that seeks to strike terror into the hearts of men, outface, cause to cower down by superior sternness, horror, abstract for concrete

51 **That great**, that shape their behaviour by the pattern of their superiors

52, 3 **and put resolution** Malone quotes *Macb* ii 3 139, "Let's briefly *put on manly readiness*"

55 **When field** When it is his intention to lend splendour to the battle field by his presence, cp *H V* iv 2 40 "You island carrions Ill favouredly *become* the morning field"

56 **aspiring confidence**, soaring, lofty, reliance upon yourself

59 forage, seems here to have merely the idea of going forth, ranging about, which according to Florio (*It Dict*) it originally had Cp *H V* 1 2 110, "*Forage* in blood of French nobility," i e go about slaying French nobles

66 upon land, is generally explained as 'standing upon our own soil', though possibly the meaning is when an enemy has set foot upon our shores, in *H V* 11 4. 143, "For he is *footed* in their land already", *R II* 11 2 48, "Who strongly hath set *footing* in this land"

67 fair-play offers, with Dyce and Singer I have followed Collier's MS Corrector in substituting offers for 'orders' Schmidt and Rolfe interpret 'orders' as 'stipulations,' 'conditions,' comparing "order" in v 2 4, which does not seem to me a parallelism

68 Insinuation, terms which shall wind their way into the acceptance of our enemy

70 A cocker'd wanton, a pampered, effeminate debauchee The derivation of 'cocker' is uncertain , Skeat suggests that the original sense was to rock up and down, to dandle **brave fields**, insult our fields by daring to trample upon them with such parade

71 flesh soil, to flesh his sword was a military term used of a young soldier when first drawing blood hence flesh his spirit is equivalent to 'make the first display of his hardihood' in a soil, on the soil of a warlike nation like ourselves

72 Mocking spread, Johnson compares *Macb* 1 2 49, "Where the Norwegian banners flout the sky And fan our people cold "

73 And check? Without meeting with any opposition

74 Perchance peace, Possibly it may turn out (as the Bastard hopes it will, and as it really does) that the cardinal cannot make up this peace which you are so ready to accept there seems a sarcastic flavour about your

76 a purpose of defence, were ready to defend ourselves

77 Have ordering, I leave it to you to arrange matters as you think best

79 Our party foe We on our part are still (yet) capable of coping with a more powerful foe than this

SCENE II

3 precedent, the original draft of the engagement between the Dauphin and the English lords , cp *R II* 111 6 7, "Eleven he is I put to write it o er the president so full of

2 doing

1 **That having** down, that I saving the word grace et in line is unclearly set down

5 **notes,** memoranda

6 **May know** sacrament, may have to excuse for any doubt as to the terms to which we to and enforce by taking an oath; 'sacrament' meaning the most sacred of the oath administered to also entailed, the ordinary modern use of the word, ie the euchrist, as a remnant here and thus in the Roman Cathol Church is only one of several sacraments

9 **albeit,** although it be

10 **and unurged faith,** unabated loyalty; Po folio s read 'and as unurg'd faith'

13 **Should** revolt, should be obliged to have recourse to such a desperate remedy as revolt p up Trieq n l 154, 'you subtle ones, When you would bring to up er'

11 **inveterate,** deeply rooted, hence inextinguishly rooted

17 9 **O and Salisbury!** Especially in a case in which every motive urges one so patriotic as himself to fight in honourable defence of his native land. That **Cries out upon** as used as in n H IV ini 94, 'And that same word even now cries out on us,' and not as in 1 H IV iv 3 51, 'cries out upon abuses' the exclamation against us, I think, shown by the words honourable rescue and defence

21 3 **for the health** wrong, to restore our right to a healthy condition, we have no other remedy but the breaking injury to our countrymen and anarchy in what right and wrong are confusedly mixed up, the play upon **right** (that which is due) as opposed to **wrong** (that which is not due, injustice) and of **right** (that which is morally good) as opposed to **wrong** (that which is morally evil) makes the sentence difficult of explanation the very hand, the hand itself, nothing less of rious

26 **were born,** should have been born

27 **step** stranger, follow the lead of a foreign foe

28 **fill up,** complete the number of, serve as a complement to, etc Cp Oth ii 3 370, 'I do follow here in the chase, not like a hound that hunts, but *one that fills up the cry*'

30 **upon the spot,** upon the disgrace as though his tears would wash it out Dyce reads "spur" **enforced cause** this cause which we have taken up only under the compulsion of circumstances

31 **To grace,** to lend grace by our support.

32 **unacquainted**, not the standards of our own army with which we are so familiar, which we have so often followed   the words **is 't not pity (l 24) govern the whole sentence down to this point.

33 **What, here?** What, must we "follow unacquainted colours" even here? O nation,   remove ' O my country, would that you could bodily remove yourself from that quarter in which you have so long been planted

34 **clippeth**, embraces, surrounds , as frequently in Shakespeare

35 9 **Would bear   unneighbourly !** Would that Neptune's arms would take you up and carry you to some far distant region where you could forget your former existence, and fasten you to the shores of some pagan country, where, instead of engaging in a contest which is unworthy of them as neighbours, the two nations might blend in a friendly channel that blood which is now so hotly engaged in each against the other, and direct their united efforts against a common enemy] A comma seems better than a semicolon after shore   To **grapple**, to fasten as with grappling irons, or grapnels, by which in former days a ship, about to board another, locked itself with it   And   **spend**, instead of spending , the sentence ends as if it had begun, ' Where *it would be possible* for these two armies *to* combine,' etc For the omission and subsequent insertion of 'to,' see Abb § 350   Shakespeare is probably thinking here, as Malone points out, of the crusades in which France and England fought as allies against the Saracens

11, 2. **And great   nobility** And powerful feelings contending in your breast mightily disturb your naturally dignified equanimity, cp *Macb* 1 3 140, "My thought, whose murder yet is but fantastical, Shakes so my single state of man, that," etc. For **doth**, see Abb § 337

13, 4 **O, what   respect '** "This *compulsion* was the necessity for a reformation in the state, which, according to Salisbury's opinion (who, in his speech preceding, calls it an *enforced cause*), could only be procured by foreign arms , and the *brave respect* was the love of his country " (Warburton)

45 **honourable dew**, the tears that did such credit to his heart

46 **silverly**, like a silver stream, on the suffix *ly* with a noun, see Abb § 447

48 **Being   inundation** , though that is a spectacle which one so commonly sees.

50 **blown up   soul**, excited by your strong feelings as rain is blown up by a strong wind, Malone compares *Lucr* 1788,

"This windy tempest, till it ... 161 I ... lion's tide

52 vaulty top, the cope, ... "the empty heaven so high above our heads", and ... ' this ... '

53 figured meteors. Illustrated from ... to ..., ... with etc.

55 great heart, brave heart

56, 7 Commend enraged. ... such tears as these to childish eyes that ... a commotion in the mighty world with which you are familiar. Baby and grand are antithetical

58, 9 Nor met gossiping. Nor ever made acquaintance with any other mode of fortune than that which is ... at feasts, where high spirits, mirth, and genial talk animate and enliven all

61 That knit mine. Who unite your strength with mine in this undertaking. sinews in a metaphorical case is frequent in Shakespeare, always used to mean, in the sense of 'to knit together strongly,' as II ... ii 6. 91

64 And even spake. 'In ... I have now ... all angel spake for me, the holy legate approaches to give a warrant from heaven and the name of right to our cause' (Malone) Wright points out the pun upon angel suggested by nobles in l 61

67 set, ... is a seal, carrying on the metaphor in warrant

69 The next is this. after which I tell you, etc.

70, 1 his spirit church. the obstinate perversity with which he refused to recognize the supremacy of Rome has now given place to humble obedience come in, in antithesis to stood out

75 foster'd hand, reared as a domestic animal, fed by the hand as a tame animal. a domestic pet

77 And be show. And though looking terrible, be harmless

78 Your mo, with your grace's pardon, which I am confident you will grant me, I will not, etc. The formula is not intended to be peremptory, but respectfully firm. Cp. M. V. iv 1 150. "Your grace *shall* understand that at the receipt of your letter I am very sick"

79 to be propertied to be treated as a mere tool: probably with an allusion to the 'properties' of a theatre—the dresses, masks, wigs, etc. Cp. the use of the subs. in J. C. iv 1 40, "do not talk of him (Lepidus), But as a *property*"

80 **To be ... control**, to be a subordinate directed just as my superior may think fit

82 **sovereign state**, the papal power then, and till quite recently, was a temporal, as well as a spiritual power, the Pope being a prince as well as a bishop

83 **the dead ... wars**, the spirit of hostility which had died out

84 **chastised kingdom**, which I have scourged with invasion, not, I think, with any reference to the Pope's punishment of John

85 **matter**, fuel

87 **same weak wind**, the breath of your words

88 **to know ... right**, to recognize right when I saw it, to distinguish between the appearance of good and evil

89 **interest to**, Malone compares 1 *H IV* iii 2 99, "He hath more worthy interest *to* the state Than," etc , and a passage from Dugdale, to show that this was the phraseology of the time, whereas we now say ' interest *in* ', taught me what interest I had in this land, what pretensions I might make to it , see the legate's speeches iii 4 141, etc

90 **Yea, thrust ... heart** Yea, and not only showed me this, but forcibly prompted this undertaking

92 **What ... me?** What have I to do with that peace? How does it affect my claim to the throne?

95 **now it is**, now that it is

96 **Because that**, see Abb § 287

97-9 **What ... penny ... action?** i e Rome has not contributed a single penny of the expense, not a single man, not a single munition of war to support, maintain, this expedition

100 **That ... charge**, that take upon myself the expenditure incurred , for undergo, cp *W T* ii 3 164, " Any thing, my lord, That my ability may *undergo* "

100 2 **who else ... war?** Who except myself, and those who are bound to render me service, if called upon, have to bear the burden of this war? i e none else have, etc

104 **Vive le roi !** For the sonant *e* in Vive, cp *H V* iii 5 11, " Mort de ma *vie* ' if they march along " In one of Heywood's Epilogues we have the line—" But *Vive, vive* le Roy, *vive* la Royne," where the final *e* must be sonant twice at all events , so Marlowe, *Massacre of Paris*, sc xii 1 86, has " *Vive* la *messe* ' perish the Huguenots " Abbott, § 489, gives other instances **bank'd ... towns**, probably, sailed past the banks of the rivers on which their towns stood Others explain it to mean landed

upon the bank. Schmidt thinks that from the context there may be an allusion to card-playing, and that by buried their towns is meant, or that *to set, put forth their hand* correct.

105, 7 Have I not set? Have I not the same in my hands, and shall I throw up my cards as a loser? *this match, this contest in which it is now my joy to get the better of him.* the

set, a set is any number of games agreed upon between the combatants beforehand, 'yielded is here perhaps, give over the set which will then be yielded, i.e. give over the set and content myself beaten.

109 the outside, the surface of things

111, 3 Till my war till I have won such glory as was promised in when in sanguine expectations of the results I gathered together this force. the promise of glory is perhaps as much that made by his ample hope as by the legate's words. For drew, cp. above, iv 2 118. in head of war, there seems to be the idea of things gathered to a head, brought to a point.

111 And cull'd world, and chose out these very spirits from among all those I might have got together, it being the flower and top of French chivalry

113 To outlook, to outstare, cause to cower before you etc. Cp. above, v 1 49, ' *outface the brow of bragging horror* "

116. Even in the jaws, in the very jaws

118 the fair world, that courteous treatment which is always accorded to ambassadors

121 how you him, what terms you have to rule for him.

122, 3 And as you tongue And, according as your answer is, I shall know what rejoinder my instructions authorize me to make

124 wilful opposite, obstinate in his hostility

125 will not entreaties will not accommodate himself to, etc. To temporize is to observe the time and accommodate oneself to it, thence, to come to terms generally

126 flatly, plainly, in round set terms. It is strange that this idea of thoroughness should belong, though in different ways, to 'flat,' 'round,' and 'straight', in 'flat,' the notion is of what is level, in 'round,' of what is complete, in 'straight, of what is without any twisting. On "round dealing," Bacon, *Essay on Truth*, Abbott remarks, " *Round* was naturally used of that which is symmetrical and *complete* (as a circle is), then of anything thorough. Hence (paradoxically enough), 'I went *round* to work,' *Hamlet*, ii 2 139, means, 'I went *straight* to the point'"

129 in me, by my mouth cp. i 1 3, 'In my behaviour '

130 and reason should and there is good reason why he should be well prepared, it is well that he should, etc

131 apish, fantastical, with this term applied to Lewis, cp *R III* 1 3 49, "Duck with French nods and *apish* courtesy"

132 This masque, this masquerading in arms, this buffoonery of invasion, **harness'd**, armed, as 'harness' frequently for armour Skeat (s v *Mask, Masque*) has shown that the primary meaning of 'masque,' as an entertainment, was that of buffoonery, the wearing of a mask "being (from an etymological point of view) an accident" unadvised revel, this farcical imitation of war

133 This sauciness, this youthful freak of impudence, **unhair'd**, *i e.* unbearded, is Theobald's correction of 'unheard' Malone compares v 1 69, above, "shall a *beardless* boy, A cocker'd," etc, *Macb* v 2 10, "many *unrough* youths, that even now Protest their first of manhood," and *H V* iii Prol 22, "For who is he whose chin is now enrich'd With *one* appearing *hair*"

136 From out territories, clean out of the length and breadth of the land

138 take the hatch, leap over the hatch, the half door, in order to hide yourselves from his anger, cp *Lear*, iii 6 76, "For, with throwing of my head Dogs *leap* the *hatch* and all are fled" To take, *e g* a hedge or a ditch, is, as Steevens points out, a hunter's phrase Cp *W T* iv 3 133, "merrily *hent* the stile a"

139 concealed wells, wells that offer concealment, passive for active participle Rolfe explains "wells in out of the way places," but wells wherever they were would afford equally effective concealment

140 litter, the straw which is strown over the floors of your stables

141 pawns, things pledged to a pawnbroker, which he, being liable for their restitution, locks up in some safe place, —"'F' *pan*, 'a pane, piece, or panel of a wall, also a pawn or gage' Cot —Lat *pannum*, acc of *pannus*, a cloth, rag, piece The explanation of this peculiar use of the word lies in the fact that a piece of cloth is the readiest article to leave in pledge" (Skeat, *Ety Dict*)

142 To hug with swine, to make your bed with swine, *i e* in the pens in which pigs are kept **sweet safety**, safety which is sweet wherever it may be obtained, even if in vaults and prisons

143 to thrill, to quiver, shudder

144 Even at crow, Collier's MS Corrector alters this to, 'Even at the crowing of your nation's cock' "Malone," says Dyce, "refers this to 'the caw of the French crow,'—a sense which the words may very well bear Douce on the other hand, says that the allusion is to the crowing of a cock,—gallus meaning both a cock and a Frenchman, but would Shakespeare (or any other writer) employ such an expression as 'the crying of the crow [of a cock]'"

116 to scobled here. If it showest itself so victorious when on your soil the soil of a foreign country, is it likely, that here, on its own native soil, it should have been no enfeebled.

117 in your chambers, penetrating into your very houses.

119, 50 And like   nest. A I like an eagle, careators his nest, ready to swoop down upon all who threaten injury to his brood. Staunton points out that the verb to 'tower,' as is primarily of the flight of an eagle, which, etc., seems formerly to have denoted not merely soaring to a great height, but to flying spirally. He also quotes from Drayton's *Polyolbion*, and from Beaumont and Fletcher's *Chances*, is 1, instances of soose, in the technical language of falconry, for to pounce down She it shows that *nosy* is from the Low Lat. *nidus*, a nest, of a bird of prey, and has no connection with 'code,' as a common derivation, *i.e. cry*, inferred, thus causing the word to be written *eyrie* or *eyry*

151 ingrate revolts, ungrateful revolters, rebels, used also by *Cymb* iv 4 6, "receive us For barbarous and unnatural revolts"

152, 3 You bloody   England, you unnatural sons of your mother country who, like Nero (who is said to have murdered his mother by ripping up her womb), would mutilate her who bore you

154 pale visaged maids, Rolfe compares *Ind. part*, *R III* iii 1 95, "Change the complexion of her maid pale peace."

155 tripping, walking daintily

157 neelds, Shakespeare's contracted form of 'needles,' as in *M N D* iii 2 204, *Per* iv Prol 23

158 bloody inclination, murderous thoughts

159 thy brave, your bravado threatening words, cp *I S* iii 1 15, "Sirrah, I will not hear these braves of thine"

160 outscold us, outdo us in the matter of scolding

162 with such a brabbler, in converse with a noisy, quarrelsome, fellow

164, 5 and let   here We do not care to answer you in words, our answer, justifying our interest in the land, and our presence here, shall be given by our drums and trumpets

169 even at hand, i e so close at hand are our forces.

170 all as loud, fully as loud

172 **rattle**　ear, startle the atmosphere around us , welkin, from A S *wolcnu*, plural of *wolcen*, a cloud

173 **mock**, imitate

174 **halting legate**, this legate who halts between one resolution and another

175 **Whom**　need, whom John has employed as his agent more for amusement than because he had any need for his interference

176 **in his forehead**, Rolfe quotes *R II* iii 2 160, "for within the hollow crown That rounds the mortal temples of a king Keeps Death his court, and there the antic sits," etc

177 **A bare-ribb'd death**, cp Milton, *Comus*, 562, "And took in strains that might create a soul Under *the ribs of Death* " office, function, duty

179 **this danger**, i e that you threaten us with

SCENE III

the day, the battle, as above, iii 4 116

4 **my heart is sick**, I am sick at heart, utterly despondent

8 **Swinstead**　"Halliwell reads 'Swineshead,' which is unquestionably correct , but Shakespeare copied the mistake from the old play　Swineshead is in Lincolnshire, about seven miles southwest of Boston　It is now a rural town, but was then a seaport　The abbey, about half a mile east of the town, was founded by Robert de Gieslei in 1134　It was a large and magnificent structure, but nothing is now left of it　The mansion known as Swineshead Abbey stands near the site, and was built with materials from the ancient abbey" (Timbs, quoted by Rolfe)

9 **supply**, reinforcements , frequently in Shakespeare, both in the singular and the plural

11 **Goodwin Sands**, "or the Goodwins (*M of V* iii 1 4) are dangerous-shoals off the eastern coast of Kent, not far from the mouth of the Thames. Tradition says that they were once an island belonging to Earl Godwin, which was swallowed up by the sea about A D 1100" (Rolfe)　They are quick-sands rather than shoals

13 **coldly**, with little spirit　retire, transitive , not retire of themselves, of their own accord

15 **welcome**, give that glad reception which it deserves

16 **Set on**, set out for　litter, a portable bed , these were of

two kinds, that borne on the shoulders of men, was proher of India, and that borne by horses, the poles being attached to collars and to straps round the hind quarters " Matthew of Westminster informs us that John was conveyed from the Abbey of Swineshead in *lectica equestri* —the horse litter" (Knight) - straight, at once

SCENE IV.

1 stored. well supplied. cp. *H. 1 m. 5* 71, " To new store France with her valiant warriors"

3 If they too, re all our hope depend upon their success

5 In spite of spite " come the worst that may notwithstand-ing anything that may happen' (Schmidt) cp *3 H VI ii 3* 5, "*In spite of spite alone I keep a hill* "

6 sore sick, dangerously ill

7 revolts, see above, v 2 151

8 When names When things went well you did not speak of us in such terms, then no compliments were too great for us though Melun did not as his next speech shows, mean the word revolts for a taunt, Salisbury in his answer takes it for one.

10 bought and sold, literally made the subjects of barter, just as may suit the convenience of others, hence, betrayed, as frequently in Shakespeare

11 Unthread rebellion "Shakespeare was evidently thinking of the *eye of a needle*   Undo (says Melun to the English nobles) what you have done, desert the rebellious project in which you have engaged In *Coriolanus* [iii 1 127] we have a kindred expression, 'they would not *thread the gates'* Our author is not always careful that the epithet he applies to a figurative term should answer on both sides 'Rude' is applicable to 'rebellion.' but not to 'eye'" (Malone) To the passage in *Coriolanus* Dyce adds *R II v 5* 17, " It is as hard to come as for a camel To *thread* the postern of a small needle's eye " There is, as has been pointed out, a plain allusion to *Matthew*, xix. 24, " It is easier for a camel to go through the eye of a needle than for a rich man to enter into the kingdom of God "

12 And welcome faith. Receive back into your hearts that loyalty which for a while you have driven away

14 lords On account of " he " in the next line the Camb Edd propose 'lord' for lords, taking French as singular, and in sup-port of their suggestion refer to *H 1 iv 1* 80, "*the French* might have a good prey of us if *he* knew it " loud, *i e* with the discharge of cannon

15 He, i e Lewis

17 moe, According to Skeat, the distinction between *moe* (or *mo*) and *more* is that *moe* referred to number, *more* to size

19 Even   altar, on that very same altar, the treachery being made all the more glaring thereby

21 May   may, can this, etc , the original sense of 'may', see Abb § 307

22 within my view, staring me in the face

23 but a quantity, i e a small quantity only , cp *T S* iv 3 112, "Away, thou rag, thou *quantity*, thou remnant", ii *H IV* v 1 70, "If I were sawed into *quantities*, I should make four dozen of such bearded hermits' staves as Master Shallow "

24 Resolveth   fire   Melts and loses its form when placed near to the fire   "This is said in allusion to the images made by witches   Holinshed observes that it was alleged against dame Eleanor of Cobham and her confederates 'that they had devised an *image of wax*, representing the King, which by their sorcerie, by little and little consumed, intending thereby, in conclusion, to waste and destroy the King's person '   *Resolve* and *dissolve* had anciently the same meaning   So, in *Hamlet* [i 2 30], 'O that this too too solid flesh would melt, Thaw and *resolve* itself into a dew'" (Steevens)   The practice spoken of by Steevens is also referred to in *R III* iii 4 70-4   For the expression in the text cp *T G* ii 4 201, 2, "Which, like a *waxen image* 'gainst a fire, Bears no impression of the thing it was "

26 What in the world, i e nothing could possibly, etc

27 use, profit, possibly with a reference to the word as meaning the interest on money

29 live   truth, that my only hope of eternal life is by being true in this , another jingle between true and truth.

31, 2 He is   east   He will have broken his oath if he allows you to live to see another day

33 6 But even   expire, not only will he not allow you to live to the dawn of another day, but this very night, this night whose pestilential gloom is already enveloping the bright light of the sun, now weary of its daily task, this ill-fated night, your breath, will pass from your bodies   The image is here of the cap of smoke which forms at the top of a flame of fire , and there is perhaps an allusion to the cover put over a helmet when not in use   Contagious is used again of darkness in ii *H IV* iv 1 7, "Breathe foul *contagious* darkness in the air "

37 rated, "The Dauphin has rated [i e appraised] your treachery and set upon it a *fine*, which your lives must pay" (Johnson)   Treason, when not against the sovereign person, could be condoned on payment of a fine

41 3 The love   this   The love I bear to him, and the consideration that my grandfather was an Englishman, move my
conscience to confess this to you with a view to saving your lives
The line for that   Englishman is taken from the old play,
and its insertion perhaps accounts for the pleonasm for that, or
because   Either 'The love of him, and the consideration that,
etc, lead me,' etc, or 'because of my love for him and because
(for that) my grandsire was, etc, I am led,' etc, would have
been more logical

44   In lieu whereof   in return for which confession, cp. M 1
s 1 262, "In lieu of this let me that he with us." The literal meaning of the phrase is 'in place of,' i e, a substitution, not
restitution or recompense, but Shakespeare always uses it as here.

45 rumour,   'a confused and indistinct noise" (Schmidt), cp
J C ii 1 15, 'I hear a breathing noise, like a fray.'

47 part   separate, divorce

49 beshrew my soul,   may my soul be accursed

50, 1 But I   occasion, if I do not love the appearance of this
occasion, cp. gladly welcome this opportunity   for the which,
used when there are two possible antecedents, see Abb 3 270

51 untread   flight, retrace the steps by which we acted as
traitors to our king, cp above, l 11, "Unthread,' etc

53 And like   flood, and like a river which has risen above
its proper level, but afterwards states itself and shrinks back to
it, etc, for retired, see Abb

54 Leaving   course   abandoning that extravagance of action
to which we have given way

55 o'erlook'd,   looked over, exceeded, cp above, ii 1 24,
'Like a proud river peering o'er his bounds"

60 Right, plainly   'bright' was proposed for right by Collier's
MS Corrector, and is approved by Knight   Dyce, quoting the
opinion of an eminent physician, remarks, "Mr Collier tells us
that 'Bright' is to be understood in reference to the remarkable
brilliancy of the eyes of many persons just before death; but if
that lighting up of the eye ever occurs, it is only when comparative tranquillity precedes dissolution,— not during 'the pangs of
death', and most assuredly it is never to be witnessed in those
persons who, like Melun, are dying of wounds—of exhaustion from
loss of blood,—in which case, the eye, immediately before death,
becomes glazed and lustreless'

60, 1 New   right   There is now before us a new flight (ie
back to the king), and one that in its newness is a happy one
since its object is the restoration of the ancient rightful
government

SCENE V

2 blush, i e with shame at the sight

3, 4 measur'd   retire, retreat in a cowardly manner, that retreat being all the more disgraceful that it is made over their own soil **bravely   off,** in a triumphant manner did we quit the field

5 needless, no longer needed for use against the English, they having abandoned the field

7 And wound   up   For tottering, Steevens reads 'tatter'd', Dyce, 'tattering', holding, with Gifford, that tottering was merely the old spelling of the word   Staunton, keeping tottering, thinks that "*tottering* or *drooping* colours, after a hard fight, contrast becomingly with the *spreading, waving* colours of an army advancing to battle." Singer renders the word *wavering, shaking,* Fleay (*apud* Rolfe) *waving,* quoting from *The Spanish Tragedy,* "A man hanging, and *tottering* and *tottering,* As you know the wind will wave a man." **clearly,** is explained by some as 'stainlessly,' by others as 'completely,' with which meaning Dyce proposes 'cleanly,' a conjecture made by the Camb Edd also, but with the interpretation of 'neatly'   If we knew what clearly meant, we should be nearer knowing what tottering means   If tottering = 'tattered,' it is the active participle for the passive

11 again fall'n off, have revolted from the Dauphin as they did from John

12 supply, see above, v 3 9   **wish'd,** looked for, desired

13 Goodwin Sands, see above, v 3 11, and cp *Cymb* iii 1 21, 2

14 shrewd, bitter, accursed

18 The stumbling night, the darkness which caused us to stumble, lose our way

20 keep   quarter, keep good watch at your posts or quarters, Rolfe compares i *II VI* ii 1 63, "Had all your *quarters* been as safely *kept*", cp also, "their *quarter'd* fires," *Cymb* iv 4 18

21. The day   to morrow, i e I shall be up before daybreak to take the fullest advantage of whatever may offer, **adventure,** the chances that may come in my way

SCENE VI

2 Of the   England, one belonging to the English side

4, 5 why   mine' Dyce, adopting a suggestion made to him by Mr W W Lloyd, gives these words to the Bastard, considering this distribution "absolutely necessary." If given to Hubert, they will mean, I have not asked you, 'Whither dost thou go,' and you had no right to put such a question to me'; but Mr Lloyd's suggestion removes all difficulty.

6. a perfect thought, a correct, sound, thought.

7 I will believe, I will at all risks confidently believe.

10. 1 Thou Plantagenet. As you are so ready to believe me a friend, you may show your friendship in return by believing that on one side of my family I belong to the line of the Plantagenets.

12. 3 Unkind shame O, treacherous memory, thou and the darkness of the night have put me to shame. Schmidt explains eyeless (Theobald's correction of 'endless') by "infinite, excessive, that is, extremely dark". Flmy, quoted by Rolfe, thinks it means 'starless.' The stars being the night's eyes, as the sun is the day's. Delius, retaining 'endless,' renders it "boundless, infinite, and compares 'eternal' in *J C* i. 2. 160, "There was a Brutus once that would have brook'd The *eternal* devil to keep his state in Rome As easily as a king"; *Oth.* iv. 2. 130, "some *eternal* devil"

14. 5 That any ear That my ear should fail to recognize with perfect certainty any inflection of your voice.

16. sans compliment without any further bandying of civilities.

17, 8. Why out. Why, here am I looking for you in the darkness, that is the first thing I have to tell you, brow of night, "as we say, in the face of day" (Fleay, *apud* Rolfe).

18 Brief, then news? To come to the point, then, what is the news that you are seeking me out to deliver?

21, 2. The very wound, the very sting, that part which especially pains.

23 The king monk, "Not one of the historians who wrote within sixty years after the death of king John, mentions this very improbable story. The tale is, that a monk, to revenge himself on the king for a saying at which he took offence, poisoned a cup of ale, and having brought it to his majesty, drank some of it himself, to induce the king to taste it, and soon afterwards expired. Thomas Wykes is the first who relates it in his *Chronicle*, as a report. According to the best accounts, John died at Newark, of a fever" (Malone).

24 broke out, broke away, hurried off from amidst the confusion.

26, 7 The better this, that you might be the better able to prepare yourself to meet this sudden emergency than if you had been left to hear of it by chance, and some time after the event.

As Rolfe says, at leisure means 'at other people's leisure' For to the sudden time, on the use of 'to' before nouns, meaning 'with a view to,' see Abb § 186

28 **who   him.** In days when there was so much danger of poison being administered, it was the custom for kings to have each dish of which they partook tasted by an attendant, who was called the 'taster,' and "whose office it was to *give the say* [*i e* the assay] (*prelibare*), to taste and declare the goodness of the wine and dishes" (Dyce, *Gloss*).

29 **resolved,** resolute, determined, his resolution being shown in his not hesitating to drink of the cup, though knowing it to be poisoned, in order to induce the king also to drink of it

30, **suddenly,** immediately, cp *A Y L* ii 2 19, "do this *suddenly* "

32 **Who,** for other instances of the inflection of 'who' being neglected, see Abb § 274

33 **Why   back,** Dyce, following Malone's suggestion, reads, " Why know you not the lords are all come back," and puts the note of interrogation at company, **brought,** we should now use the perfect instead of the aorist

36 **about,** in attendance upon

38 **And tempt   power !** And do not try us so severely as to give us more to bear than we are capable of bearing

39 **my power,** the forces I was bringing with me

40 **flats,** stretches of flat country common in the eastern counties **taken   tide,** swept away by the tide   " On the 14th of October, 1216, as the king was attempting to ford the Wash at low water, and had already got across himself, with the greater part of his army, the return of the tide suddenly swept away the carriages and horses that conveyed all his baggage and treasures , and the spot is still known as ' King's Corner ' It was on the same night that the king arrived at the Cistercian monastery at Swineshead, and was taken with the fever of which he died " (Rolfe)

42 **well mounted,** though well mounted, on a powerful horse

44 **or ere,** for this reduplication, see Abb § 131

SCENE VII

1 **the life   blood,** the essential part of his blood

2 **corruptibly,** "*i e* corruptively   So, in his *Rape of Lucrece,* [1854], 'The Romans *plausibly* did give consent'—*i e* with acclamations " (Steevens) , on the termination *ble,* used in

an active sense, see Abb § 115   pure brain, which hitherto was clear

4, 5 Doth   mortality   see the account of Falstaff's death
II 1' n 3   mortality, mortal life

6 9 and holds   him, and is firmly persuaded that if he were brought, etc , the burning quality, etc , would be allayed, or, that bringing him into, etc , would allay the burning, etc - fell, cruel fierce, death

10 orchard (*orgeard*, a ord of worts or vegetables), garden, is usually, if not always, in Shakespeare, the word was at one time written *hortyard*, under the mistaken idea that it was derived from *hortus*, a garden, which singularly enough is said to be related to the latter syllable, *yard*   "John did not die at Swineshead for Swinstead) as here represented   On the day after he arrived there   though very ill, he was conveyed in a litter to the Castle of Sleaford, and thence on the 16th of October to the Castle of Newark, where he expired on the 18th, in the 49th year of his age and the 17th of his reign" (Rolfe).

11   rage, rave

12   even now, but a moment ago

13, 1 O vanity   themselves, O strange caprice of sickness, the continuance of the fierce extremes of pain at last prevents the body from being sensible of them, ie there is a point beyond which the capacity of feeling pain cannot go

16 insensible, this is Hanmer's emendation , some editors retain the reading of the folios, 'invisible', which Malone explains as an adverb , Knight gives 'unlooked at, disregarded' as its meaning, Flea putting a comma before the word, says that death is "visibly acting while preying on the body, but invisible when he attacks the mind ", and Wright also refers 'invisible' to Death.

17   the which, see Abb § 270

18   fantasies, the older and fuller form of 'fancies.'

19, 20 Which   themselves   Which as they crowd and try to force their way into that stronghold, the last to yield to death, destroy themselves   Malone quotes *II VIII* ii 4 185, "which force'd such way That many maz'd considerings did throng And press in with this caution "

21   cygnet, the young of the swan

22 Who chants   death, for allusions to this belief, cp. *Lucr* 1611, *Phœnix and Turtle*, 15, *Oth.* v 2 247, *M I* iii 2 11   For Who, personifying an irrational antecedent, see Abb § 264

23, 4 And from , rest   And uses the last weak strains of its voice to accompany the departure of the soul from the body , the soul finding rest in heaven, the body, in the earth, an allusion to the service performed over the dead with an accompaniment of music from the organ, organ-pipe, windpipe, throat

26 that indigest, that chaotic mass, so the adjective, = formless in *Sonn* 114, 5, "monsters and things *indigest*"

28 elbow-room, room to move about in

29 It   out, it refused to depart from the body while it had no other outlet than doors and windows

30 so   summer, such fierce heat

32 scribbled form, I am as a rude figure, portrait, drawn, etc

33 against, when placed near, cp above, v 4 25

35 ill fare, in answer to the Bastard's "How fares," etc, the King says, 'I have taken poison, which is but ill fare'

36, 7 And none   maw, Steevens quotes from Dekker's *Gul's Hornbook*, "the morning waxing cold, *thrust his frosty fingers* into my bosome", and Malone from *Lust's Dominion*, "the cold hand of sleep *Hath thrust his icy fingers in my breast*"

41 comfort   cold, it being warmth that is generally spoken of as comforting, cp above, iv 1 107, "the fire is dead with grief, *Being create for comfort*"

42 cold comfort. "There is a play upon the phrase, which was ironically used, as it still is, in the sense of small comfort Cp *T of S* iv 1 33, 'whose hand   thou shalt soon feel, to thy *cold comfort*'" (Rolfe)   so strait, so niggardly

44 virtue, some property that would give relief

46-8 Within   blood. My inside is as a hell in which the poison is shut and set to prey upon my blood which is condemned beyond all hope of reprieve

50 spleen of speed, fierce activity

51 to set   eye, to close my eyes, as is done after death, the eyes naturally remaining partially open

52 The tackle, that by which my heart was braced up   Cp *Cor* iv 5 67, "though thy *tackle's* torn, Thou show'st a noble vessel"

53 the shrouds, the rigging which holds the masts in their place

55 to stay it by, to support it, another nautical term, the stays being also large ropes supporting the masts

56 holds, does not give way

58 module, another form of 'model,' i e the mere outline, ground-plan, confounded ruined

O

59, preparing hitherward, "For the eclipse of _Rich. II._, v. 1. 37: 'prepare thee hence for France'; and _Cor._, iv. 5. 110: 'Who am prepared against your territories' (Delius).

60 Whoro knows, on the insertion of the pronoun after a proper name, see Abb. § 247. Walker thinks that the original reading "God" was altered to heaven on account of the statute of James against profane swearing, answer him, meet, oppose, cp. _Cor._, i. 2. 14, 'We never yet made doubt but Rome was ready To answer us.'

62 upon advantage, in the hopes of gaining by the movement.

63, 4 Were good. This occurrence, which has already been related, happened to the King himself

65 dead news, deadly news.

66 but now ... thus, a moment ago a mighty King, now but a clod of clay, as in l. 64

67 run on ... stop, metaphors from a clock

71 To do ... revenge, to perform the office, not of burial, but of revenge, cp. _II. H. n. d._ 157, "Tarry, dear cousin Suffolk,' My soul shall keep thee company to heaven ... Tarry, sweet soul for mine, then fly abreast'

73 still, ever

74 you stars ... spheres, you nobles who have returned to your allegiance, and now move in that orbit out of which for a time you had wandered.

75 Show now ... faiths, give proof of your loyalty being equal once more

77 To push ... land. To thrust out of this land, which is faint with the suffering it has undergone, those destructive powers which have brought shame upon it

79 straight ... sought let us instantly attack the Dauphin, or he will attack us

82. Pandulph. "It was not Pandulph, but Cardinal James Guala, who opposed the intention of the Dauphin to invade England" (French, S. G.) at rest, resting himself peacefully

84 offers ... peace, offers of peace to us

86 With ... war with the intention of abandoning this war upon us

87, 8 He will ... defence He will be more likely to give up the idea of continuing this war when he sees us strongly armed to resist him, so therefore let us show our strength

89 Nay, ... already, Nay, there is no fear of his endeavouring to prolong the war, for his departure has already to a certain extent been begun

91, 2. and put   cardinal   and left it to the cardinal to arrange matters with us

94   post, go with speed

97   With other princes, Walker thought that princes was a corruption, the transcriber's or compositor's eye having been caught by the word prince in the preceding line   The Camb Edd think that the mistake may be in the word prince, for which it would be easier to suggest a substitute than for princes

98   Shall wait   funeral   Shall accompany as mourners, etc

99   At Worcester   "A stone coffin, containing the body of King John, was discovered in the cathedral church at Worcester, July 17, 1797" (Steevens)

102.   The lineal   land '   That royal dignity and glorious sway which you have inherited

104   I do bequeath, I offer, generally used of something left by will to heirs, etc

106   tender, offer, as frequently in Shakespeare

107   To rest   evermore '   To continue without stain for, etc

108, 9   I have   tears   My heart is full of kindly feelings towards you, but is unable to express them except by tears

110, 1   O, let us   griefs   The time has already beforehand exacted a large tribute of griefs from us, therefore let us now pay it so much as is due and no more

114   But when   itself.   This logically can only go with did lie

115   her princes, her chief nobles   are   home, have returned to their allegiance

116, 7   come   them.   Let the rest of the whole world attack us, and we shall meet it boldly in the shock of war

117   rue, suffer, cp in *H VI* iv 1 40, "Why knows not Montague that of itself England is safe, if true within itself?"

GLASGOW. PRINTED BY ROBERT MACLEHOSE AT THE UNIVERSITY PRESS

MACMILLAN'S
ENGLISH CLASSICS:
A SERIES OF SELECTIONS FROM THE WORKS OF THE GREAT ENGLISH CLASSICS,
WITH INTRODUCTIONS AND NOTES.

The following Volumes, Globe 8vo, are ready or in preparation

ADDISON—SELECTIONS FROM THE SPECTATOR. By K DEIGHTON, late Principal of Agra College 2s 6d

BACON—ESSAYS By F G SELBY, M A, Principal and Professor of Logic and Moral Philosophy, Deccan College, Poona 3s, sewed, 2s 6d
The *Schoolmaster*—"A handy and serviceable edition of a famous English classical work, one that can never lose its freshness and its truth"
—THE ADVANCEMENT OF LEARNING By the same Book I, 2s, Book II, 3s 6d

BURKE—REFLECTIONS ON THE FRENCH REVOLUTION. By the same 5s
Scotsman—"Contains many notes which will make the book valuable beyond the circle to which it is immediately addressed"
Schoolmaster—"A very good book whether for examination or for independent reading and study"
Glasgow Herald—"The book is remarkably well edited"
—SPEECH ON AMERICAN TAXATION, ON CONCILIATION WITH AMERICA, LETTER TO THE SHERIFFS OF BRISTOL By the same [*In the Press*

CAMPBELL—SELECTIONS. By CECIL M BARROW, M A, Principal, Victoria College, Palghát [*In preparation*

COWPER—THE TASK By F J ROWE, M A, and W T WEBB, M A, Professors of English Literature, Presidency College, Calcutta. [Book IV *in the Press*

DRYDEN—SATIRES By J CHURTON COLLINS, M A [*Dec*, 1893

GOLDSMITH—THE TRAVELLER and THE DESERTED VILLAGE By ARTHUR BARRETT, B A, Professor of English Literature, Elphinstone College, Bombay 1s 9d THE TRAVELLER (separately), sewed, 1s THE DESERTED VILLAGE (separately), sewed, 1s
The *Educational News*—"In the book before us every justice is done to the genius of the poet The introduction gives a very good outline of his life, and the notes teem with all manner of information, and it would be difficult to point out any omission on the part of the editor The volume would make an admirable class book"
The *Scotsman*—"It has a short critical and biographical introduction, and a very full series of capital notes."

GRAY—POEMS By JOHN BRADSHAW, LL D, Inspector of Schools, Madras 1s 9d
Dublin Evening Mail—"The Introduction and Notes are all that can be desired. We believe that this will rightly become the standard school edition of Gray"
Schoolmaster—"One of the best school editions of Gray's poems we have seen"

MACMILLAN AND CO., LONDON.

HELPS—ESSAYS WRITTEN IN THE INTERVALS OF BUSINESS. By F. J. ROWE, M.A., and W. T. WEBB, M.A. 1s. 9d.

The Literary Herald—"These essays are indeed, two... of tolof gather... The... instruction 'A work... a while'... to a certain extent... The in... instruction, though brief, is full of point."

JOHNSON—LIFE OF MILTON. By K. DEIGHTON. 1s. 9d.

MACAULAY—ESSAY ON LORD CLIVE. By K. DEIGHTON. 2s.
—ESSAY ON WARREN HASTINGS. By K. DEIGHTON. 2s. 6d.
—ESSAY ON ADDISON. By Prof. J. W. HALES, M.A.
[In preparation.

MILTON—PARADISE LOST, BOOKS I and II. By MICHAEL MACMILLAN, B.A., Professor of Logic and Moral Philosophy, Elphinstone College, Bombay. 1s. 9d. Books I and II. separately, sewed, 1s. each

The Times of India—"That kind of commentary the editors child often find a source... They are easy, concise, and to the point... with as the same time they are suppos... are useful for those... books to whom Milton is... also the... must not be a..."
The Schoolmaster—"The best... to a... title of...of... in upper classes of English schools."
The Educational News—"For higher classes these are no less... for reading, analysis and grammar... the use of these books of Paradise Lost may... best as a great induc... to a study of our literature in..."

—L'ALLEGRO, IL PENSEROSO, LYCIDAS, ARCADES, SONNETS, &c. By WILLIAM BELL, M.A., Professor of Philosophy and Logic, Government College, Lahore. 1s. 9d.
The Guardian—"A careful study of this book will be as educative as that of any of our best... themes..."

—COMUS. By the same. 1s. 3d.
The Dublin Evening Mail—"The introduction is well done, and contains much sound criticism."
The Practical Teacher—"The notes include everything a student could reasonably desire in the way of... elucidation of the text, and as the same... are presented in so clear... in a fashion that they are likely to attract the reader instead of repelling him."

—SAMSON AGONISTES. By H. M. PERCIVAL, M.A., Professor of English Literature, Presidency College, Calcutta. 2s.
The Guardian—"Miss... are learned literary... His introduction is equally masterly, and for... all Latin... about the poem."

SCOTT—THE LADY OF THE LAKE. By G. H. STUART, M.A. Principal and Professor of English Literature, Kumbakonam College. 2s. 6d., sewed, 2s.

—THE LAY OF THE LAST MINSTREL. By G. H. STUART, M.A., and F. H. ELLIOT, B.A., Assistant Professor of English, Presidency College, Madras. 2s. Canto I, sewed, 9d. Cantos I-III, and IV-VI, 1s. 3d. each
The Journal of Education—"The text is well printed, and the notes, wherever we have tested them, have proved at once scholarly and simple."

—MARMION. By MICHAEL MACMILLAN, B.A. 3s., sewed, 2s. 6d.
The Spectator—"... His introduction is admirable alike for point and brevity."
The Indian Daily News—"The present volume contains the poem in 500 pages with more than 100 pages of notes, which seem to meet every possible difficulty."

—ROKEBY. By the same. 3s., sewed, 2s. 6d.
The Guardian—"The introduction is excellent, and the notes show much care and research."

MACMILLAN & CO., LONDON.

SHAKESPEARE—THE TEMPEST By K DEIGHTON, late Principal of Agra College 1s 9d

The *Guardian*—"Speaking generally of Macmillan's Series we may say that they approach more nearly than any other edition we know to the ideal school Shakespeare The introductory remarks are not too much burdened with controversial matter, the notes are abundant and to the point, scarcely any difficulty being passed over without some explanation, either by a paraphrase or by etymological and grammatical notes"

The *School Guardian*—"A handy edition of *The Tempest*, suitable for the use of colleges and schools generally Mr Deighton has prefixed to the volume an introduction on the date, origin, construction, and characters of the play, and has added a pretty full collection of notes, with an index of reference to the passages of the text in question The 'get up' of this series is a model of what such books should be"

—MUCH ADO ABOUT NOTHING By the same 2s

The *Schoolmaster*—"The notes on words and phrases are full and clear"

The *Glasgow Herald*—"The notes occupy a larger space than the text of the play, and are supplemented by a valuable index to the notes, so that if one remembers any notable word he can find at once a reference that leads to the proper explanatory note"

—A MIDSUMMER NIGHT'S DREAM By the same 1s 9d

—THE MERCHANT OF VENICE By the same 1s 9d.

The *Practical Teacher*—"The introduction is a good summary of the play, and the notes are precise, clear, and, we need hardly add, full A student who has mastered the contents of this volume will have a thorough acquaintance with the play, and be prepared for any test of his knowledge of it to which he may have to be subjected"

—AS YOU LIKE IT By the same 1s 9d

—TWELFTH NIGHT By the same 1s 9d

The *Educational News*—"This is an excellent edition of a good play"

—THE WINTER'S TALE By the same 2s

The *Literary World*—"The Introduction gives a good historical and critical account of the play, and the notes are abundantly full."

—KING JOHN By the same 1s 9d

—RICHARD II By the same 1s 9d

—HENRY IV, Part I By the same 2s 6d, sewed, 2s

—HENRY IV, Part II By the same 2s 6d, sewed, 2s

—HENRY V. By the same 1s 9d

The *Scotsman*—"The text is excellent, the Introduction is sufficiently learned, and elucidates not this play alone, but the dramatic scope of the Lancastrian tetralogy, and the notes are very full, very explanatory, and not often superfluous"

The *Educational Times*—"We have examined the notes with considerable care, and we have found, in almost every case, that a full and clear explanation is given of each difficulty The notes are clear and comprehensive"

—RICHARD III By C H TAWNEY, M A, Principal and Professor of English Literature, Presidency College, Calcutta 2s, 6d., sewed, 2s

The *School Guardian*—"Of Mr Tawney's work as an annotator we can speak in terms of commendation His notes are full and always to the point.'

—CORIOLANUS By K DEIGHTON 2s 6d, sewed, 2s

—ROMEO AND JULIET By the same 2s 6d, sewed, 2s

—JULIUS CAESAR By the same 1s. 9d

The *Guardian*—"Of *Julius Caesar* and the *Merchant of Venice*, edited by Mr K. Deighton, we can speak in terms of almost unqualified praise The notes are admirably suited to the use of middle forms, being brief, numerous, and accurate. Besides affording evidence of scholarly attainments on the part of the annotator, they show a perfect knowledge of the limits of a schoolboy's capacity, and a rare ability to explain away his difficulties in a simple and interesting manner"

MACMILLAN AND CO, LONDON

SHAKESPEARE—HAMLET. By K. Deighton 2s 6d, sewed, 2s.
—MACBETH. By the same 1s 9d.

The text of these plays is given with a careful collation of the Quartos that reappear later ... at all the still more important variations of Macmillan, with full notes and explanations ...

—KING LEAR. By the same 1s 9d.

—OTHELLO. By the same 2s.

—ANTONY AND CLEOPATRA. By the same. 2s 6d, sewed 2s.

—CYMBELINE. By the same. 2s 6d, sewed 2s.

The "Athenæum" ... is ... as ... for ... complete ... in ...

SOUTHEY—LIFE OF NELSON. By MICHAEL MACMILLAN, B.A. 2s 6d, sewed, 2s 6d.

The ... Nelson ... is a ... Macmillan ... and Co ...

SPENSER—THE FAERIE QUEENE. Book I. By H. M. PERCIVAL, M.A. 3s, sewed, 2s 6d.

TENNYSON—SELECTIONS. By F. J. ROWE, M.A., and W. T. WEBB, M.A. 3s 6d. Also in two Parts, 2s 6d each. Part I. Recollections of the Arabian Nights, The Lady of Shalott, The Lotos Eaters, Dora, Ulysses, Tithonus, The Lord of Burleigh, The Brook, Ode on the Death of the Duke of Wellington, The Revenge.—Part II. Œnone, The Palace of Art, A Dream of Fair Women, Morte d'Arthur, Sir Galahad, The Voyage, and Demeter and Persephone.

The Selection ... is ... and the notes are admirable.

The notes of ... Rowe ... It is all and a wide circulation in English schools ... The ... a very valuable amount of helpful and reliable information ... with the poems themselves ... illustrated ... Value ... in reduction gives the value ... ever ...

The Literary World—"The book is very ... able and will be a good introduction to the study of Tennyson on a wider ground.

—ENOCH ARDEN. By W. T. WEBB, M.A. 2s 6d.

—AYLMER'S FIELD. By the same. 2s 6d.

—THE PRINCESS. By P. M. WALLACE, M.A. 3s 6d.

—THE COMING OF ARTHUR and THE PASSING OF ARTHUR. By F. J. ROWE, M.A. 2s 6d.

—GARETH AND LYNETTE. By G. C. MACAULAY, M.A. 2s 6d.

—THE MARRIAGE OF GERAINT. GERAINT AND ENID. By the same. 2s 6d.

—LANCELOT AND ELAINE. By F. J. ROWE, M.A. [In preparation.

—THE HOLY GRAIL. By G. C. MACAULAY, M.A. 2s 6d.

—GUINEVERE. By the same. [In preparation.

WORDSWORTH—SELECTIONS. By F. J. ROWE, M.A., and W. T. WEBB, M.A. [In preparation.

MACMILLAN AND CO, LONDON.